HOMELESS HERO

UNDERSTANDING THE SOUL OF HOME

MIKE TAPSCOTT

abbott press®

A DIVISION OF WRITER'S DIGEST

Abbott Press books may be ordered through booksellers or by contacting:

Abbott Press
1663 Liberty Drive
Bloomington, IN 47403
www.abbottpress.com
Phone: 1-866-697-5310

Because of the dynamic nature of the Internet, any web addresses or links contained in this book may have changed since publication and may no longer be valid. The views expressed in this work are solely those of the author and do not necessarily reflect the views of the publisher, and the publisher hereby disclaims any responsibility for them.

ISBN: 978-1-4582-1064-7 (sc)
ISBN: 978-1-4582-1066-1 (hc)
ISBN: 978-1-4582-1065-4 (e)

Library of Congress Control Number: 2013912798

Printed in the United States of America.

Abbott Press rev. date: 08/29/2013

DEDICATION

To Bowtie Bob, a man I also know as my father.
By his own definition, Bowtie Bob is a simple man. This simplicity of character taught me what I first knew about humanity. My father is kind, giving, patient, loving. His work ethic is based on living and acting to the highest limits that his humanity and his humility will allow. Bowtie Bob is known for the bowtie he always wears. It matches his general style of dress—suspenders and all—that he wears to work at his volunteer job at a homeless shelter in Albuquerque.

This is where *hero* and *homeless* began for me.

I once asked him if he saw the good he was doing at the shelter. I wondered if he actually saw people's lives change. He responded, "Not really."

"Then why do you do it?" I asked. After all, isn't the point to make a difference?

He responded in a compassionate, gentle, surrendering, yet unrelenting tone, and with no judgment, no indignation: "Because it's the right thing to do."

My father did not mean that statement in a moral sense. He never cites morality for the reason to do something, or anything. So I knew he must mean something else.

But what?

It was my desire to answer that question that inspired me to write this book.

TABLE OF CONTENTS

PROLOGUE...xi

THE ORDINARY WORLD..1

CALL TO ADVENTURE 5
   ME, HOME: Monday, January 5, 2009, 10:00 a.m........................ 5

REFUSE THE CALL 12
   MOVIE WORKSHOP, LDRC: Saturday,
      January 10, 2009, 1:00 p.m. 12

CROSS THE FIRST THRESHOLD...19
   DON, LDRC: Monday, January 12, 2009, 9:00 a.m. 19
   CLARENCE, LDRC: Monday, January 12, 2009, 11:00 a.m....... 24
   DWIGHT, LDRC: Monday, January 12, 2009, 1:00 p.m............. 27
   JESSICA, LDRC: Monday, January 12, 2009, 3:00 p.m.............. 29

TESTS, ALLIES AND ENEMIES 32
   DAWN, MOVIE, LDRC: Saturday, January 17, 2009, 1:00 p.m. 32
   SCOTT, CLIENT, LDRC: Monday, January 19, 2009, 1:00 p.m....34
   JESSICA, LDRC: Monday, January 19, 2009, 4:00 p.m. 40
   DAWN, MOVIE, LDRC: Saturday, January 24, 2009, 1:00 p.m. 43
   ROSS, CLIENT, LDRC: Monday, January 26, 2009, 9:00 a.m.......44
   DAVID, CASS: Monday, January 26, 2009, 11:00 a.m................ 48
   RUNNING DEER, CLIENT: Monday, January
      26, 2009, 1:00 p.m. 54
   JESSICA, LDRC: Monday, January 26, 2009, 3:00 p.m............. 58
   LARRY & RONNIE, EX-CLIENTS, LDRC:
      Tuesday, January 27, 2009, 1:00 p.m. 62

MOVIE WORKSHOP, LDRC: Saturday,
January 31, 2009, 1:00 p.m. 67
AMY, ST. JOSEPH THE WORKER: Monday,
February 2, 2009, 9:30 a.m. 70
COMPUTER CLASS, LDRC: Monday,
February 2, 2009, 11:00 a.m. 74
NANCY, THE NEW ARID CLUB: Tuesday,
February 3, 2009, 2:00 p.m. 78

THE INMOST CAVE **86**
ME, HOMELESS FOR A DAY: Monday,
February 9, 2009, 10:00 a.m. 86

ORDEALS..**117**
JON, COMPUTER CLASS, LDRC: Monday,
February 16, 2009, 9:00 a.m. 117
TONY, CLIENT, LDRC: Monday, February 16, 2009, 10 a.m. ..117
JESSICA, LDRC: Monday, February 16, 2009, 1 p.m. 124
HECTOR & PETER, MAGELLAN HEALTH
SERVICES OF ARIZONA, INC.: Tuesday,
February 17, 2009, 6 p.m. 125
JESSICA, LDRC: Monday, February 23, 2009, 10:00 a.m. 127
HECTOR, MAGELLAN HEALTH SERVICES
OF ARIZONA, INC.: Tuesday, February 24, 2009, 1 p.m. 128
LAURA, LDRC: Tuesday, February 24, 2009, 3:30 p.m. 132
JESSICA, LDRC: Monday, March 2, 2009, 1 p.m. 141
MICHAEL, CLIENT, LDRC: Tuesday, March 3, 2009, 1 p.m.....142
ART CLASS, LDRC: Saturday, March 7, 2009, 9 a.m. 146
THE NEW ARID CLUB: Saturday, March 7, 2009, 11 a.m...... 148
MOVIE WORKSHOP, LDRC: Saturday, March
7, 2009, 1:00 p.m. 151
JESSICA, LDRC: Monday, March 9, 2009, 1:00 p.m. 155
ARTHUR, CLIENT, LDRC: Tuesday, March
10, 2009, 1:00 p.m. 155
BRIAN & SEAN, PHOENIX POLICE
DEPARTMENT: Tuesday, March 10, 2009, 6 p.m. 161
A WEEK OFF: Monday, March 16, 2009 171

REWARD **172**
   JULIA, CLIENT, LDRC: Monday, March 23, 2009, 1:00 p.m. 172
   RUNNING DEER, AUTOBIOGRAPHY:
     Monday, March 30, 2009, 1:00 p.m. 177
   SCOTT, MSVA: Monday, March 30, 2009, 2 p.m. 183

THE ROAD BACK **187**
   LINDA & JEFF, LDRC CAFÉ: Monday, April
     6, 2009, 2:30 p.m. 187

EXPERIENCE **192**
   JESSICA, LDRC: Tuesday, April 14, 2009, 3 p.m. 192
   TERRY, LDRC, MSVA: Tuesday, April 14, 2009, 4:30 p.m. 194
   SCOTT, CLIENT FOLLOW-UP: Monday,
     April 20, 2009, 1:00 p.m. 198
   ARTHUR, CLIENT FOLLOW-UP: Monday,
     April 20, 2009, 2:00 p.m. 199
   RUNNING DEER, CLIENT FOLLOW-UP:
     Monday, April 20, 2009 3 p.m. 202
   BILL, CASS, MSVA: Tuesday, April 21, 2009 12 p.m. 204
   FATHER ERIC, ANDRÉ HOUSE: Tuesday,
     April 21, 2:00 p.m. 208

RESURRECTION **214**
   ARLENE, HSC: Wednesday, April 22, 2009, 10:00 a.m. 214
   CHAPLAIN DAVE, HIS HOME: Thursday,
     April 23, 2009, 11:00 a.m. 222
   DAWN, LDRC: Monday, April 27, 2:15 p.m. 227
   WOMENS' WORKSHOP, LDRC: Tuesday,
     May 19, 2009, 9:30 a.m. 230
   WOMEN'S WORKSHOP, LDRC: Tuesday,
     June 16, 2009, 9:30 a.m. 236

RETURN WITH THE ELIXIR **243**
   BEN, CASS: Monday, June 22, 2009, 1:00 p.m. 243
   TILLIE, CLIENT, LDRC: Tuesday, June 30, 2009, 11 a.m. 247
   JESSICA, LDRC: Monday, August 3, 2009, 9:00 a.m. 252
   ME, HOME: Thursday, December 31, 2009, 5:00 p.m. 258

EPILOGUE **261**

EDITORS' NOTES **263**
    TYE RABENS 263
    MARY L. HOLDEN.. 265

PROLOGUE

WHEN MY FATHER RETIRED FROM his job as a well-respected environmental scientist, I thought he might take up golf, travel the world or just watch a lot of TV. Instead, he started volunteering five days a week at a homeless shelter. I was shocked, to say the least. Who retires from 30-year career to work at a homeless shelter for free? Who fantasizes about that day when they won't have to work anymore so they can work some more at no pay and with the homeless?

Further, he admitted to me that he didn't feel his volunteering there made much of a difference. This was a solution-driven, results-based man. He wouldn't have lasted a day as a research scientist otherwise. What had happened to my father? Was he truly (as I had always suspected) crazy?

My lack of understanding only grew. During my first visit to the shelter where he worked, I had the opportunity to talk with some of the homeless persons there. I was 39 years old, and it occurred to me that I had never spoken with a homeless person before. I did not even know what the term meant.

I was also shocked to learn that many of the homeless people I spoke with seemed no different from you or me. And that scared me a bit. I'd always assumed there was a difference between them and us. That difference kept me from being "one of them," from being homeless. If there wasn't a difference, or if I didn't know what that difference was, then I could just be one chance occurrence or one unforeseen mistake away from being homeless. I had just left a stable job of 13 years for reasons I didn't fully understand. The decision, I worried, could easily be that unforeseen mistake.

But the emotions ran deeper still. I sensed some kindred feeling when I spoke to the men at the shelter. They were a reminder of a feeling of emptiness—of being out of place—that I only then realized had followed me for much of my life. At times, when things were good, I hardly noticed it. But even during good times, the emptiness had always been there.

It was that night, couched safely in my parent's home—the home I had grown up in, that I pondered my first real interaction with homeless persons.

How did they get there? Why did my father work there? What was keeping them there? I didn't have good answers to any of these questions, which led to an even greater concern: I really didn't know what homelessness was. I was 39 years old, yet I couldn't hold a discussion with someone about homelessness beyond the fact that these persons had no homes.

As a person who prides himself on being knowledgeable about the conditions of the world and, more importantly, the causes of those conditions, it bothered me that I didn't know or understand anything about what I was witnessing. I had literally never thought about "it." I had just chalked "it" up to bad luck, mental illness, drug addiction or just plain laziness. But the brief time I spent with the men at my father's shelter had already poked holes in such sophomoric theories.

Bad luck couldn't explain why someone stayed homeless. True, some of the men seemed a bit "off," but so have a lot of the people I have met and even worked with. Drug addiction seemed like a factor for some but may have been more of a symptom than a cause. (And again, many of the people I used to work with in corporate America had drug addictions.) As for laziness, many of the men worked very hard, harder than I was accustomed to. It just didn't seem to get them anywhere, and of course, I didn't know why.

My simple visit with my father had left me with a myriad of complicated questions. What made them homeless and me not? Did they deserve their lot? Why did the entire issue scare me to think about or to get close to? I think many of us at some time in our lives have asked at least a few of these questions. But most of us, myself included, have never really answered them except by assigning some unexplored blanket answer. They're crazy. Lazy. On drugs. Unfortunate.

I knew that in order to properly answer any of those questions, I would have to understand the subject they all stemmed from. I would have to understand what the term "homelessness" really means. At the time, I just knew that I did not know.

So it was over a family dinner of steamed artichokes—a dish my mother had made for us hundreds of times—that the idea came to me. I would interview homeless people, and also those like my father who worked with them, in order to discover answers to the questions of homelessness. What the term *homeless* really means. That simple man, that innocuous visit, that familiar dinner and that small idea are what started this book.

THE ORDINARY WORLD

M Y INTENT FOR THIS BOOK was to research homelessness in a brand new way so that by the end, my readers and I would have a real understanding of what the word means—and not just in a technical sense. This book grasps at the emotional scope and depth of the concept.

I started by reading a couple of books on the history of homelessness in America, hoping that an understanding of the past would lead to an understanding of the present. I learned that homelessness has been a phenomenon in our society since the dawn of Western culture on this continent. It was also present in European society long before we colonized the North American continent. But interestingly enough, the homeless population exploded during the Industrial Revolution and has basically not subsided since.

Some of the books I read suggested that the birth of large industry fueled the exponential increase in the rates and numbers of homeless persons in America. Factories employed large numbers of people, and then because of seasonal demands, increased efficiency, or economic conditions, laid them off. These workers then were released in large numbers into the cities that could hardly reabsorb them.

In addition to the powerful flux of supply and demand during this period, there was also a change from rural to urban lifestyles. Farm life was disappearing—for it was also becoming industrialized—and city life was growing. If you wanted to work, you needed to move to the city. Some of these books on the history of homelessness in America suggested that this change further fueled homelessness, as many persons were just not suited for factory work, but it was the only work to be found.

The introduction of interchangeable parts created a move toward greater conformity in our society. As all mechanical parts had to conform, it was not unreasonable to assume that those who made them had to do the same. To many, repetitious tasks done for long hours inside dark, stuffy buildings simply did not suit their nature, and they often couldn't or wouldn't hold down such jobs.

And of course, wars occurred. More importantly, wars ended. At the end of each war in U.S. history, there was a surge in homelessness as soldiers returned and couldn't find work or were unable to work.

These theories made sense to me, but they still didn't give me an understanding of what homelessness means today. They instead focused on the many academic aspects, possible historical causes, facts and figures. While useful, this background research doesn't explain why Joe X or Jane Y is on Z Street corner today.

I couldn't just write off the idea of homelessness by blaming it on modernization. Factory conditions today are far better than during the dawn of the Industrial Revolution, but homeless numbers are not. City life is better, too. We've had a century to adjust. And not all homeless people are veterans. The causes just could not be that simple.

Still, the research I did had value to inform me that homelessness affects many different types of people and has many different causes. I had a new appreciation for the diversity of the issues I was about to tackle. But I still felt that I was looking in through the peephole of some front door, trying to get a feel for the house inside. So I kept reading, finding books that documented the stories of homeless persons. Their stories were fascinating and sad. I felt great sympathy for the individuals and got lost in detail after shocking detail. After all those stories, I thought I'd have a pretty good understanding of homelessness.

But I didn't.

I was still left with a feeling that I didn't know the people behind these stories. Most important to understanding homelessness is witnessing the people, knowing their stories personally and coming to learn how they are related. What connections allow all these different people to fall under the category of homeless? And what does that category even mean?

Socially, I realized that the people I came in contact with most days were all basically the same. This is not to say that they made the same amount of money, dressed the same, and thought the exact same thoughts as me. Rather, I mean they all made money, bought their clothes in retail stores, and digested roughly the same media. The choice in my world for tonight's dinner is to eat in or eat out. Pondering those two options leaves no room to consider a third: don't eat at all. Or a fourth: eat, but out of a trash can. Like me before I started to research, you may not notice these givens in our similar worldview, because they seem so ordinary. To this extent, I remained blind to the larger picture.

From this, my plan to understand homelessness emerged. I thought I'd begin by interviewing homeless persons and those who work with them—not about their stories, but about who they really are and what they think about homelessness. After all, if anyone knows what homelessness is, these people do. It started as a hunch, a shot in the dark. I wanted an answer to my question but didn't even fully understand what I was asking.

Unlike other books on the homeless, I did not want to interview people without shelter about the details of their lives. Instead, I wanted to interview them on their thoughts on life. I wanted to find out what makes them different from—or the same as—you and me. And since insight is a mater of perspective, I was fairly sure they would have new insights due to their different perspectives. I hoped to gain a new vantage point—the vantage point I needed to properly interpret the histories and stories of homelessness. By the end, I might actually understand the concept of homelessness itself.

There is no growth in understanding unless you dare to look into the unknown and outside your usual reality. If ours is the ordinary world, theirs is a special world—not necessarily better or worse but running parallel. While a real part of our society, the homeless are anything but part of our daily lives. Even if we see them daily, we don't know them. Just how separated or connected the homeless really are from the rest of us was yet another question I could not answer. Were these worlds really separate, or was I just blind to the connections?

Speak to the average, normal, and ordinary and you will learn what you already know: the average, normal, and ordinary. If you think about it, this is what we do most of the time. We speak to people who share our general worldview. But homelessness is a whole other world, and to us who have housing, it is anything but ordinary.

Unsatisfied by facts and histories, I was determined that my book would focus on the philosophies of those who dare to live outside the norm and those who dare to work with them.

I considered that the special world could teach me a lot about the ordinary world.

Ordinary World. Photo by: Steven Sable.

CALL TO ADVENTURE

ME, HOME: Monday, January 5, 2009, 10:00 a.m.

IT IS THE FIRST DAY of the rest of my life, a day that seems quite uncertain at the moment. I awake with a rush of worries and concerns. This feeling is all too familiar lately. I recently left my corporate job, no longer able to justify staying in a position that demanded long hours and was of little personal interest. I don't know where my next paycheck will come from or if I might also be homeless in the near future.

But today, I have an appointment to meet with Jessica Berg, the executive director of the Lodestar Daily Resource Center (LDRC), LLC, in Phoenix, Arizona. From what I've gathered, LDRC is a type of central services center for homeless persons. The director was very receptive to the idea of my book. She felt that interviewing willing clients would give them a much-needed voice and act as a type of therapy. She also hoped it would help to raise public awareness—that is, if it ever got published. We both know that is a long shot—but my whole life feels like a long shot at the moment.

So I have a contact, and an accommodating one at that. It has taken me weeks of e-mails and phone calls to find someone interested in my project, so I should be excited to get started. But instead, I awake in a less-than-great mood. My back had gone out in a bad way a few days earlier, and I don't even want to try to get out of bed. I wonder how long I will suffer its crippling effects. The last two times this happened, it was months before I could get out of a chair properly.

I lay in bed now, belabored over feelings of unemployment, injury, and loneliness from a recently ended relationship. I'm not sure I want to start writing a book—and will there be a book anyway? I only have a glimmer of an idea of what I am looking for.

Curiosity may not sell books, but for me, it's what writes them. So I pry myself out of bed, shower, and leave my middle-class home in northern

Phoenix to head downtown. As I turn off 7th Avenue onto Washington Street, things start to change.

The buildings, if anything, improve. Downtown Phoenix has been well attended to by city planners in recent years. There is the Carnegie Library, a turn-of-the-last-century red brick structure in the center of a beautifully maintained park with large old trees towering above. Located across the street is the quaint Arizona Skies Café and Coffee Bar. The capitol is just a mile in front of me to the west, and other well-maintained civic buildings are all around.

The people are what I most notice changing. All of a sudden, there they are: homeless persons, or those whom I presume to be homeless. Their numbers increase as I turn onto 12th Avenue; they number in the hundreds by the time I reach LDRC. I have to slow my Honda Fit down to a crawl so as not to hit anyone.

I pass through the sea of people, through the open gates, and am struck by the sheer size of this place. The LDRC is just one building on what I now realize is a very large spread called the Human Services Campus. I was expecting a single building like the shelter where my father volunteered, but I feel as if I'm traveling out of the orbit of the ordinary world and entering a strange new one. It occurs to me that we spend billions of dollars looking for life on other planets when we don't even recognize all of the life right in our own backyards. I have lived in Phoenix for 18 years and never known this place was here—in the middle of downtown.

The Human Services Campus looks like a typical community college campus. Stepping out of the car, I feel like an urban astronaut on this cool January day. One small step for man, one giant step for a man with a hurt back. The smell of cigarette smoke hits me at once. I look at the other cars in the parking lot, mostly the cars of homeless persons seeking services there. My car sticks out like a sore thumb. I know it's brand new, but this is the only time in my entire life that my car is the nicest, most expensive one in the entire parking lot. In Scottsdale, my car would be one of the least expensive in the parking lot. No one seems to notice, but I do.

I walk across the lawn toward the front doors of the LDRC located in the center of the campus. Laptop bag over my shoulder, strolling toward the institutional double doors, my feeling of being out of place increases. I am struck by the diversity surrounding me. Each person here is radically different from his or her neighbor. They each dress in a way that is completely unique to everyone else. It is as if every single person is from a different era, past and/or future.

I've lived a lot of life in my 39 years and am therefore shocked to feel so ill at ease, nervous, alien. And it is all coming from me. The people I pass by greet me with smiles, hellos and even sometimes hollow indifference, but no animosity—not even curiosity. Not one single person looks at me as though I don't belong here. And I've been in places where they make it very clear you don't belong. For some strange reason, that type of fear bothers me much less than my present alienation. The fear of danger bothers me less than the fear of being an outcast, of not fitting in.

The atmosphere changes as I enter Lodestar Day Resource Center through the double institutional style metal doors. It smells warm and stale in here—not exactly filthy, but like wet dirt. In certain Scottsdale locations, one is overwhelmed with aromas too, each sweeter and sappier than the last. I tell Ryan, a young guy at the front desk, that I have a meeting with Ms. Berg and take a seat in one of the few available chairs nearby. There are two rows of colored plastic chairs—maybe 20 in all—with additional seating in the form of a very long bench built into the dividing wall between the reception area from the large main lobby. The wall is less than four feet high, so I can easily crane over it to view the many round tables and chairs beyond. Two of the center's walls are entirely made of thick glass and framed with metal. They do little to mitigate the industrial atmosphere.

And of course, the lobby is filled with people, looking as though they are from every place and space as they are filling every place and space.

I am immersed in the sounds of hundreds of conversations, culture shocked as I try to take it all in. I look down a long hallway that extends from the lobby to the right. It ends in double doors, and staff members occasionally enter or exit through them, whipping out an access card before disappearing. As I watch, the left one opens and out walks a young, petite woman in her thirties, with a fashion sense that could be described as 'professional bohemian.' She looks at the waiting area from a distance for a brief moment before her eyes land on me. She smiles knowingly. I don't know if it is the look on my face or fact that she recognizes everyone but me.

"Michael?"

I smile and nod. Her voice is sweet, relaxed.

"I'm Jessica Berg."

She looks like she might belong behind the counter of a boutique coffee shop—not an attribute I would expect from someone who deals on a daily basis with the rugged realities of the homeless, whatever those realities are.

Jessica speaks quietly, clearly, and with great articulation. She is excited to share. I have the crazy thought that she has the power of a fairy: delicate and light, yet also charming, strong and fearless.

As we walk together amongst the clients, Jessica explains that the Human Service Campus is arguably the first homeless campus formed in the United States. In November 2005, Maricopa County decided it might be a good idea to group a number of homeless-related organizations and services together in the same geographic area. The 25,000-square-foot facility known as the LDRC is meant to be the liaison point for directing people to the resources they need. On a sprawling 11-acre campus, that is no small task.

Jessica explains that the name Lodestar comes from one of the main contributing foundations (Arizona State University Lodestar Center for Philanthropy & Nonprofit Innovation), and is also a term for a guiding star, a tool used by sailors for navigation. Lodestar is a point of reference, a guide in choppy seas. Clients can come to the LDRC and get directed to various other service organizations on and around campus, not to mention what seems like a plethora of services offered by the LDRC itself. Jessica further explains she refers to the homeless people they serve as *clients* because she and her staff work for them, just like any other business. Apparently it's about "service, not charity." And no, I don't fully get what that means.

The campus has five anchor agencies: Central Arizona Shelter Services (CASS), Maricopa County Healthcare for the Homeless, Northwest Organization for Voluntary Alternatives (NOVA)—Safe Haven, St. Joseph the Worker, and St. Vincent de Paul.

The campus is a massively ambitious operation meant to coordinate and address every aspect of the immediate and long-term homeless challenge. It's truly astounding in it's scope and vision. And Jessica hints that the LDRC helps clients navigate the campus and even life itself.

All of the main five agencies stand alone as separate entities under LDRC's umbrella. Jessica explains that she has no authority over much of the campus, even many of the agencies located within the LDRC building. The campus is a "campus of cooperation," she says. If that's the case, I instantly see why Jessica is perfect for the job. Her real title should be CEO of Cooperation.

Jessica continues walking me around the LDRC and I continue to feel overwhelmed. I expected to see a shelter that housed and fed a few hundred homeless people. I am now in the center of a gigantic homeless campus with hundreds (perhaps a thousand) of homeless persons. Up until this point in my life, I've never seen a total of a thousand homeless persons in my life and never more than a dozen homeless persons in the same place.

When I got in my car just an hour ago I was wondering if there was really a book idea to be found here. But now Jessica is spewing out more relevant information than I can record. The side questions are endless. I only wonder which ones to pursue.

I could write a book about Jessica alone. This woman is eclectic. Before holding this position she was an art therapist, summer camp director and she earned degrees in public administration and art therapy, which as she says "is ironically a great combination" for what she's currently doing. That is, if anything could prepare one for what she's doing. Nowhere else in the country does a nonprofit effort quite like this one exist.

I ask her point blank if she likes her job, which she has now been in for two years. She lights up in a rosy, Christmassy sort of way. "Yes! I love it!"

"Doesn't it get draining? Frustrating?" I ask.

"Well sure, of course, sometimes." What bothers Jessica most is when people don't work together. "We have to get rid of egos here and stick to the goal, and for the most part that's what we do," she says.

Jessica leads me into her office behind double doors at the end of a hallway. I'm finally able to lower myself into a chair (I hate looking disabled) and open my laptop to take proper notes. I'm already upset at the wealth of information I failed to capture on tape or paper.

"So Jessica, how do you do a job that's never been done before?" I ask.

Jessica explains that one of her hobbies is improvisation. "The first rule of improv is: yes, and . . ." This is her guiding principle, her lodestar. She continues, "In improv, you never deny what you have been given. You only look as to what you can add to it."

This approach makes sense, because the LDRC in many ways is an improvisational concept. It is the newest agency on the campus (the other agencies existed in other locations prior to the creation of the campus), and they are still defining and discovering the identity of LDRC beyond simply coordination of services.

Before I can ask another question, a woman enters into the office— casually—but like a woman on a mission who is not unprepared to kick some ass if necessary—as her cowboy boots imply.

"You're going to love Dawn," Jessica says by way of introduction. She explains that Dawn Shires started as a volunteer but now wears many hats at the LDRC, namely as the volunteer coordinator. While being on staff means a paycheck, I assume no one works here for the salary.

Dawn says hello, but seems too busy to talk.

"What's the movie this week?" Jessica asks her.

Dawn replies with a smart-alecky grin and a New Jersey accent: "Now you know I'm not going to tell you that."

"Movie?" I venture.

"Yeah, people try and trick me into telling them what the movie is going to be," Dawn replies.

I try again. "Movie?"

Dawn catches herself, realizing that I have no idea what she's talking about. She sits down and, at 60 M.P.H., explains that every Saturday she holds a movie workshop for the homeless.

It sounds like a cute idea, but impractical. I'm not quite sure what all the people in that lobby need, but I'm pretty sure it isn't a movie workshop. Still, it's obvious to me that Dawn is not into cute and is very into practical.

Seeing my look of confusion, Dawn lays out the objective of the workshop. Essentially, she carefully picks movies that feature a hero who has to conquer some great obstacle. Then, she leads a group discussion about the movie and how the hero overcame his or her challenges.

The point is "to get them to identify with the character and see that they are their own vehicles for change," Dawn says, still in rapid-fire mode. She is trying to get the "head, heart and will aligned" for each client who attends the workshop.

By this point, I feel overwhelmed. Dawn keeps talking faster and starts dropping phrases like, "your state of residence is not your identity," "trigger event" and "strategic thinking."

My head is whirling. I was not expecting these impassioned persons to be staffing this place, this place that exploded from a small shelter in my mind to a giant campus in reality—a campus that I didn't even know existed, and right in the middle of my city. And I definitely did not expect to see such radical approaches to changing human behavior put into practice while housing, job assistance and dozens of other services are provided simultaneously.

Suddenly, I feel like I might cry. Not just because I saw all these depressing looking people on the way in. (I did.) Not just because I feel so out of place. (I do.) And it's not even exactly that I have been feeling depressed myself lately (though I have). It's because these women are so damn impassioned about what they are doing! And I'm assuming, they, like the rest of us, have plenty of their own struggles to deal with. It is such a contrast to the "woe as me" feelings I woke up with.

Fighting back the unexpected tears, I ask Dawn why she does it. She seems confused, almost exasperated. "Does anyone even have to ask that question? It's my gift. It's what I've always done. That's what we do here. We share our gifts."

I ask her what her education was for doing all this, and she almost scoffs at the question. "It's just what I've always done since I was fourteen." She seems to imply that if the questions and problems are about life, then life is the necessary educational background. Especially when you're trying to fix something that no one has ever fixed before. There are no formulas, no schools on ending homelessness. These people at Lodestar are navigating their own course.

I ask if I can come to the movie on Saturday and Dawn is fine with it—not ecstatic, just fine. She doesn't seem to care if anyone notices what she is doing. I ask her if she ever feels down about her progress. (I ask for my research, but also for my own emotional state.)

Dawn again replies with that surprised of course look. "All of the time. I feel like people aren't making enough progress or I'm not helping enough people. But then I remember that I'm contributing, and what is supposed to be happing is happening. The timing is not up to me."

I tell Dawn and Jessica I have to conclude the interview and digest everything, setting up a later date to talk. I need a game plan for how to proceed. I've been complaining about the bills, my ex-wife, my ex-girlfriend, my hurting back . . . and these people have been changing lives! I'm not even sure which direction to take the book, because this brief visit to LDRC has already blown all my ideas out of the water.

This place is not as sure, simple, typical, or small as I might have thought.

Jessica and Dawn make me consider the power of passion. They gave me the call to adventure.

And frankly, our first meeting scared the shit out of me.

REFUSE THE CALL

MOVIE WORKSHOP, LDRC:
Saturday, January 10, 2009, 1:00 p.m.

I'M EXCITED ABOUT TODAY'S VISIT to the Human Services Campus, and yet, feeling like I might really not be up for all this. The problems and solutions seem bigger than life—or at least much bigger than me—after talking to Jessica and Dawn. Can I capture this enigma on paper? It's weird and disturbing to be surrounded by something but still not understand it.

I am somewhat more comfortable this time setting foot onto the Human Services Campus lawn than on my first visit. The LDRC closes every day from 11:00 a.m. to 1:00 p.m. I arrive about 15 minutes before 1 and stand outside with the clients as we wait for the center to reopen. I notice a long line forming in front of a window to the right of the main entrance. One of the clients, a man who says he is from Ohio, sees the look of curiosity on my face and explains that they get their mail here. The LDRC has its own post office? He asks if it is my first time here. Apparently I still stand out.

What is your address? The LDRC hosts the only sanctioned homeless post office in the United States serving 5,000 individuals. The ZIP code is 85007. Photo by: Ashton Romano.

Mr. Ohio is about 30 years old and looks like a college student with sunglasses and a small backpack. He says arrived on campus just nine days ago. He has been homeless for two months and wanted to move to a place that had warm weather. You might assume that many homeless people would do the same but per capita, Arizona is right at the national average for homelessness.

I ask Mr. Ohio how things are going for him so far.

"It's going pretty well," he replies. "Especially considering that I am bipolar and have social anxiety."

This man seems clean cut, well spoken, well educated. As for social anxiety, doesn't everyone have that? The admission of bipolar disorder might scare some off, but to me he is kind, articulate and welcoming, and we chat until the doors open. For me, it's nice not feeling like such an outsider any more.

The LDRC doors swing open promptly at 1 p.m., greeting us with a waft of bleach smell. They mop the floors twice a day here. A couple hundred people migrate into the huge lobby. Some sit down on small bench near the front of the main desk, where I'm told they will often remain until being ushered out at closing time, almost four hours later. But if a client doesn't go to the front desk for information or past it for activities and services, one of the staff will eventually engage the person. Their main purpose at LDRC is just to acknowledge a person's existence and guide them toward assistance.

People veer off in all directions after entering LDRC. I follow a crowd past the front desk and across the large lobby behind it, toward a glass door set in a glass wall in the back. The door opens unto a small café area with a service counter. It seems odd to me: a café in a homeless services center? Classroom doors line the adjacent hall, to the right of the café seating area. In search of the movie workshop, I open one and am greeted with the smell of popcorn.

Besides that, it appears to be a typical classroom: plain walls, a whiteboard, some tables, some chairs. I want to sit in back. My idea is to observe, take notes, but not get involved, to remain objective like a scientist or a journalist. But my old laptop has no battery life left and the only outlet for it is in the front row.

Dawn hardly notices me as she sets up the projector. I plug in my laptop as people quietly shuffle in. They run out of folding chairs, and a client aid brings in more chairs to accommodate the still-growing group. Eventually there are at least 60 people in the small room. The popcorn machine is popping away and the client aide passes out bags of salty goodness to everyone, along with bottles of Gatorade that had been donated to the center. With us all packed together, the clean bleach smell dissipates and is replaced by that wet dirt smell, now intermixed with popcorn.

Dawn has notes already on the whiteboard and a matching handout:

Hero's Journey

1. Heroes are introduced in THE ORDINARY WORLD, where . . .
2. . . . they received the CALL TO ADVENTURE.
3. They are reluctant at first or REFUSE THE CALL, but . . .
4. . . . are encouraged by a mentor to CROSS THE FIRST THRESHOLD and enter the Special World, where . . .
5. . . . they encounter TESTS, ALLIES, AND ENEMIES.
6. They APPROACH THE INMOST CAVE, crossing a second threshold . . .
7. . . . where they endure the ORDEAL.
8. They take possession of their REWARD and . . .
9. . . . are pursued on THE ROAD BACK to the Ordinary World.
10. They cross the third threshold into EXPERIENCE, then undergo . . .
11. . . . a RESURRECTION, and are transformed by the experience.
12. They RETURN WITH THE ELIXIR, a boon or treasure to benefit the Ordinary World.

The "Hero's Journey" is a pattern of narrative identified by the American scholar Joseph Campbell. Dawn has figured out how to use it in this "workshop," a class that draws viewers who might just come in for the "entertainment." Dawn is lively and commanding. She engages the crowd by asking us first to guess the movie. "It's a 1989 drama with and incredible sound track."

There are many guesses and I can see Dawn straining to hear each person as they call out. None are correct.

"It's got Morgan Freeman and John Gielgud and Stephen Dorff in it."

Still many more people try and guess, but none are successful. To be honest, I have no idea myself.

Dawn's last hint: "Set in Africa."

By now almost half the class is volleying excited guesses around the classroom. Dawn diplomatically receives each attempt. Finally she tells us it is "The Power of One." And by now everyone is pretty excited to watch it, including me. Everyone feels a part of the workshop, the class, the community. She's done a great job at engaging the crowd and building anticipation. Now that she has everyone's attention, Dawn discusses what is on the whiteboard and the handout before the movie begins. With the command of a college professor, she dictates that she wants us to look for each stage of the hero's journey.

"This is a powerful movie because the hero loses everything before he becomes who he needs to become," Dawn says. "The hero always has the decision to make as to whether to follow a particular path or not."

That hit close to home. I started a few days ago wondering if this project was worthy of my time. Now I am wondering if I am worthy of the project. This place feels a little too important, too life-or-death.

Dawn lists too many things to mention. She focuses on how the hero overcomes problems, and also that "the hero receives rewards from overcoming those challenges and then shares those gifts with others."

Then, there are bonus questions: "What is the role of hope? What is the purpose of all these losses? There has to be a reason for this tremendous loss!" she hammers in the last point.

The room eventually grows quiet and Dawn starts the movie, which is about apartheid and one man's challenge to make a difference in a world of prejudice and the suffering that comes from it. It's a powerful movie with many important messages. Dawn obviously selected it for a reason.

Halfway through, Dawn stops the movie. She once again has our attention. I've forgotten I'm here to do research, and instead get completely engaged in the discourse. So much for remaining objective.

Dawn asks questions of the group to identify what steps of the hero's journey the main character has gone through thus far. As the clients identify the steps, Dawn discusses the value of each one as an integral portion and process of the entire journey. She makes few statements, answering questions with more questions. Dawn doesn't preach—she draws out. The overall lesson appears after a long discussion: how to overcome fear. And, I've noticed that Dawn purposefully switches from talking about the main character to generalizing about all of us, talking about "we" instead of "he."

I can relate to so much of what she is talking about. And, judging by the looks on the faces around me, I'm not the only one who connects to the material. Dawn is aware, not only of what she is doing to get us to relate to the hero in the movie, but also of what to do with that emotional connection. She teaches to the heart, not the head. We switch between referring to the hero in the movie and to us as individuals, as though they are synonymous.

"When does he face his fears? How does he learn to overcome his fears?" Dawn asks us all. "What is the bigger enemy that we are really being faced with?"

"Racism," members in the class say.

"Yes," says Dawn, "this is the beginning of apartheid. But what else?" The point is that our own personal fears must be overcome before outside problems can be conquered. I can see on the faces of some of the students that they get it, that they are thinking about their own fears. I sure am. The LDRC movie workshop proves itself to be quite the amazing experience. I *know* all the stuff we are talking about, but have never *felt* it like this before.

She gives us a 10-minute biology break, and I have my first opportunity to use the bathroom in the lobby. I'm a little apprehensive. This is a restroom that is utilized by hundreds and hundreds of people a day. People are shaving in the sinks. A guy in the corner is injecting insulin. While the space is not unbearable, it makes me appreciate the privacy of my own bathroom. I wonder—when was the last time one of these people pooped in privacy?

When I reenter the class, Dawn is talking about courage. We all get fired up about how the hero stood up for the rights of others. After riling us up in discussion she asks, "Why will people stand up for others, but not for themselves?"

Professor Dawn has us.

Most of us have stood up for someone else at some point in life. But I can hear the gears whirling—everyone is starting to think about why they won't do the same for themselves. And I'm sure I see a twinkle in Dawn's eye. While this is an open, loose forum, it is also very calculated and directed. And it's working. I ask myself: Why are we willing to die for those we love, but still be so afraid to live for ourselves?

Dawn, as if she knows she has us hooked, quietly reels us in. Her voice lowers. We have to strain a bit to hear. "We stand up for others because we love them and identify with their worth. So we must do the same for ourselves, because there must be worthiness in us."

Her voice rolls off into silence, a silence that is met by our silence. Finally, Dawn starts the movie again.

I quickly get reabsorbed along with everyone else. And there is this line in the movie that strikes me because it reminds me of what they seem to be doing at LDRC. A character makes the point that "Inclusion, not exclusion, is the key to human survival."

Is that really true? Most of us would like to say it's true. But is that because we should? How much excluding of others do *I* do without even thinking about it?

I feel overwhelmed. No one can tell, of course, because as a man, I've spent almost 40 years learning to pretend that I don't have feelings. But if I were more comfortable with myself, less in control, I would be crying right now. I wonder if I will feel this way every time I'm at the LDRC?

Finally it ends. Not the feelings, but the movie.

"So . . . what did you think?" Dawn asks.

The class members give many responses: what they hated, loved, identified with, wished they could change. But they are all emotional responses, emotional and thoughtful, head and heart.

"There is a path, if you want to accept the challenge," Dawn says. She continues to lead the class through the remaining steps in the Myth of the Hero. "There are rewards for accepting and overcoming the challenge. The hero receives gifts and they are multiplied when shared with others, when given back to the community. But if we don't follow our path, the myth becomes meaningless."

Maybe this should be inspiring me to say yes to this book project, to commit to it fully. But if anything, the movie workshop leaves me feeling open and vulnerable.

Dawn should write this damn book! This is way too big and complex a subject for me to capture. I need to get a job. I can't even capture this movie workshop. I can't even capture this one class of this movie workshop.

Under the guise of composing my notes, I stay in the classroom late to compose myself. As I close my laptop and look up at Dawn, she asks me how I liked the workshop. I'm almost speechless.

"Amazing," I say, "truly amazing!"

I've been to a lot of movies and I've taken a lot of college courses. This group of people was one of the quietest groups I have ever sat with through a movie and one of the most engaged with whom I have ever taken a college class.

Dawn makes me consider that true understanding is getting things from one's head into one's heart.

CROSS THE FIRST THRESHOLD

DON, LDRC: Monday, January 12, 2009, 9:00 a.m.

J ESSICA HAD SUGGESTED INTERVIEWING DON because he met both
of my criteria: A staff member at the LDRC who works with homeless
clients, and a former client himself.

I wait for Don in the computer lab in one of the LDRC's many small
classrooms. It has eight computers on which a client volunteer teaches
typing and basic computing skills. Other times, it is open to clients so
that they can search for jobs and check email—necessities in the 21st
century.

The room is not in use for the next two hours, so I've been given
permission to conduct my first interview here. I sit waiting in what used
to be a nice ergonomic office chair, now worn with broken springs so that
it tilts to the left and leans dangerously far backwards. Most of the chairs
in the room look to be in similar states of wear. It makes me think of the
hundreds of clients I had just walked through to get to this computer lab.

Don enters the room. He is a wiry man with a ponytail who seems
short but is a deceptive six feet tall. The weight of the world seems to have
compressed him down a bit. Don looks healthy, but his skin is the type I
am all too used to seeing in the Southwest. He has rancher's skin, parched
by the sun and hot, dry winds.

I introduce myself and ask him how he is doing—typical small talk,
a greeting to which we don't really expect an answer, but apparently not a
light question around here.

"Not great, but I've been worse," Don says. He asks me the same and
listens to my answer.

This gives me a chance to study his face. He has kind but sad blue eyes
and they are a little small for his face, a little sunken in, the kind of eyes
that have seen too much. But they are clear and clean like they are open to
the world. They look like bright blue eggs resting in small white nests.

I explain my project, which is just to learn about homelessness . . . I think. He seems calm but apprehensive.

Don opens up. He is 59 years old and had been homeless before, but now lives in a trailer far from the LDRC. He rides his bike to the bus stop every day. Don does odd jobs, but mainly works in the mailroom.

"Lots of different ways people become homeless. There's all kinds out there," Don says, gesturing behind him, as if to the people right outside the doors. "What's here is just a small piece."

Because I still don't know the campus well, Don explains that there are two different places here for people to sleep. Central Arizona Shelter Services (CASS) houses 400 persons each night. The other major location is for overflow that staff prefers to call the Outreach Facility. It sleeps another 300-plus. Don says the Outreach Facility has a more negative perception among clients: "It's pretty bad over there. Dirty, dangerous." Don has slept in both, and a whole bunch of other places.

Don was a trucker from Illinois. He got in trouble in Arizona for something that he does not mention. I don't ask. They didn't process the charges and three years later, he got in trouble in Illinois and was sent back to the Grand Canyon State. He served almost three years in an Arizona prison and is now on probation, with at least five years to go.

"Sorry for rambling a bit," Don says, like a strong, silent type catching himself in a moment of chatty weakness. "I don't know if that's what you are looking for."

"I want you to ramble. And remember, I don't know what I'm looking for."

He nods and continues to explain that while in prison he lost everything: job, house, family. This is a common theme of those who've been imprisoned. Few employers (or spouses, for that matter) are going to hold your place or position for you until you get back. And who's going to make your house payments in the meantime? Don has 26-year-old twin sons who live elsewhere in the country. He talks to them every week and loves them dearly. "They're doing well, but I can't go live closer to them because of my probation," Don says. This too is a common theme. "It's been five years since I seen my one son, and two since the other."

I can't imagine not being able to see my twins, who are now 14.

From what I can gather, Don's greatest pain comes from the shame over being in prison coupled with the reality of not being able to see his kids. I ask him if he had any money when he got out and he explains that he had about $50 from working in the prison at 15 cents per hour for three years.

"When you get out they just drop you off at the parole office and tell you to go to the homeless shelter," Don says. "I think you'll find that half the people on campus are fresh out of prison."

This can make the area around the Human Services Campus a dangerous place, Don explains: "People still have that prison mentality. Some guy cut ahead of some people in the food line. And a guy cut his throat."

I ask Don how common this is, and he replies that during a couple months' period there were five or six people killed. Death also comes in the form of heatstroke and dehydration during the Arizona summers, he adds. But an increased police presence in recent years has cut down on violence and crime among the homeless.

Next, Don tells me about the differences in attitude among the agencies on campus.

"They are nicer [at LDRC] than the staff at CASS, but that just might be because CASS is dealing with a rougher group of people," Don says. "But here, the staff and volunteers seem, I don't know, more experienced. CASS might be rougher because you have just too many people in a small space and a lot of them still have that prison attitude."

Keeping the topics fresh, I ask him about his job in the mailroom. "I try and get out personal letters first, then the checks," Don says. "Those personal letters are often the only contact these people have with friends and family. That is more important than even the checks. People are lonely. If it wasn't for my weekly phone calls with my sons and the staff here, I would feel all alone."

Don talks about working in the café and at the clothing bank. There, he figured out a way for the organization to save a bit of money. They put together packages for persons moving into housing. They buy things like pots, pans, dishes and utensils, as well as other household sundries so people won't have added expenses while trying to transition into their new lives.

"When we get people into housing, we want people to stay there," he says. "Even in CASS, they want you to stay there the full six months so you can be successful when you move out, so you can save up enough money and be ready." Don realized that the clothing bank received many of these household items, but passed them on to the Salvation Army because they only deal with clothing. He started taking these items to help compile the care packages for the newly housed. He concludes in an Eeyore sort of way, "It's not much, you know. But every little bit helps."

His attitude of non-attachment to good deeds makes the fact that Don has practiced Buddhism for about eight years less surprising.

"I just see so much misery. I just want to cry," he says. "I've pulled myself away from that, but I still don't want to be here. I don't consider Buddhism a religion. I believe strongly my religion is Kindness. Like the Dali Lama says, all religions are the same. All people are equal in my mind, because we all want the same thing, to be happy and to be free from suffering. It makes me feel like everyone is my family."

Don pauses; maybe he is unsure how much more talking with me to allow.

"Everyone in this world has been someone's mother at one time, so you should treat them that way, like they're your mother," he continues. "When you feel that way, you can get by the anger and talk to others and then they smile. It helps. I think I've turned a lot of frowns into smiles and I think it helps. I used to see differences in people. I used to see different races, but not anymore. Colors don't make any difference. I don't notice it. Since I've been here, I've gotten deeper and deeper into that."

I'm noticing a definite change in Don since he started talking. He is more optimistic and sure of himself. It reminds me how much it helps to just talk to someone who is really listening. Don seems to telepathically agree with my thoughts.

"We all need help and guidance," he says. "Hell, I do. I'm on disability insurance because of depression. That's why I'm here, because it helps with my depression. When I don't work here, I get depressed. This place is the best part of my life . . . except for my kids."

I explain to Don that I want to ask him three questions, but I'm leaving their interpretation up to him. I reassure him that there are no right or wrong answers; they are just meant to give the reader insight into him as an individual.

What is the meaning of life?

That's a difficult question. I think the meaning of life is for people to get along and be happy, for people to get away from anger and hatred. And it's happening gradually. But you still see so many wars and most are fought because of religion. I guess the meaning to life is like the word Buddha is—to awaken from your delusional state of mind, which is conditioned to you as you grow up. When you can awaken to that then there is a calmness to that. If everyone could learn this, then there would be no wars. There would probably be no homeless. The rich would not be bitching about taxes. I can't say I'm all for socialism, but I think we should move closer to it.

What are your thoughts about society and/or societies in general?

This society is too materialistic and too self-centered. A lot of societies are that way. I think the poorer a country is, the less under dictatorship, the more they take care of each other. When there are bad feelings and a large population of people, everything seems to break apart. It's like Lehman Brothers, all these people lost this money and these guys walk away with all this money. I've drove a truck for 14 years. I've been all over the country. This is worst I seen in this town of homelessness. I've always lived in smaller towns. I hear L.A. is worse but I haven't seen it. In small towns there's always someone to help you out. When we do the mail, letters from home are the first thing we pull out because that's the most important.

Who are you?

I'm a father. I'm a family man. I lost my wife to divorce because of the trouble I got in and drugs and alcohol. I'm a hard worker. I've been off drugs for seven and eight years. I try to be kind. I try to be helpful. I do what I can. I try not to be selfish, but I still am sometimes. I pray to be free from anger, jealousy, hatred.

I ask Don if there is anything else he would like to tell me, anything at all.

"I think this place is a wonderful place and it gets better all the time," he says of LDRC. "I think they are setting some pretty aggressive goals to end homelessness in three years . . . We're hidden back here. You can go anywhere in town and just look at bus stops and see what you see. Every bus stop has someone there. Every bridge has blankets under it. Just look and see. It's everywhere. I have run into entire homeless camps hidden throughout the city."

Don ends by again apologizing for rambling on and getting off the point. And again, I reassure him that he did not do either.

As the trucker saunters out I think of what a brave man he is. Who could face such feelings and continue to get up each day and try? Don is trying. He isn't giving up.

Don makes me consider that there is not much difference between the courageous person and the coward, except that the courageous person keeps trying.

CLARENCE, LDRC: Monday, January 12, 2009, 11:00 a.m.

While I wait for Clarence, another LDRC staffer who used to be homeless, I read a handout lying on the large meeting table in front of me. It's for a sobriety program, and the section concerning depression has a test to determine if you might be depressed.

"If you said yes to two or more of these questions then you might be depressed," the handout reads. I take the test in my head, and say yes or possibly yes to ten questions. I know I've been a bit down lately, but am I depressed? I hate the word to begin with—it says too much and too little all at the same time.

There is a knock at the door, saving me from more introspection. I remember that a lot of the doors around here self lock and assume it must be Clarence.

I open it and see a man twice my size. "Clarence?"

"That's the name they always seem to use for me."

He has a sober look on his face and does not return the smile I shoot his way. He doesn't look angry. I simply don't know what he is feeling. I can't read him.

I ask Clarence if he's familiar with my book project already, and his response is brutally honest.

"What's this book going to do for this place if it sells?"

I get a bit defensive. I don't mind discussing this with him, but I assume he means money and I have no intention of giving any proceeds from sales of my book to this organization. Worse yet, I assume when he finds this out he will not want to be interviewed. I explain that my book is a long shot in the first place, and even if it sells, not a dime is going to the LDRC.

"No, not the money," Clarence answers in a deep, powerful, compassionate voice. "What's it going to do for the people? From the dirt poor in boxes to the persons who are rich in their million dollar homes, this is affecting everyone. It's affecting everyone to the point that giving a person a dollar doesn't help anymore. But the situation is, behind the dirt, the smell of urine, the dirty clothes, you see a human being. It could have been you. God created all of us. We are all one. We are all the same. For me to go out and help someone, it truly is helping myself."

Wow! That was not what I expected. I respond that what I am trying to do is help others to understand homelessness. Clarence seems satisfied.

"I was incarcerated for 23 years," he begins. "I was addicted to crack for 20 years. I slept in the streets. I spent my last dime on drugs." Clarence pauses, his voice sauntering and deep. "It all came down to the same thing. I had lost my way. You can't tell me from a person who is SMI (Severely or Seriously Mentally Ill), from a college grad, because they are all on this campus. We forget that, that there is a human being behind the story. They need love and that's what we are here for."

When Clarence says the word "love," it vibrates. Yet there is a great sternness to the big man, as though love is serious work to him. Around here, love is an honest, steadfast, hardworking thing.

Clarence explains that he flew into Phoenix in 2004, running from himself and his addictions. But he quickly reverted to his old lifestyle of drugs and hustling in "the zone" [slang for this area of town].

"My spirit was broke, man," Clarence says. "I was still getting high for a few months, but then I started going to groups and being around people who had made it. I started getting money away from me by spending it on bills instead. Then . . . I was clean for one month. One month turned in to six. Six months turned into two years . . ."

As Clarence talks about his sober years adding up to eight, he makes it sound easy and I know it couldn't have been. Maybe he just doesn't like emphasizing himself, and all the hard work he put in. The big guy is definitely all about other people.

Clarence says he has always wanted to be a counselor, so when Jessica offered him a job at the LDRC, the choice was easy. He seems thankful to be helping the same people he used to get high with, because he knows how to treat them with love, respect and honesty.

As the story changes from past-tense to the present, Clarence's voice becomes deeper, more sermon-like: "You have to become part of the family here. What you are seeing here is a transformation!"

Tears are starting to form again. I'm used to it. I think Clarence will understand. He's seen more life than ten people put together.

"You just need to do what's right for today," he continues. "We are empowering people to take their lives back and we are joining hands to help each other live. And I have days where I get mad but I have so many more days when I have someone tell me that I helped them, when I get a card, when I get a hug."

In full Southern preacher mode, Clarence brings home his message: "What's going on in our country right now is that people are having to go back to the basics. Back to the basics! Where we have to love our neighbor as ourselves! As ourselves! And that's what's going to change the economy, change everything! Not money, not the color of your skin."

I explain to Clarence that while I think he has basically already answered them, I have three more questions I must ask, the three questions I will ask everyone I interview.

What is the meaning of life?

I think the meaning is to know that you've been given the privilege of making a difference in someone else's life; that you have been given the opportunity and responsibility to help others get to that next level. You have been given the opportunity to just love and to teach others to love. And to love unconditionally.

What are your thoughts about society and/or societies in general?

We've been raised in a capitalist society where it's all about the dollar bill. In the past, the people accepted what we were told is the truth. But that no longer is. People are examining the truth. People in all walks off life are loosing what they had because of what you said, some politician or what have you. Now they are starting to believe in each other. They are starting to meet their neighbors. So many people don't even know their neighbor's name. Just saying hi to your neighbor makes a difference. All those things bring about change. People are learning about how to live with each other again and not isolate.

Who are you?

I think of my self as the prodigal son. I was lost. I was raised in a middle class family. My whole family has a background in law enforcement. I was rebellious and made decisions that caused me to loose 20 years of my life. I have regrets, but I really don't, not really, you understand? Because right now I am becoming all I was meant to be, which is a messenger for others. My job is to tell others they are loved and God loves them. I learned how to love. I learned how to be in love with me and I learned how to love those around me.

I ask him if there is anything else he wants to tell me, to share with readers.

In his ever deepening, ever powering voice, Clarence says: "The greatest key to anybody's life is learning how to be sincerely humble. If you can be humble, there is nothing you can't conquer!"

Crying. I can't help it. Of course he knows. Clarence knows that everyone has struggles and is humble enough not to think his are any greater than mine. I don't know how, but this seems to be a key to the man's strength.

I stand up to shake his hand.

"No man," Clarence says, and gives me a great big hug. It feels like hugging an oak. It feels like coming home.

Clarence makes me consider the power in humility.

DWIGHT, LDRC: Monday, January 12, 2009, 1:00 p.m.

Dwight, another ex-client of the campus, is now its facility coordinator. To me, he is the man with the keys who let me into the two previous meeting rooms. Dwight reminds me of a black version of my father. He is jollier and more slender, but they both share the same height (5'8"), humility and kindness. Dwight looks much younger than my father who is now 71 years old. Ultimately, the association is more in my heart than in my eyes. I feel instantly comfortable with Dwight.

Dwight sports a worn baseball cap and an equally worn, patchy beard. He's full of energy, but not a nervous energy. He walks fast everywhere he goes, like a hard-working man on a mission—presumably to find more hard work. By the time of our meeting, I had already raced behind him on several occasions trying to keep up as we moved from one room to the next, preparing for the interviews.

We sit and talk about the ever-changing concept of this book. Dwight is relaxed, but his inexhaustible energy causes him to fidget in the chair every few minutes, like he isn't used to just sitting and talking.

Dwight talks in a gravelly tone that is pleasant to listen to, like the sound of a plane flying far overhead. It would be annoying if it were too close, too loud. But subdued, it's pleasant and relaxing.

"Homelessness is a state of mind," Dwight begins. "It's just something that society says. This whole planet is ours. We feed them, we house them, so they are not homeless. They are not homeless. The planet is our home. When I was homeless it was because I did not forgive myself and did not love myself. Everything we do is a choice. Homelessness is a choice not to be responsible for [oneself], first and foremost. And forgiveness is the key. If you never forgive yourself, you will always have homelessness."

Dwight says he bases these thoughts on his eight to nine years of being homeless, as well as what he's experienced as "the maintenance man around here."

"Homeless is people not operating in faith," he concludes. "They don't have enough faith to be responsible."

That last remark sounds eerily like my father's advice to me. Partly, it's the sound of Dwight's voice, but there's something else, something about this place, that's getting to me. I'm looking at my own life, failures and successes, and the times when I lost faith in myself.

"How did it all change for you Dwight?" I ask, returning from my thoughts to the interview.

"God allowed me to look at myself," he replies. Faith seems to be a common theme around here. "I got on my knees and surrendered to God. I surrendered to where I was at, right then. And He put people in my life and what I needed in my life to grow. I had to go through all that pain . . ." Dwight slowly shakes his head, ". . . when I surrendered to the spirit of God, God inside me, as I knew Him, not as anybody told me He was, I realized that I was valuable and always was. I had always been valuable, but didn't see that because of the choices I had made."

Dwight's voice may be gravelly, but his speech is also loose and intelligent. It's a pleasure to listen to and learn from.

"Life ain't about us," he continues. "Life ain't about us! It's about my relationship with God and my fellow man. How can you love God and not your neighbor? I see God everyday cause I look in the mirror. And I come to work and see other people. I see people's lives turning around. But we have to constantly work through bitterness, malice."

That's it! I think to myself. That's why he reminds me of my father. Then he says, "Because it's the right thing to do."

"Homelessness is a mindset. I've come to that conclusion," Dwight says. "I can't give what I don't have, but you've got to give to get. It's like going to the bank. You got no business going there if you haven't put anything in there," he concludes, finally laughing as well.

Dwight seems to be winding down. He's moving less and less, like a racecar shifting into neutral. But he still summons the energy to answer my final three questions.

What is the meaning of life?

That's a good question. The meaning of life is to understand that I am the most valuable thing in the universe, next to God, and to share the love of God with everyone. If I apply the will of God to me, then everyone who comes into contact with me is blessed. The meaning of life is to walk in his grace and his mercy.

To enjoy this beautiful planet and love one another. To say, "Thank you for letting me breathe." To know whatever I go through today is OK. Each and every day is OK. Life is the love of God. You love Him and your life will be fulfilled.

What are your thoughts about society and/or societies in general?

You are told as long as you don't get caught, it's OK. When it comes to the physical, society is great. It gives you stuff. But when it comes to the spiritual . . . it ain't worth a damn! It ain't worth a damn! They always feed you negative information. Just watch the news on five different stations. They never tell you anything good. Society, in its mindset, ain't worth a damn. They tell you drugs are illegal but then they sell drugs. They have medicines that have more side effects than illegal drugs. Don't drink and drive, but go to the stadium and drink beer . . . and they sell it with sex. The world is corrupt. Society is just doing what they do. Society ain't worth a damn!

Who are you?

Damn, these are good questions. I'm a spirit that lives in a body and wants to do the will of God. That's it. That's all I am.

Dwight causes me to consider that faith is a choice.

JESSICA, LDRC: Monday, January 12, 2009, 3:00 p.m.

Jessica has a nurturing confidence about her, a calm that I look forward to experiencing again. Maybe it can help make sense of everything I am feeling and thinking. First, this place itself, and now these interview subjects—I don't know what I expected, but this wasn't it.

Jessica has agreed to meet with me every week. She has faith in my project, even if I do not. She is willing to invest her time, despite knowing I'm an unpublished author. The thought of doing it all for nothing is one that has gone through my head every day of every book project I have ever worked on, this being number three. Jessica might be doing this all for nothing, too, but she doesn't seem to wrestle with this same inner debate.

I want to explain how amazing her three staff members were, and how talking to them made me more aware of how unaware I am. Which is something—I guess? I still don't have an answer to my original question. Instead, the question has expanded in complexity. All I end up saying is, "Clarence gave me a big hug."

Jessica knowingly laughs and nods a bit. "He's something else."

She's excited about the immediate benefits of my project for clients and staff. And while she hopes it will raise public awareness one day, she also expresses that it might help the public to know what's going on down here at LDRC. Jessica believes that the general public needs the campus as much as the campus needs the general public, although I don't fully understand why yet.

In the meantime, she thinks the interviews might be cathartic and give perspective on her job as director. Jessica explains that she's always on the lookout for a new outlook so she can see life and problems from a new angle—and view herself more honestly.

"How accurate is the number 14,000 for homeless persons in Maricopa County?" I ask today. "I've heard or read that the actual number is quite controversial due to how hard it is to count the homeless."

"There's not enough attention paid to it to make it controversial," she replies, finishing with a sarcastic smile.

Jessica explains that 14,000 is a very accurate number—as a minimum. Every year they do a street count, locally and nation wide. All the shelters report, and in addition social workers divide the county into grids and drive around doing a manual tally of every person they see living on the streets. They're not allowed to go into abandoned buildings, etc., so they miss some, maybe a lot. No one knows for sure. But the number comes from actual people counted, so it's anything but inflated. About half of that 14,000 is in Phoenix. Seven hundred or more people sleep in one of the campus shelters every night, though the campus itself provides services for many more. Besides that, a woman's shelter and a family shelter are located nearby. Many people staying there come to the campus for services, along with the countless others who sleep under bridges, in parks, fields and abandoned buildings or unknown locations.

"You seem so calm," I tell Jessica. "How much time do you spend here? How consuming is your job?"

"It used to be pretty crazy, but now I've learned to pace myself," she says. "And now I have a great staff. Chaplain Dave told me to pray every day that I get done what has to get done. The rest can wait till tomorrow."

"What was the best thing that happened last week at work?" I ask.

She talks about a Friday night barbeque and music jam. People from the community hosted the barbeque, which was "great" according to her. Jessica believes that homelessness is a community problem and requires a community solution. The clients loved it, which was "great too." And many people from the community were really moved by what they do here, which was "super great!" Jessica finished the story looking like a girl opening gifts at her own birthday party. "It's affirmation that what we are doing is important."

Jessica says she's also happy that after being out sick for three days, she didn't fall too behind on work. "It made me realize how well run things are in general and how staff was willing to step up," she says. "It was affirmation that I'm on the same page with my staff and they care."

I decide to change the subject. "Where does the LDRC's funding come from?"

"It's a fairly equal distribution of government, private and foundations. And I like it that way." She likes to diversify the funding of the organization, because it provides stability should they lose funding from any one source. "And it's more than that," she continues. "It fits in with my overall philosophy that this is a community wide problem and requires community wide involvement."

"How do you decide what to fund or what not to fund?"

"It's a tough call because there are a lot of things we are doing way beyond where we started," Jessica says. "The beginning idea was to greet people and get them connected to services and get them housed. And people come with ideas and descend on us and I have to decide if it's furthering our mission. I have fears too about having to pull in programs, but I can't even fathom where to cut because it's all pieces of the pie."

Jessica explains that having a supportive board of directors helps. The board is a mixture of government officials and community members. They give her free reign—as long as she stays within the budget. The 150-200 hours of work volunteers put in every week certainly helps Jessica do this. (LDRC also has 11 full-time and seven part-time paid staffers at the time of this interview.)

As we continue chatting, I get a feel for this woman who is my main contact for this entire project. Talking with Jessica is like throwing stones into a pond. There are ripples of excitement and yet each stone is seamlessly absorbed into calmness, and an infinite patience awaits the next throw. She's full of enthusiasm, yet serene and pensive.

This isn't just an interview deflection technique, either. Jessica interacts this way with clients and staff as they drift or storm in and out of her office as we talk. She definitely has an open door policy. All of us throw stones in that pond, some gently plopping them in, some heaving great boulders. All are received the same.

Jessica makes me consider the importance of community.

TESTS, ALLIES AND ENEMIES

DAWN, MOVIE, LDRC: Saturday, January 17, 2009, 1:00 p.m.

E NTERING THE SECOND WEEK OF Dawn's six-week course, I'm in better spirits all around and I think it's due to a Dwight-inspired decision to be humble. (Translation: Quit whining and get to work.) My back is miraculously better, too. When my back had gone out in the past, it meant months of trouble. This time it started feeling better the minute I started being humble. I still have feelings of depression, or just general crappiness, but overall I am more positive. That alone seems proof enough that I'm at least headed in the right direction.

I walk across the campus, through the atmosphere of smoke, through the crowds of people, through the doors of the LDRC. Clarence is at the front desk. I say hi to him, thank him for his help and tell him that it was great information for both my book and my back. Our interview truly changed my life. His face lights up like the warm glow of a fire that is fueled by an undying source of faith.

"Ah man, that wasn't me, that was all God," Clarence says.

"Well, it changed my life. Thank you."

I continue toward the classroom, entering into the smell of popcorn and the sound of laughter. A "Bugs Bunny" cartoon is on-screen and it brings back childhood memories of Saturday mornings and cereal. By the client's comments, I gather it does the same for them—childhood and home.

More people are gathered than last week. Chairs are pushed even more tightly together to make space for the additional students. I have to take a seat in back, unable to sit in the front by an outlet. I will have to take notes by hand. I hate taking notes by hand. I have the handwriting of a doctor and I can type faster than I can write. Transposing notes sucks when you've been raised in the world of cut, paste and spell check.

But again I am reminded to keep my mind on the task at hand. Tomorrow that task will be someone's oily body. I just got a job as a massage therapist, something I had done on and off for 18 years. It will be half the hours I used to work, and half the pay. But I'm thankful for a change and the job will be essentially stress-free while leaving me plenty of time to write.

I look around and a see a sign I didn't notice last week. I don't know how I missed it because it is rather large. It reads: *When seen from a distance your problems are somehow much smaller than mine.*

I feel free and safe to ponder this thought, surrounded in a blanket of laughter as the cartoon plays on. How long has it been since I really laughed? Not my forced intellectual laugh of 'yeah that's clever,' but the laugh of a child. Not thinking, just reacting. And how can these people be laughing? They're freakin' homeless! I still have a lot to learn.

Dawn, to everyone's disappointment except for Serious Me, turns off the cartoon. She has us guess the name of the movie again. This week it's "Ray," a movie about the life of Ray Charles. She continues with the standard presentation of what we are to look for as it pertains to the journey of the hero.

Dawn sure doesn't talk down to her audience. Maybe that is part of treating people with dignity. I also know she believes that learning means figuring things out for oneself.

As I watch the movie, one line strikes me. Ray's mother tells him, "Never let nothing or nobody turn you into a cripple." It makes me think, as I'm sure Dawn intended it, to that we all have liabilities. Ray Charles was blind, and he never let that hold him back.

Dawn stops the movie halfway through and asks what Ray Charles's trigger event was. She explains that a trigger event is a traumatic event we are often afraid to face. For Ray, it was witnessing his baby brother drown and failing to save him. He goes blind just nine months afterward. Dawn hints that maybe he went blind because he could not face the fact of the event, then asks us to identify the future subsequent events that continue to trigger this memory and how they relate. Dawn is a damn good teacher: stern, funny, smart, patient, always with a game plan.

Our Damn Good Teacher talks about turning points, or the moments in which we make decisions that change the course of our life, for better or for worse.

Then she asks us to identify Ray's demon, his crutch, and the method he used to deal with it. The musician was a heroin addict for a good portion of his life and many people in the class answer that his crutch was drug use. Dawn corrects them: That was the *method* he used to deal with his crutch, which was guilt. I've never thought about needing to deal with the crutches we create, which we originally created to deal with our demons. Crutches for crutches . . .

My demon is the fear of not being loved, of being alone. My trigger events are anything that makes me feel irresponsible or less than perfect. Didn't you get love as a child when you were responsible and perfect? I know in my head that's not true; I was a loved child. But I don't know that in my heart.

As for guilt, it's my crutch too. I choose to feel bad about not being a conformist and following my dreams instead of fully admitting, without apology, that I am doing what I want to do. Somehow, my guilt is an insurance policy against my possible failure.

And what excesses do I use to help me deal with my crutch? God, these workshops are powerful!

After the movie, I have a few minutes to speak with Dawn in private. She explains that she wanted to introduce the drug theme this week, but knew she couldn't do it too blatantly. Dawn's purpose is to open people up to grow, not shut them down to whither, so she tries to go in through some sort of personal back door for each person.

I ask Dawn if she believes in the myth of the hero—if she believes that this is how life really works, or, is she just trying to use the concept to free people from their predicaments?

"Both."

Most important is that she really believes life has a built-in magical quality to it; that life could work like the myth of the hero.

**Dawn makes me consider that facing one's fears
may be the key to living one's dreams.**

SCOTT, CLIENT, LDRC: Monday, January 19, 2009, 1:00 p.m.

My new plan is to come to campus every Monday and Tuesday to chat with clients and interview those who are interested. With this general approach in mind, I have no immediate plans to interview Scott when I meet him. But we have instant rapport when he and I discover that we are both writers, although neither of us has been paid for anything we've written. But at least Scott has a poem in print and shows me a copy. "Of course," he tells me, "they don't pay for poetry."

He's written a series of vignettes on the homeless, which he shares with me. Each focuses on an aspect of the homeless situation, such as: personal relationships between the homeless, eating experiences of the homeless, sleeping on the streets, networking within the homeless community, and so on. They are well written, clever, and have catchy titles.

Scott is a slim man with grey hair and a thick, well-trimmed mustache. I explain my project, and his voice takes on a sad tone in telling his life story. "One thing I learned in prison," Scott, who was incarcerated for three years, begins, "you lower your level. You turn down your empathy. You hope for the best, but expect the worst. If you are going to stay strong, you have to turn your empathy level way down."

If events like moving towns, or breaking up with a boyfriend or girlfriend can be psychologically traumatic, Scott asks, how much worse is prison, where you suddenly have no control over food, shelter, clothing, education or relationships?

Scott doesn't *look* homeless, whatever that means. He is dressed casual and clean, with a red baseball cap, glasses, worn jeans, tennis shoes and a bright white T-shirt. He looks like anyone you would meet in line at the grocery store. He does not look like he slept on a floor last night (but he did, in the Outreach Shelter).

Later in the interview, Scott leans over and quietly offers a confession of sorts that he asks me not to put into print. He adds at the end that he believes that he is narcissistic, that he lacks a social conscience, and that this is an intrinsic flaw in him.

"So you don't care about people?" I ask.

"I do care," Scott says. "But sympathy does no good for people and just because I lack sympathy, does not mean I don't care."

Scott continues that he has empathy as opposed to sympathy, but the longer he talks, the more apparent it is that he mostly lacks empathy for himself. Scott seems to feel a lot of guilt for the type of person he thinks he is.

Maybe this is why Scott needs to write. His writing organizes the scattered thoughts of his mind and acts as an outlet to express pain. He continues circling around on his ideas of narcissism, sympathy and empathy.

There's also a noticeable lack of continuity with Scott's conversation. I try to steer him back to the subject of homelessness. "You were saying that there's plenty of food."

Scott continues in his sad, thoughtful tone as though we never veered off course. "Yeah, you can always find something to eat or to wear, but you may not always have a roof over your head," he says. "But part of the spiritual component is that it's hard to use those services. What enables me to go on is to have a vision larger than myself. One is my writing and the other is Madison Street Veterans Association, homeless vets helping vets. Terry (Terry Araman, who is on the LDRC staff) will give you the straight skinny. Vets in the shelter were the ones who created it. To our knowledge, it's the first one in the nation. Within three months, Colonel Strickland [head of Department of Veteran's Affairs] gave us $5,000. One of the ways I see my way out is to tie myself to two sets: homeless vets and Native Americans."

The Madison Street Veterans Association (MSVA, a new division of the LDRC) is a grassroots organization of homeless and formerly homeless veterans, recognized by the Arizona Department of Veterans Affairs, the local VA, DAV, American Legion and Veterans of Foreign Wars Posts. As Scott said, it is also perhaps the first organization of its kind in the nation. They have received start up funds from the Arizona Department of Veterans Affairs, The Catholic Charities of Human Development and private donors.

Targeting assistance to a specific community helps prevent viewing "the disenfranchised population" as a single group, formed by a single cause. Scott says this mindset is part of the problem in social justice today.

"Say single mothers have been 'disfranchised.'" Scott's tone is now philosophical. "How many women are still married because if they left that relationship, they would have no place to go? Or men, for that matter? But the numbers are higher for women. These women have to prostitute themselves to keep from being homeless. I just talked to an abused woman in the shelter. She's thinking about going back to her abusive relationship."

"Why?" I ask.

"They've got all these rules over there [in the women's shelter]," Scott replies. "The alternatives aren't that good: choice between crappy life in the shelter or occasional beatings. The whole gist of all this is, 'Don't we prostitute ourselves in today's society for the illusion of security?'"

He's got a point, I think. That's what kept me at my corporate job for years.

"And it is an illusion," Scott continues. "Many people are just one paycheck or one catastrophe away from being homeless and don't even know it. And the title of a story like that is something to the effect of

'Prostituting America.' It's quite common with men too who put up with a trophy wife who they don't like. But that's more fluff."

Scott continues to riff on these theories. He's having fun discussing ideas with someone. I notice something else unusual about how Scott talks: His comments are spoken with sterility, as theoretical concepts without any feeling behind them, a sign of his muted empathy. That is not to say Scott doesn't have any feelings, but he communicates without feelings, as though he has been numbed.

Once again, Scott veers off in the middle of an idea to focus on his own life. Scott has been homeless for a year, due to alcoholism since age 18 and a diagnosis of bipolar disorder and depression since 1971.

"See, I had a double whammy," he says. "So if I don't exercise responsibility for myself, I will go out on binges and trash myself."

Scott says he "exercises responsibility" by going to meetings at New Arid Club (a division of the LDRC), a peer run Alcoholics Anonymous facility on campus, every morning. His voice grows loud and optimistic as he shares plans for designing his own rehab program some day. I wonder how much of Scott's clever language I can trust as he begins talking about limiting your negative inputs.

"I don't associate with people who have SMI or are currently drinking or using," he says. "I try to identify any negative self-destructive behaviors and try to eliminate them, except for smoking cigarettes and drinking coffee. I love the taste of coffee. My fiancé sent me a Starbucks card."

"You have a fiancé?" I have to ask.

"We've been off and on for 25 years," Scott says. "She's married four times and me twice. One thing I've learned is, never marry a women you meet in the psych hospital."

Where do I go with this? I think desperately to myself before blurting out a question.

"Does your fiancé live out here?"

"No, she lives in Spokane, Washington." Moreover, both Scott and his fiancé are still legally married to other people. The story only gets more confused from there, so I eventually shift the topic away from their unusual relationship.

After some questioning, Scott opens up about his military service. He applied for a VA pension for disabilities incurred long after he was discharged. Scott is hoping to be accepted for "degenerative joint disease, pacemaker, and/or bipolar depression," and believes that he will get about $931 a month.

I don't ask him why he doesn't get a job. I feel like asking the wrong question might just give me the wrong answer. I still want to learn what homelessness is beyond the typical definitions. Scott tells me that he does work odd jobs as a painter and handyman. It sounds as if getting a job is only half the battle. Keeping it is the other half.

Scott makes some interesting points about why we are seeing an increase in troubled military personnel returning from The Gulf, Afghanistan and Iraq. He feels that we sent "video gamers to war." We sent a generation of young men and women that have grown up in a more cushioned time and a time when issues are not as "black and white" as they were when he grew up. So they are coming back very mentally disturbed.

"Did you see action in the military?"

He replies with a Cheshire Cat sort of smile. "No. I went to Italy, drank wine and chased women when I was in the service."

My interest in his ideas, which range from aliens to politics, seems to cause Scott to really open up to me. He is like an attention-starved child. His thoughts increase in speed and in their disjointedness as he hurries to get them all out, sensing that I will somehow limit his time. Once again, Scott leans forward and talks quietly, as if telling me a secret.

"What I've done is try to get involved," he confides. "It's not what you know, it's who you know." Scott continues on for some time, giving me examples of how his connections with others give him certain "luxuries." Knowing the right person, for example, to get into the computer room off hours so that he can check his emails every day instead of just on days when it's open for that purpose. I'm struck by how valuable certain things are to him—things that I don't even give a second thought to.

Then, he's changing gears once again. "I don't care what I do now; I just need to make money."

It has been two and a half hours and I see no end in sight. Scott feels talking with me provides him with some "balance through contact with a non-homeless person and the outside world." Finally, after assuring him that we will talk again, I ask Scott my three questions.

What is the meaning of life?

I want to be able to ah, ah, make this, to make, to have a positive impact on the people I have had experiences with. I want to leave a legacy that he was a help, not a hindrance. He helped further the human condition along. That term is vague but to be a help, not a hindrance. If my writings have positively affected one person, if they cause them to pause then . . . And that all ties into something bigger than ourselves. Without this we are like black holes and suck shit into ourselves. And there is no limit to the shit we can suck into ourselves.

What are your thoughts about society and/or societies in general?

As a result of being homeless I have come to a new understanding of my responsibility to, um, to, um, walk in that vision larger than my self. Not only to be self-supporting for myself, but those in my arena of care, my network of others. But the bottom line is like the Dali Lama says if you can't love everyone, don't hurt them. You can't give away something you don't have. I know that now. I have actually lived a charmed life. I used to have it all. It hasn't always been like this and it won't always be like this, but even in the good times I was mixed up with depression, self condemnation, remorse and drinking. And for years I thought if I had the right woman, car, job . . . I know now, change comes from the inside out not the outside in. So this time in my recovery process I have to find a way to contribute by helping myself and helping others.

Who are you?
I'm defined by what I will ultimately accomplish before I die. So to answer that question . . . it's impossible for me to answer it and it will only be answered after I'm passed on.

As Scott walks away, he turns and asks if we can collaborate on a project together, sometime. I tell him that I don't think I have the time, but that I would like to include one of his poems in my book if he's interested.

"Never been impressed with poems in non-poem books," he drawls in that vaguely Texan accent. "What are they trying to do, make it all artsy crafty? 'Oh, isn't it cute, the homeless man wrote a poem.'"

"You've got a point," I concede.

He comes back and leans way over towards me, quietly, "That's the danger. If you write it in such a way that you trivialize it."

Scott makes me consider that spirituality can't be intellectualized.

JESSICA, LDRC: **Monday, January 19, 2009, 4:00 p.m.**

Scott made me think about the issues of employment for the homeless. He seemed employable to me, though eccentric. So I ask Jessica in our weekly meeting if she would tell me her general thoughts about employing the homeless. I know there has to be more to the subject than I have considered thus far.

Humble as always, Jessica insists she's not really the person to talk to about this and refers me to Amy at St. Joseph the Worker.

"Will you give me some insight so I at least know what to ask?" I ask her.

"I think a lot of people . . . a lot of non-homeless people think: why don't they just get a job?" Jessica begins, after some hesitation. "But there are a lot of factors in getting a job and keeping a job. You need a phone, good teeth, nice clothing, an address."

She pauses again, accumulating passion before continuing. "And then living on the street for some time, there are some social skills that disappear. You're not always good at presenting yourself as a person who is ready to be employed. There's job training of course, but there's not emotional training that's also needed. You know what I mean?"

Jessica is careful and slow in putting together her next thought. "And there's something more than just getting a job. There's not enough emphasis in this country about doing something you care about. Take me for example. I've had jobs that didn't fit me and was depressed and not happy. It's not just about making money, it's about satisfaction."

She shoots me a perplexed, questioning look, as if to say, does that help?

"That's what I was looking for, Jessica."

I reflect back on my own job experiences, given what I've just heard. In all the jobs I've landed, the interviewer probably made up his or her mind about me in the first few minutes of our meeting. My appearance and a few well-spoken sentences made all the difference. I've even gotten a job that required a college degree, which I do not have. They simply assumed I had one based on the way I acted.

"What was the best thing that happened last week?" I ask Jessica, returning to the interview.

She talks about seeing a performance by Playback Theatre, a group of actor-volunteers who act out a client's story. They get to see the story of a piece of their life acted out before their eyes. I ask her why that stood out this week.

"I like knowing that's happening," she replies. "I've heard a lot of stories. It's what we are trying to do. It helps people connect with people, with themselves."

"You sound like it gave you warm fuzzies."

"Significant warm fuzzies, I would have to say. One of the goals is to offer the clients engagement."

"Engagement?" I want to hear more.

"Homeless adults are so often used to being ignored in society, invisible," Jessica says. "They may ask someone for some 'spare change,' and the reaction is often nothing. No eye contact. No words. No acknowledgement of their existence. During Playback Theater, they see their stories acted out. They receive validation as a human, they become visible, valuable."

Jessica pauses again, and I see she's crying. She apologizes, explaining that even after two years, she still gets choked up over just speaking about what goes on here.

"So that's why you can't just put someone in a house when they feel invisible; that's why we have to do all this other stuff," Jessica says, looking up and wiping her eyes. "Why even live in a house if you are invisible?"

We both just sit there, in silence, for about a minute. A minute is a long time to not only think about the meaning of 'invisible person,' but also to feel it.

Jessica, in an act of mercy, moves on. Her face begins to light up with child-like enthusiasm as she describes "the other cool thing about last week." The LDRC had a full staff meeting, when everyone looked at the center's goals and strategic plan and based personal goals on them.

"And this makes you happy, why?" I ask.

"I feel like that's a lot of what I'm supposed to do," Jessica says. "I want to make sure everyone feels passionate about their jobs and is a part of the big picture. I want to make sure that they understand how every little part of what they do aids in ending homelessness."

These meetings are also a chance for Jessica to stay in touch with her team, keep her finger on the pulse of the LDRC. She has a pleased expression on her face, as if her work for the week is complete.

"It was good to see how they, for the most part, all got it," she says of her staff. "Even if they work in the post office one day a week. That is helping to end homelessness, and everyone seemed to get that."

"What was the worst or hardest thing that happened last week?" I ask.

Jessica explains that she gets frustrated sometimes with all the meetings, even if they are a success.

"I need to be patient enough for people to find the light for themselves, but sometimes I have to just tell them, to make sure we are on the same page," she says. "There's a balance there I'm still learning."

"How do you do it, Jessica? How do you stay so calm and humble?"

In response, she hands me a piece of paper. It reads:

The Two Wolves

An old Cherokee chief is teaching his grandson about life.

"A fight is going on inside me," he said. "It is a terrible fight and it is between two wolves. One is evil—he is fear, anger, envy, sorrow, regret, greed, arrogance, self-pity, guilt, resentment, inferiority, lies, false pride, superiority, self-doubt, and ego."

"The other is good—he is joy, peace, love, hope, sharing, serenity, humility, kindness, benevolence, friendship, empathy, generosity, truth, compassion, and faith."

The grandson thought about it for a minute and then asked his grandfather, "Which wolf wins?"

The old Cherokee simply replied, "The one you feed."

Jessica tells me she tries to live this every day. She tries "to feed the right wolf."

"I definitely think I've learned to reprogram my brain," Jessica says. "I learned not to waste any time on useless banter. Especially now, I know that's just stuff I'm making up in my head. Who knows if it's true or not? It's really fascinating to know all that and call others on that. My relationships are so much better, personal and work ones. I have very little tolerance for people making up negativity and wanting to talk about it."

With that, we bid adieu until next week. The interview actually took a long time, being frequently interrupted by staff in need of Jessica's guidance. But I walk out with a smile on my face. Still waters run deep, and they make for a refreshing swim.

Jessica causes me to consider that maybe homelessness is a symptom—a symptom of the disease of invisibility.

DAWN, MOVIE, LDRC: Saturday, January 24, 2009, 1:00 p.m.

The Human Services Campus (HSC) is swamped with people and cars today. I've never seen it this busy here. As I pass The New Arid Club, I notice they are hosting some sort of open house. And CASS right next door seems to be having a "party" for the homeless. There is a local restaurant serving food, and two live bands. It's quite the lively scene and, if anything, changes the landscape of the HSC from what everyone is used to.

They open the doors of LDRC for the afternoon and I move quickly to the movie room so I can get a seat near an outlet (I don't want to take notes by hand again). I find the door to the movie room locked and I can see through the small institutional window that the room is dark.

Dawn finds me and says the movie has been cancelled. It just didn't make sense with The New Arid Club's open house and CASS's client appreciation event: "No one would show up."

"I'm crushed. I've been getting a lot out of these movie days," I say.

She smiles, perhaps pleased, and explains that they will resume next week. The movies don't go in any particular order, anyway; the six-week series is just to get clients to commit, work on follow through, and be rewarded with Go-Getter Bucks that are worth a dollar in each in the Get Goin' Café (which is yet another service of the LDRC).

"Dawn, can I ask you a quick question about the movie workshop. I get the fear thing, really get it thanks to you, but I don't understand what you mean by will?"

"People have learned not to make choices as individuals. I did it to my own children until I learned this. I tell my kid, 'we're going to the store, get dressed.' The child responds, 'no.' I say, 'GET YOUR CLOTHES ON!' I don't give him a choice. I don't say, 'which pants do you want to put on, this one or this one?' The problem is we label these two-year-olds that say no as non-obedient. And again when they are teenagers and start saying no, we label them as rebellious."

Dawn explained further that the point is not that kids don't learn to make good decisions; they don't learn to make decisions, period. They don't learn that their decisions matter because they are constantly overridden. So they don't learn to exercise their will. I'd never thought about this. As a parent we're always obsessed with making sure our kids make the right choices, not teaching them to choose. How many people here simply have been trained that regardless of what they do, it just won't matter?

"Do you think prison furthers this? I'm not saying we should or shouldn't put people in prison but it's a place where decisions are made for them."

"Well we always have a choice to make; that's my whole point. But yes, prisons do this, so does the army and so does our schools, when they tell us 'you will learn this way and you will be graded against others instead of as an individual.'"

Dawn causes me to consider that not everyone has the equal ability to choose.

ROSS, CLIENT, LDRC: Monday, January 26, 2009, 9:00 a.m.

I met Ross about a week ago while talking with his friend Stormy, who is a veritable icon around here. He seemed to be one of the images I used to conjure when I thought of "a homeless person." Stormy has been on the streets for years and is full of ideas. He carries most of his belongings with him in a large backpack. You can almost always find him on the HSC during the day drinking coffee, rolling cigarettes, talking or dozing off somewhere.

My original intention was to interview Stormy, an older gentleman with a big white beard and a mustache yellowed near the mouth from nicotine stains. But he did not want to do a formal interview. He was more than happy to speak with me for hours on end—and did—but he refused to let me take notes or tape our conversations. He has a general mistrust for anything mainstream. He doesn't sleep on campus at night, because Stormy likes his freedom and chooses to sleep somewhere off site, somewhere out there . . .

During a long and seemingly endless conversation with Stormy, one that I was continuing in hopes that he might change his mind about an interview, Ross quietly mentioned that he wouldn't mind being interviewed.

In the hours I had spoken with Stormy, Ross did not once interject. You have to listen very carefully when he speaks, because he does so in a low monotone. In other words, Ross is the complete opposite of Stormy.

Ross looks to me like someone who one would think of as "homeless." He has a medical problem with his foot and is currently in a wheelchair. (There are lots of people here with medical issues.) He has long and straight black hair with a beard to match. His shoes are worn, his jeans are dirty and he wears an army fatigue jacket. There must be something about that jacket and wheelchair that I associate with homelessness.

I'm not suggesting a true connection beyond the fact that there are a lot of homeless vets. According to the National Coalition for Homeless Veterans 23 percent or homeless persons are veterans. And 89 percent of them received honorable discharges.

"So Ross, tell me about yourself."

Ross seems very downtrodden. He's never looked me in the eyes.

"Pretty much I was a whipping post and it didn't matter whether I was right or wrong; I always got the blame for someone else," he says, quietly, while looking down at his feet. "And it went on through the military. People point their finger and lie instead of talking to me. And at the end of it, I got married. And this supposed friend of the family turned my family against her because of religion, because of her being Mormon. After my wife left, [the marriage] was annulled and six months later and I was out looking for work. This same friend of the family used her daughter as a set up and lied, stating that I molested her. The sheriff's department picked me up at 1 o'clock. They believed her, not me. The judge put me into the state penitentiary for 10 to life behind it, for that lie. They couldn't find any proof of it. And the judge made the statement with it that he was going to make an example of me. And I spent four years of a 10-year sentence that I didn't have to do."

"How did you get out in four years?"

"The judge said the only way I was to get released was to get a degree and my diploma. I got an associate degrees in both industrial and architectural drafting and I got my high school diploma and a certificate in blueprint reading."

Ross falls silent. I gently nudge him into sharing more. He admits to being homeless since 1980. He's had jobs, but can't seem to hold them down for more than six months. Three trips back to state penitentiary haven't helped either, though Ross blames his arrests on circumstance and prejudice.

"Like in California, five cops who always come around to hassle the homeless," he says, "and it always seemed like every time I tried to better myself, they take me down and give me a hard time. I was helping a friend—or I thought he was a friend. I was helping him get his car running. He couldn't lock his car. He asked me to hold on to some prescription medication for him. I was sitting down enjoying my coffee when two of the local cops drive by and then come back up behind me and hit their lights. For no reason."

Ross tells his story slowly, shaking his head, never looking up from the ground.

"They ask me if I had any drugs and I told that I was holding a prescription for a friend. For that I was put in jail for 30 days and put on a drug diversion program. Two months later [the police] pulled a traffic stop behind my van and one of them, for no reason at all, said 'I want to arrest this guy' and the other one told him that I was not in the computer. At that point, I sold my van and got a ticket to come here."

"Why Phoenix?" I ask.

"Because the police department doesn't mess with people like they do in California," Ross tells me. They respect people here as long as they keep their nose clean and do what they are supposed to do and I just got a belly full of it."

He's been in Phoenix since July 2008, and currently sleeps in the Outreach or Overflow. They are one in the same. And by either name, it is just a warehouse with a parking lot and a fence around it. When the warehouse fills up, they use the parking lot.

Ross says he can do manual labor ranging from hay fields, to welder's assistant, to forklift operator. "I've done just about everything there is to do," he says. Ross has tried to go through the job services programs on campus, and looks for work on career listings sites on the public library computers. But bad luck and/or his trust issues seem to sabotage every opportunity.

"[I'm seeking] physiological help for me to see what I am doing wrong in society's eyes," Ross says. "I might have to play a damn game with society so I can get what I want. Course that in turn would make my whole life a complete lie."

Currently, he is also trying to get his military rating for PTSD (Post Traumatic Stress Disorder), which would determine how seriously he is disabled and how much he is entitled to receive in disability. He feels only then can he support himself and clear up his California warrant. And he does seem shell-shocked to me, as well as a whole bunch of other things.

"Society wants me to be what they expect me to be and I don't know what that is," Ross adds, which seems to sum up all the life stories he's just told me. "I want to be true to myself and do something or better myself, and they don't want it. They think I'm strange. The way I see it, if a person doesn't enjoy what he wants to do, and try and better society by doing it, then he's spinning his wheels and no one wants to hear about it or see it."

Ross continues to illustrate his central message: He doesn't fit in. At one point he asks me, "How do you think I'm supposed to be?" I sense that he really wants me to answer. And I can't. In a way, I am struggling with that same conformity issue. Ross's case is very complicated and very sad, and yet I think all of us often ask ourselves what others expect of us.

"Frankly, I don't know Ross."

He looks lost, sad as he nods his head.

"Can I ask you three more questions?"

"Sure," Ross agrees, in his fatigue jacket and with downcast eyes.

What is the meaning of life?

That's a deep question. As far as I'm concerned, the meaning of life is more or less creating a society where one can live and prosper in, a society where people accept people as they are and not for what they want you to be. It's almost a utopian type thought that I have. But I know that will never happen. The corruption and mistrust has been inbred for years and it starts right in school. The separation of different societies, different beliefs, mistrust, hatred, uh, lying all that starts there in the school. And that's why the world is so screwed up like it is. That and the government intervenes on it too.

What are your thoughts about society and/or societies in general?

The first question actually answered the second one pretty much; but as far as people becoming aware of what's going on, then it will change.

Who are you?

Who am I? Well according to different people: I'm a traveler looking for something, looking for truth, for answers, something to believe in other than myself. That's about all I can think of right now.

I get down on my knees in order to look up into his eyes so I can properly thank him. Ross still makes it difficult. It is as if he is deeply ashamed. I tell him how much I appreciate his time and honesty.

Ross simply shrugs his shoulders. "Maybe that will help someone. I don't know."

**Ross makes me consider how important it is for us to
be included, to fit in, and yet still be individuals—
and how the two are sometimes in conflict.**

DAVID, CASS: Monday, January 26, 2009, 11:00 a.m.

Central Arizona Shelter Services (CASS) is one of the five main anchor
agencies of the Human Services Campus. At four stories tall, it is the
largest building on campus, towering over the single-story LDRC to its
right.

I enter through the shelter's doors, only to be greeted by a metal
detector with four persons manning it. They check my laptop bag and have
me pass through the body scanner before proceeding.

It is not the tight security that strikes me, but the building's structure.
The ceilings are two stories high. The walls are a very pale yellow and the
floors are unfinished cement. It feels a bit like prison and very different
from the LDRC. I can tell you don't just stroll in and out of this place.
There is a three-sided front desk with three women working behind it. All
the doors leading from this reception area are closed, and the place feels
relatively empty.

I inform the front desk that I have a meeting with David Bridge, the
Director of CASS. The woman behind the desk seems in no hurry to
contact Mr. Bridge. After waiting several minutes, watching her do little
to nothing, she makes a phone call to inform him I am here.

After some time, a tall and well-dressed man appears from behind
metal doors. David looks to me like your average corporate executive, grey
suit and all. He greets me and starts to give me a tour of the facility by
leading me through a door to my left. He talks as we walk, filling me in
on the building's history:

CASS is a 20-year-old institution and has roughly 100 employees
between its two locations, only one of which is located here on campus.
There is another one serving another sector of the community far away. We
are in a 54,000 square foot facility that provides beds, case management,
help with employment and dental work for the 400 persons who sleep here
each night. David is also in charge of the Outreach Shelter located across
the street, which sleeps another 300-plus persons.

There are three levels to CASS. David explains, if a homeless person
is working on their action plan to get income, get housed and "address

barriers to their self-sufficiency," they move up levels, assuming a bed is available. That is a big issue here: There are not close to enough beds.

At level one you get a mat on the floor for the night and indoor facilities such as bathrooms and showers. David insists that it's no picnic but it is a step up from the Outreach building and definitely from the parking lot of the Outreach Facility.

Being a mixed-gender facility, 100 beds here are for women. David doesn't know why, but in the 11 years he's been at CASS, the number of homeless women they serve has gone up from 10 percent to 30 percent.

People can sleep in the Outreach Shelter for as long as they like, but once inside the three-level CASS system, they have a six-month limit. David says that 80-90 percent of their clients are new to the facility—meaning clients don't keep returning.

David has a very straightforward manner, yet everything he says to me seems wrapped in empathy. He spouts facts and statistics, but then comments on how those facts affect individuals. In this blended tone, David says that though CASS cleans its bathrooms every day, "Can you imagine sharing a bathroom with 400 other people?"

And level one is only an indoor sleeping arrangement. You are outside in the morning at 5:30 a.m. and not let back in until 3 p.m. David's explanation for this is in part that it's not good to lie around all day; it just makes the clients get more depressed. Personally, being up at 5:30 a.m. and turned out onto the street sounds depressing to me.

He leads me into another gymnasium-sized room that is level two. At level two, you get a shared cubicle. The walls are only about four feet high, so I can see into each squared-off space as I peer across the vast empty room. At level two you still have to leave during the day, although there is a recreation room now available. David walks me through this room. There are men sitting at tables reading and playing board games. Another advantage of level two, he explains, is that you have a place in your cubicle for your possessions. From the way he says it, I can tell that's a pretty big deal to the clients. As I witness this, I wonder how much time I spend acquiring, storing, cleaning, organizing all my stuff?

At level three, you have more or less your own space and can even be in your "room" during the day. This level is mainly for persons who have employment, who are thus demonstrating movement towards self-sufficiency. As David tells it, the reality is that many of the jobs their clients get are not 9 to 5, and so this stage allows the luxury of sleeping during the day. Level three is also made a priority for veterans.

I question David if veterans get special treatment. He's not defensive at all and says that veterans are the one group you might argue gets some sort of special treatment around here—although he insists, "it's a weak argument." Essentially, everyone is the same here. Even veterans have to be out in six months.

"So would the Outreach Shelter be level 0 and the parking lot be level negative 1?" I press.

David says that while he would not refer to it that way, I am basically correct. The Outreach Shelter is a more recently created overflow shelter because the 400 beds provided in the main building simply do not meet the needs of the community. The inside provides some beds and many mats, with two bathroom facilities. The outside furnishes nothing but a couple of portable bathroom facilities in a fenced in parking lot. But it does provide a relatively safe place for the homeless to sleep, because CASS hires off-duty police officers to guard the shelter at night.

David, caring but far from impractical, makes no excuses for this shelter. He does not pretend that it is a good place to be, only that it is a step toward possibly something better and a Band-Aid to helping prevent deaths. He tells me they formed the Outreach Shelter five years ago when about 30 persons died on the streets during a brief period of time.

David points out that one of the greatest functions of the Outreach Shelter is exactly what the name suggests. It reaches out and helps to get homeless people into the system of assistance. Clients can see the gated area from the streets and while some are leery of institutions, they might enter it and then might eventually want to get to the main facility and seek help on their way to self-sufficiency.

When a client enters the main building for the first time, the staff meets with them to formulate a plan for the homeless person to become self-sufficient. The first part of that plan is income. David tells me that for one reason or another, only about 40 percent of the clients here are employable. If employment is not an option, they look next to what benefits the client might be eligible for. Often this step takes some time, and the person is left waiting to be accepted or denied for particular benefits. The final portion of the plan is addressing barriers to self-sufficiency. Common barriers for this community are: medical issues, substance abuse, past legal problems that still need to be resolved, transportation, clothing and help with hygiene/personal appearance.

That's where the dental team comes in.

David leads me to a single story arm of the building where dentistry is performed. It looks like a typical dental office, a state of the art nine-chair dental office. The homeless often have chronic dental pain and infections that go untreated.

The office was founded and is run by Kris Volcheck, DDS, MBA. Since it's inception in 2001, the office has provided millions of dollars in free medical care and has engaged the time and talents of hundreds of volunteer dentists, dental hygienists and dental assistants. Dental labs from across the state and country have contributed as well by donating all the restorative appliances. This provides all patients with x-rays, cleanings and education on proper oral hygiene—and for patients who are following their case plan, restorative dental services. David comments on how important looks are to getting a job and adds: "When you look better, you feel better."

CASS's dental office serves homeless adults and children and is the only office of its kind in the nation. Dr. Volcheck has won numerous awards for his efforts and is currently working with India's dental clinic at the Sri Sathya Sai Institute to duplicate the success of the CASS clinic in India. Oh, and he saves the community millions of dollars because if they weren't treating these issues, emergency rooms would be doing it.

I'm a bit overwhelmed by this one man's efforts and those who are associated with him. Like Jessica and so many others no this campus, I could write a book about him alone.

As we head upstairs to David's office, he says that one way or another, CASS gets about 80 percent of their clients housed. This, of course, means that 20 percent don't get housed and are back out on the streets at the end of the six months (although they can sleep at the Outreach Shelter).

David is still explaining the system here. CASS only deals with single men and women. Families stay at UMOM, a homeless agency located off-campus but nearby. David points out that there is a disservice done by thinking of their clients as single and UMOM clients as family. For example, he explains that many of CASS's single—unmarried—men and women have children who are being taken care of by someone else.

"So, the single population here is very connected to family populations," David concludes. "You can't really separate the two. We should think about it with continuity and try to reduce it. It's the same way you can't really separate the homeless from the non-homeless. It's part of the fabric of who we are.

"And homeless is just a label," David continues, voice lowering. "But it's not a label, it's a phase. There is a movement to end homelessness. You are never going to end it, but you can reduce or shorten the phase. And once someone wants to make a change, you don't judge people. You don't know what you would do in that situation. There are probably four times in my life that other people helped me out with a car or some money or I would have been homeless too. So I can empathize. I can't judge!"

David makes a strong point here: Everything we get is from the society in which we are immersed. Even if we think we worked hard for a degree or a promotion, we did so in an environment that supported the possibility of such rewards. He implies that it's not a level playing field. While we all live in the same country, we really don't all live in the same environment. It really is *whom* we know; not what we know.

"David . . . is it just me, or why does it seem like there aren't many elderly persons around campus?" I ask.

"I think only about five to six percent of the homeless population meets the definition of elderly," he answers. "It could be because they have access to income through Social Security. And it could also be because life is so hard on the streets. Chronic homelessness lowers your life expectancy by something like 20 years."

That's a sobering thought and statistic.

I try again to get a sense for all this, this whole place at once. In response to my perplexed look, David suggests I do an immersion. That is when you come and spend the night at CASS posing as a homeless person, so you can get a feeling for what it's like. He's making it sound like no big deal. But I don't like the idea. It sounds wimpy because what's the big deal of spending one night here . . . but I hate not having privacy. So sharing a bathroom with 400 other people? That does not sound like fun to me.

Later in our talk, David mentions that one group they will not be housing as of June 30, 2009 is sex offenders. There are apparently many complicated issues when it comes to sex offenders, the greatest of which is concern over the possible safety of women and children present on campus. But David explains that it is much more involved than just that and he non-judgmentally made these comments: "The sad thing is, if it were not for their record, they would be the easiest to house. They are not your typical felon population. They are often well educated, have good skills, are employable. And they really follow their programs. But there are not many housing options for them." He pauses. "We had a guy once who received his sex offence charge when he was 18 for having sex with his 16 year-old girlfriend. He had a home, but his probation officer would not let him live in it because there was a 12-year-old girl in the house. But this happened a long time ago. The guy has not re-offended and his case did not suggest that he's a predator."

"So this guy owned a home and was homeless?"

"Yes."

"And it doesn't matter how long ago the offence occurred?"

"No. A lot of our sex offenders have life-time probation."

The current system often sentences sex offenders to roam the streets because they can't get housing or work, which doesn't seem like such a good idea if we are concerned about keeping these people out of our communities.

While it's hard to make a case for "improved treatment" of sex offenders, something about this scenario seems wrong as well. Yet another impossible question I'd never have imagined just a month ago.

For now, I change the subject and ask David about a sign I saw concerning the homeless registering to vote. It said that in half the states in the U.S., you have to have an address to vote. David confirms this, adding that a lot of homeless are registered to vote and use CASS's address to do so.

"I'll tell you what: If they did decided to vote as an organized group, they could change this community."

It's time to ask David the three questions.

What is the meaning of life?

I wish I knew. For me on some level it's the golden rule. It's not really the rule; but leave the world better than you found it. Treat others as you would like to be treated. Be kind to others . . . I'm trying to figure out that one myself.

What are your thoughts about society and/or societies in general?

Necessary. I mean you need it. It's necessary; everyone needs a sense of belonging. You may think you're independent, but there are always a lot of other people involved in getting you were you are at. The key is to make it one that nurtures instead of destroys.

Who are you?

Well, on the demographic level, I'm a father. A homeowner. I'm a social service worker. Then it goes to religious. I'm a son of God and I've been entrusted with stuff. And I've been blessed. I have had that community. I have had that support and the least I can do is give some of that back. I know that sounds cliché.

David causes me to consider that we are anything but independent.

RUNNING DEER, CLIENT: Monday, January 26, 2009, 1:00 p.m.

Last week, while I roamed around campus, I met Running Deer when he asked what I was doing here. He sounded very interested in contributing, even setting a date and time with me, which was a bit unusual. Many people tell me they are interested in being interviewed but have a "when we get around to it" sort of attitude. Around here, time seems to slip away or disappear altogether. But I find Running Deer, as scheduled, at the locked front doors of LDRC.

The doors don't open promptly, however, the situation gives us a few minutes to chat outside. Running Deer is in a wheelchair, and I discover he didn't just wheel over from CASS. He came from his "home," an overpass many bus rides away, to meet me today. He is not approved for housing or any sort of benefits yet, and says he and cannot get a job because of his back injury and being in a wheelchair.

Running Deer is part of the 20 percent who don't get housed.

It took Running Deer hours to get here, and he came because he felt a sense of duty to do so. He is dressed in dirty jeans and a T-shirt. He says he was born in California but has a bit of Texas twang to his voice. His face—relaxed, calm—is weathered with deep lines. And despite his name, he does not look the least bit Native American. "I've gone through a lot in my life and I feel if I can give my story so people can hear it, so it helps, it's true, so I don't care if you use my name," says Running Deer, now 63 days sober.

"How do you stay clean?" I ask.

"I've found it's easier to stay clean if I pray and read the Bible and stay involved in everything in my church," he replies. "I'm going to school and working on my associate degree and getting my food handler's license."

Running Deer takes the bus two days a week to school. His schooling and books are paid for by a Maricopa County grant. I can't believe he's living under an overpass while doing this. But Running Deer doesn't stay on topic long enough to receive my praise. I had already noticed that speaking with him requires very careful listening, because the threads in his conversations tend to come loose.

Running Deer is working on getting benefits claims from six years in the Army and getting an MRI done so he can be cleared for back surgery. It becomes apparent that there is a big discrepancy between him and the Army about the length of his service and the conditions of his discharge. Running Deer used to hop around to different manual labor jobs—everything from mechanic to logger—but now needs to find something that's easier on his back and that supports his quest for sobriety.

He explains, "From the age of three 'til 10, I lived in a real abusive atmosphere: sexual [and] mental. The thing that makes life that much harder for me now is back in 2001 . . ." he gives a lengthy and complicated explanation for a series of events that ultimately lead to him having ". . . a couple of sex charges brought against me and I served six years. Now getting help from anywhere is almost impossible because they don't want any sex offenders. I stay at an overpass over by the church I go to. I can't go to work because of my back. I've been working on getting disability and SSI. But they say I haven't worked long enough to get anything." He shakes his head slowly. "I don't know how that's possible because I've been working since I was five years old, and that with the time in the service."

Even around here, Running Deer has it tough.

"CASS tells me because of my past, they won't let me in," he continues. "I went down to Saint Vinny's [St. Vincent de Paul is one of the campus's anchor agencies] to see where I might be able to go to get some help until I get on my feet and she told me there is nowhere in the state of Arizona that is going to help me. They wouldn't even let me shower. Most services pick and choose whom they help. I hate to be like that, but that's how I see it."

Running Deer is not currently using, but still considers himself "a meth addict."

I feel a strange empathy toward this man. How is he staying clean under these circumstances? I wonder. For me it's just that when I miss my girlfriend I can easily just go drink a beer.

Running Deer returns again and again to his faith, and how belief in God has saved him from an even worse place. "I've been going to church ever since I was a little kid," he says. "Even though I knew God existed, I was headstrong and wanted to do things my way. I didn't have any patience. Now I think I am more serious than I've ever been. I think I hit rock bottom. I was sick and tired running around looking for dope, dumpster diving. Now I don't have to worry about all that. I've become more reliant on Christ and doing it in a real way. Now things seem to happen for me, sometimes without me even asking."

Running Deer still has many hurdles to clear on the path to recovery. "I have contracted hepatitis C but I have to be clean for six months before they will treat it," he tells me. (Your liver has to be in good shape before undergoing the treatment for hepatitis C.) "I've attempted suicide four times in my life. Because of my mother destroying all my relationships, and drugs. But now things are good with my family. So we'll see how that goes. I know I'm not going to mess with it, because I'll screw it up."

Running Deer explains that he has been homeless since 2003, and his drug use, particularly methamphetamines, really got out of control during those first six years.

My interview with Running Deer slowly turns into a soliloquy, and I just let him talk.

"I guess growing up on the streets as a kid, fighting, skipping school and getting into trouble was fun when I was young, but now? I look around and see people fighting over ground they don't have no ownership over. I've seen people that would kill someone for .10 cents in their pockets. And you have to ask, what is the reason for all this madness? In the past I let things outside me get into me. I couldn't stand the hatred and violence. Now I don't worry about stuff outside me. If you start worrying about everything outside of yourself you are going to drive yourself mad. Then you look for an escape to get away from it, and that's what I did with drugs."

Running Deer says he used crystal meth because it made him active and seemed to break up the depression. This man is so truthful about his past, repenting but ready to move on. Why he doesn't lie about the sex offence charge in his past so he can get a job? I wonder—then ask. Running Deer answers with the honesty only possible after one has received a huge dose of reality in his or her life: "Everything you do in the dark will come into the light," he says. "So you don't want to lie. If you are straight up honest, most people will deal with you. I used to be a habitual liar. But I learned the hard way that lying will get you nowhere. My situation is bad enough already. I don't want to make things any worse. One thing about staying clean is being honest. Sometimes honesty is painful and embarrassing, but in the long run, you'll know you can trust me."

Running Deer rambles on for some time about what a disposable based society we are. We don't fix things when they break; we just throw them out and buy a new one. I finally conclude our conversation by asking the three questions.

What is the meaning of life?

It's like in a car. You got the motor and the car. The car can't go nowhere without the motor. Well it's pretty much the same with life. I'm the motor for that car out there. And someone who's down or depressed, I can be the motor for them.

Life is about caring for other people. It makes you feel good when you can make someone's day. That's what the meaning of life is about. It's not about personal gain. It's about wanting to see someone else get where you are at. It's like a ladder.

What are your thoughts about society and/or societies in general?

Well society has lost a lot, because people in society have gotten so wrapped up in the livin' for themselves that they don't look at reality no more. They don't know what reality is no more. They just get up in the morning and try to make ends meet. So they look for that answer in money or dope. They don't stop to take inventory on what reality is. The reality is you were born because God created you and in the end you will go back to the earth. In this life you only have two choices, whether you go to heaven or hell. Everyone wants to control everything outside of them instead of what's inside them. And that's my thoughts on society.

Who are you?

I'm a nobody. Personally my opinion is this. I'm a person struggling in this life like everyone else. Until I learned that I was nothing and that there was a creator in my life, I was nothing. I was always just trying to get from one place to another. I am just here to be a servant. In order to be a good leader you have to be a good servant first. You can't learn to be a leader until you learn to be a follower. I didn't know that a long time ago. I just wanted to get ahead. Nothing in this world means anything to me unless God is there. I don't want to start thinking I'm better than anybody else or I'll screw it up. I'm just someone who got it right this time. So if I was to say anything about myself, I would say I'm a nothing.

Running Deer makes me contemplate our disposable approach to things, and more so, people. Where do they go when society throws them away?

JESSICA, LDRC: Monday, January 26, 2009, 3:00 p.m.

Outside the office, I find Jessica explaining to a new intern what working at LDRC is like. As example, she uses an improvisation class exercise she just participated in. I listen in. Apparently, you sit in a circle and when someone points to you, you respond saying yes and then switch chairs with him or her. Everyone has a number, and counts off in sequence. So if your number is three, then every time you hear the number two called out, you say three. In addition, you also each have a lunchmeat name and are saying those in order as well; so for example, every time you hear salami, you say pastrami. The three games go on simultaneously. It sounds like an intentionally confusing game.

The intern, therefore, looks rightfully confused as to what Jessica means by all this.

Jessica, smiling, explains: "That's the way life is here. Lots of things happening at once and all require your simultaneous attention. And I think we all work to get good at that."

I would think you would work to reduce that. Where I see disorganization, Jessica sees value and connection. I sit down at the table in the center of the office lobby, joining them and Dawn. We are all soon proving Jessica's point as we mix and mingle our conversations. It's like a little four person cocktail party, with three or more different games going on at once.

As the intern discusses her desires and interests in working here, Dawn weaves in her own desires and interests that relate. Dawn wants to form a client woman's group that will have a focus on the individual women in the group and the group as a whole. Jessica further weaves in her ideas. They have all added ideas to the overall concept and before she knows it, the intern will be helping to form a women's group that will initially be encouraging women to speak up for themselves. The hope is that this empowerment will eventually lead them to create a group on campus that can influence decisions/conditions here.

Dawn's initial ideas seem so far-reaching. It makes me think about what David Bridge said—that if the people here organize as a political group, they would be quite the constituency, although Dawn means to have them act as a committee on the campus. Nonprofits can't push political issues.

Jessica breaks from the now frenzied conversation to go to her office for our interview. "I mean this as a compliment, but you're kind of like a fungus," I begin. "I just watched you infect that intern. And I got the feeling when talking with David Bridge that some of his more tempered and holistic ideas might have come from you."

Jessica smiles with a sort of childlike pride. "I know how powerful I am. I know I'm a fungus," she jokes before changing the subject. "I had . . . I have the most amazing parents in the world and there was no limit to what I could do and how amazing I was," she says. "But I don't know if it was that I didn't believe them or thought they just told me that because they loved me. For a while there, I was really trying to find myself. About four years ago, I was really lost. But this position just fits me so perfectly . . . I feel like someone created this job for me," she concludes.

"You always seem so humble," I respond, "so how do you rectify this pride with that humility?"

"I don't know how to rectify it," She laughs, and laughs again. "I think intellectually it's incompatible. But I don't feel at odds with it emotionally. I guess I can't rectify it. But I'm getting that feedback. I guess I'm just supposed to keep doing what I'm doing because it's having a positive effect on the organization and the people around."

I move the conversation on to something that's been troubling me lately—how sex offenders are phased out of the CASS system. My conversation with Running Deer today didn't ease my concerns, and I ask Jessica for her thoughts.

"I've met a lot of people [who] I later found out were sex offenders," she says. "I've worked with a few, and maybe I'm naïve, but I've always felt safe. I'm not excusing the behavior but . . . well, first off, society lumps in sex offenders and pedophiles." She means all pedophiles are sex offenders but not all sex offenders are pedophiles. "And there are so many levels and individual differences. For instance, being 18 and having a 16-year-old girlfriend."

"David mentioned a case like that to me, and now the guy has probation for life."

"Yeah. It is a mental disease like any other, and we don't offer them any rehabilitation in society," Jessica says. "People may hire felons; some people are very open to that, but no murders and no sex offense across the board. I'm not saying that it's excusable, but it is rehabilitatable. Most places will not hire them. Most apartments will not house them. So they are sentenced to homelessness."

Sentenced to homelessness. It's ominous, and seems impossible to resolve. All I can do for now is change the subject.

"Best thing that happened last week?"

"Well, I had a difficult conversation with an employee that went really well," Jessica says. "And I'm glad I said what I had to say, even though it was difficult."

"I hear that, but why was it difficult?" I ask. "What scares you about conflict situations?"

"I feel like I'm not going to say my truth, because I don't want to hurt someone. But this time, I just stayed true to what I felt was right. It's like that quote that most people attribute to Nelson Mandela, but it's really from Marianne Williamson."

The quote Jessica refers to is from Williamson's book, *A Return To Love*. Here it is: "Our deepest fear is not that we are inadequate. Our deepest fear is that we are powerful beyond measure. [. . .] As we are liberated from our own fear, our presence automatically liberates others."

"So I stayed true to myself." She pauses. "I think that's the answer to your other question about how I reconcile those two things."

"So, did anything bad happen last week?" I ask.

There is a long pause before Jessica replies.

"Nothing. Things have been going better and better. In a way, all that much better since we started these weekly meetings. I should be paying you for therapy."

There seems to be some benefit to having someone from the outside like me wandering around campus just talking to people, seeing what they're up to and asking them what they think. And these meetings with Jessica have been good for me, too. I get some intangible gift from her and this place, and yet it seems to help my life quite tangibly.

All this reminds me of an anecdote I saw Jessica had posted on the website for All In Campaign, another grassroots effort to end homelessness. Jessica doesn't know which quote I mean, so I remind her again. It's titled "Going up the River," from Ronald Rolheiser's book *The Holy Longing: The Search for Christian Spirituality*. Here it is:

> Once upon time there was a town that was built just beyond the bend of large river. One day some of the children from the town were playing beside the river when they noticed three bodies floating in the water. They ran for help and the townsfolk quickly pulled the bodies out of the river.
>
> One body was dead so they buried it. One was alive, but quite ill, so they put that person into the hospital. The third turned out to

*be a healthy child, who they then placed with a family who cared
for it and who took it to school.*

*From that day on, every day a number of bodies came
floating down the river and, every day, the good people of the
town would pull them out and tend to them—taking the sick to
hospitals, placing the children with families, and burying those
who were dead.*

*This went on for years; each day brought its quota of bodies,
and the townsfolk not only came to expect a number of bodies
each day but also worked at developing more elaborate systems for
picking them out of the river and tending to them. Some of the
townsfolk became quite generous in tending to these bodies and a
few extraordinary ones even gave up their jobs so that they could
tend to this concern full-time. And the town itself felt a certain
healthy pride in its generosity.*

*However, during all these years and despite all that generosity
and effort, nobody thought to go up the river, beyond the bend that
hid from their sight what was above them, and find out why, daily,
those bodies came floating down the river.*

"I bring up the story because it suggests that there are different
approaches to helping," I say. "For instance, David Bridge suggests that
building too comfortable a community here might prevent clients from
wanting to reenter mainstream society, the Ordinary World."

She looks up in frustration and dismay. "This place does not offer
enough comfort for anyone who wants to be in a home." She does agree,
however, that the wrong solutions can actually perpetuate the problem.

Jessica tells me she has shown this story to many people. One day she
emailed it to Dawn, whose office is within earshot of Jessica's. Halfway
through reading it she heard Dawn, in her loud New York accent, say,
"Why don't they just go up the river and see where all the bodies are
coming from?" Jessica yelled back to her to finish reading the quote. A
minute later, she could hear Dawn laugh from across the office.

"And I thought to myself, 'Yes! That's why I hired you!'" Jessica
exclaims.

"Just one more question," I say. "I don't even think I'm going to include
it in my book, but you mentioned last week after I had finished taking
notes about participating in a vision circle. What is that?"

"It's for putting passion into practice," she replies. "It's a support group for discovering and manifesting the possibilities of each member. You talk about your dreams and hold each other accountable for moving towards those. See that collage on the top of my bulletin board? It's from the vision circle. You can take it down. There might be some notes on the back."

I take down the collage down and flip it over. There are no notes on the back, only a date: "1/26/05." Jessica gasps and looks flushed. It takes me a minute to realize that was exactly four years ago to the day. I'm not that shocked. My entire experience has been like this since I started my book. Everything just seems to connect, just like Jessica was talking about to the intern when I walked in today.

Jessica makes me consider that life is all interrelated, but there is a big difference in dealing with things upstream then dealing with them downstream.

LARRY & RONNIE, EX-CLIENTS, LDRC:
Tuesday, January 27, 2009, 1:00 p.m.

I met Larry just the day before, when I heard him talking outside Jessica's office. He was giving Dawn $100 for repayment to the Angel Fund (a small, interest free fund they created at LDRC to help people get on their feet again) and thanking her for all her help.

"I didn't do it pal," Dawn said. "You did it."

I told Jessica that sounded like a client success story and I wanted to talk to him. It's hard finding success stories—not because there aren't any, but because people leave and get on with their lives.

Jessica introduced us. Larry looked like a biker gnome. He stood about 5'7", wore a leather Harley Davidson vest and had a small white chin-beard. He looked kind of like Popeye to me, minus the pipe.

I explained my project to him and was less than a few sentences in before he said, "Sure." I was a bit surprised because most people want to know a little bit more. So I said it would be a big help. "Yes." he responded. I explained a bit more. He continued to respond with, "Yes." He finally had to stop me, explaining that if it benefits one other person, he is all too happy to oblige. That's my paraphrase, because Larry uses simple, clear, straightforward English.

Larry asked if he might bring his fiancé Ronnie along because she too was recently homeless. "Of course," I tell him. We make plans and I look forward to the interview.

The next day, Larry arrives to the interview with Ronnie, who looks like a sweet, young grandmother. She has a pink, happy face and one of those soothing voices that always seem to imply that you are loved and everything is going to be OK. I can't believe she was homeless just a short while ago. I must still have a very prejudiced idea of what a homeless person is supposed to look like—or, for that matter, who they are supposed to be.

I ask them each to give me some brief background, explaining that it isn't really their "story" I'm after but instead, their ideas and what makes them tick.

Larry explains that almost a year ago, he was admitted into the VA hospital for trying to commit suicide. They diagnosed him as being extremely depressed, ADD and more. Larry had been a truck driver for most of his life, but also a meth addict for 25 years. He was a "functioning addict" for most of that time, meaning he could hold down a job, stay out of jail and live somewhere besides the streets. But about two years ago, his mother died and the whole drug thing got way out of control. Larry lost his license from too many unpaid fines and therefore lost his job. And with that, he lost his home, because Larry used to drive cross-country and lived in his truck.

The VA hospital sent him to CASS.

"Didn't that make you feel even worse?" I ask.

"Well, yes it did." Larry looks like Popeye, and he sounds a bit like him too.

He goes on to explain that while staying at CASS, he stopped using and they required him to go to the New Arid Club or Community Bridges, both of which help with drug counseling. Larry explains that he was working on his program so well that Jessica loaned him money from the Angel Fund to pay off his fines, get his license back and start earning money again. Dawn helped, too, by getting him some cheap monthly insurance.

So after a while, Larry was clean and going to lots of meetings to stay that way. He had his license back and even found a job driving again. He didn't have a place to live yet, but he was on his way.

Around this time, Larry met Ronnie.

I produce three pages of notes when most people tell me about their past. Larry sums his up in a few minutes. He does not derivate, does not mince or overuse words. He speaks in an uneducated, but very intelligent and logical way. His words are simple, but his thoughts are clear and concise.

He turns to Ronnie and says it probably time for her to tell about her past while he goes outside to smoke a cigarette. Larry has more energy than he knows what to do with. He's like an overactive 5-year-old in every possible way—full of energy and very silly.

Ronnie starts talking in a slow, calm, melodious voice. I feel like I am listening to a speaker at a New Age convention, not because of the content of her words but their melody. She was married for 30 years and has four kids. She met her husband in high school and was a stay-at-home mom. But Ronnie's husband was and still is an alcoholic and drug addict. He exposed her to crack.

Ronnie, the sweet young grandmother, tells me she has been a crack addict for 10 years. I am shocked! She doesn't look or sound like she's ever had a beer, let alone done something illegal. She does not fit the mold. I've got to get over this propensity towards judgment.

Ronnie continues, telling me that her husband was abusive, they were both on drugs and things started to get out of control. By now her kids were not speaking to her, either, because of who she had become.

Her husband finally threw her out of the house and she soon found out that she didn't have any friends to go to or a place to stay. Ronnie says she lived for a while in a cheap motel until a run-in with a "woman cop." The police officer was there for other reasons, but looked at Ronnie and knew she was in a bad situation.

Apparently, Ronnie was there with someone else who was most likely not the best company to keep. The police officer told Ronnie, "I don't know what's going on and I don't want to, but you had better go to CASS."

Ronnie got out of the motel situation and ended up sleeping on the streets for a few nights. She didn't know anything about survival on the streets. She was scared and had no money. And that's when Ronnie decided get off the streets and into the Outreach Shelter.

One of the good things about the Outreach Shelter is people on the streets can actually see it. It acts as a bridge from one world to another. Ronnie described the whole experience as, ". . . massive culture shock. I did nothing but cry for a week. I'm middle class. We had a Land Rover and a $250,000 house. But I lost all that. I woke up too late."

Still, Overflow looked pretty nice to Ronnie from the streets. Once there, CASS looked pretty nice compared to Overflow. That gave Ronnie aspirations to get out of CASS and into an apartment.

David would be pleased. Ronnie's situation shows how it's supposed to work.

Larry and Ronnie were friends from almost the beginning of her ordeal on the streets, but they started dating just six months ago, she says. They have both been clean for almost a year now. More than that: They are that kind of clear-eyed, in-love-with-life, glad-to-wake-up-in-the-morning clean.

Ronnie finishes her background story as Larry, with perfect timing, comes bouncing in, chuckling to himself, like a cig-loving Tigger.

"I don't care if he ever grows up," Ronnie dotes. "He makes me laugh. We finish each others sentences . . ."

". . . all the time," Larry finishes, without missing a beat. "She loves me for who I am and accepts me for who I am."

"He's street smart and I'm book smart," Ronnie chimes back.

In this back and forth fashion, they explain to me that they now live together in an apartment funded by VASH (Veteran's Association of Subsidized Housing.) It allows them to pay 30 percent of their income toward housing, regardless of the level of income.

I ask what turned them around? What made them choose differently?

Ronnie responds first.

"Determination. I never want to go back to where I had been. Once I became sober, I could see how bad I had become. My kids turned against me. I'm still repairing that. I finally felt the freedom to do what I want. I didn't realize I had that choice. Loosing everything made me realize I had that choice."

Larry proceeds in his simplistic, but honest and profound manner. "I was looking at two choices—livin' or dying," he says. "And I was too chicken to die. It was easier to fight this battle than to die. Ronnie has made it all come together. I have a daughter and a grandson. The past is gone."

"It made me realize that I was the only one who broke it and I was the only one who could fix," Ronnie continues.

I speak up in order to frame their transformation in time: "But this all took about a year. It takes a long time to get clean. Hell, it takes a long time to get a driver's license around here."

"Waiting is one of the hardest things," Ronnie agrees. "But it's one day at a time. When it was bad, my friend and I used to say 'five minutes, five minutes, five minutes.' Five minutes at a time. You deal with what's in front of you and move on."

Larry explains that he thinks God has helped him all the way. "I figure there's all these gods out there. Why can't there be a god for stoners, like me?" he philosophizes. "As long as I live by my code and be a good person, why not?"

Much like the interview, they teamed up to answer the three questions.

What is the meaning of life?

Larry: *Oh lord. Joy. Happiness.*

Ronnie: *He's right. Helping someone else feel the same joy that you feel. As long as you have faith. As long as you can stay happy, to laugh. You have to be able to laugh. Having a mate.*

Larry: *All that and sex, the glorifying of being together and waking up and seeing her smiling face.*

Ronnie: *Yes, and sex too.*

What are your thoughts about society and/or societies in general?

Ronnie: *I think society has a lot of wrong ideas about a lot of things. I think we all have a lot to learn from everyone around us.*

Larry: *It doesn't matter how old or young you are.*

Ronnie: *We have to open our eyes and our minds.*

Who are you?

Holding Larry's hand, Ronnie begins: *I'm a strong woman. I have definite ideas about things. I'm a nurturer. I'm a mother. I'm a lot different than I thought. I am willing to try anything once and if I like it watch out.*

Larry: *She sure is. We got busted in the park.*

He laughs. She blushes. I ask Larry who he is.

Larry: *Who am I? Today, today, I'm a happy man who's found the joy of his life who I've waited a lifetime for. I've made a lot of mistakes, but hopefully no more. We talk, we laugh, we have lots of sex.*

Ronnie adds, somewhat more tactfully: *We walk through life together.*

I thank them both for their time as the lovebirds leave. Ronnie, round and soft, moves in a mixture of waddle and saunter. Next to her, Larry: short, wiry, giggling and skipping beside his lover. Somehow, both keep pace with one another.

I exit the side office and enter the main LDRC lobby to finalize my notes. I want to get out there and simmer in the thick human soup of the campus. It's all here. The diversity is unbelievable. I try to find one person in the room who looks, dresses or acts like any other—and I can't find one.

A guy sits right in front of me, smiling from ear to ear because he just got some new shoes. They're brand new workman's boots. I don't know how he got them, but he sure is happy about them. After showing them off to a few friends he sits down in front of me, looking down to admire them.

There's a pride that seems to flow up from the boots and into his legs. The energy makes the man straighten out the cuffs and smooth out the rest of his pants. Finally he stands, looks at his shirt and, as a final measure, tucks it in.

Larry and Ronnie cause me to consider how well relationships work when we celebrate the differences of others.

MOVIE WORKSHOP, LDRC: Saturday, January 31, 2009, 1:00 p.m.

I'm excited as always to go to Dawn's movie workshop. But I'm also a bit sad this time. I realize that this is most likely the last one I will be going to. I need to work extra hours at my massage job on Saturdays.

But my back is much better. My feelings of loneliness are still there, but they are much better too. My general feelings about life are a whole hell of a lot better! But my finances are not. I have about $50 in the bank and a huge house payment coming due.

For the first time in my life, I must face the possibility of losing my home. Of course, I will not be homeless. I could afford a cheap apartment and continue writing, which is my main goal. I know that now, and I also know that my fear has more to it than the fear of losing my home.

"Far and Away" is the movie and this week, someone guesses it right.

Dawn explains that in this movie there are initiating events that pile up, desires that form, shifts that occur, turning points, the need for action, challenges, trials, detours, opportunities, final tests and realizations.

"There is a process between where you start and where you get to," she says. "When you make a decision, you are often tested. It rarely just works out right away for you. Those challenges show you the problems in your plan that requires readjustment. But readjustment of what? Your plan, or you?"

I feel like our teacher just planted a seed in me that will later sprout.

Running Deer sees me typing away and realizes that I need a place to plug in my laptop. From his wheelchair, he feeds my power cord under another chair and into an outlet. I ask him how his back is. He says he just got the MRI, and it doesn't look good.

This time I'm going to be a participator and not just an observer, I vow. As if I have a choice. Writing is fine, but life is where the action is. I get some popcorn and just watch the first half of the movie.

I had seen this movie before, but Dawn has given me new vision. The first half of the movie contains themes almost all of us can relate to. Tom Cruise's character's father considers him "odd." His brothers make fun of him. He doesn't conform and eventually leaves his community to follow his dream.

Dawn stops the movie halfway through. Again, it gives us time to think about what we have been experiencing and makes us hungry to see the rest.

She asks, "What was the pile up of initiating events?"

Class members throw out various answers:

"Father died."

"Tom wants his own land."

"Family house burned down."

Students contribute more to the discussion, and are received thoughtfully by Dawn, who more often than not responds with more questions.

Dawn: "What does he want?"

Student: "Joseph wants land."

Another student: "He wants freedom."

Dawn: "Right. He wants freedom and ownership. How possible is that in Ireland at the time? And what does Shannon (the Nicole Kidman character) want?"

Student: "She wants to be modern."

Dawn: "What does modern mean to her?"

The conversation bustles for some time before Dawn restarts the film. We quickly get reabsorbed in the story. When the movie ends, I have this funny feeling of completion and emotional exhaustion. It was a journey— one in which I participated.

But Dawn's not done. "Where did he detour?" she asks. The class gives various answers, but Dawn is not satisfied: "OK, but why?"

Someone says the main character lost track of his dream.

"Exactly!" The student's face lights up. We don't get a lot of "Exactly!" comments from Dawn. She's very receptive, but not overly giving of praise. We are doing very well today and in a childish sort of way, I'm feeling quite proud of our group as Dawn's lecture continues.

"Your sight can be distracted from your goal by temporary benefits, but they don't compare to what you get when you seek your true dream, your true self," she says. "The difference between a trial and a detour is trials get you closer to your dream. Detours are just spinning your wheels."

I pause for a minute as the workshop ends and everyone clears out. I want to thank Dawn for letting me attend her classes and to tell her how impressive she is. I wait for the last person to leave, but he pauses as well.

"You know, this stuff is starting to make sense," the man tells her. "I've had some shifts lately, too." He is a black man in a bright red sweatshirt with Mickey Mouse on the front of it. His tennis shoes are new, bright red, as clean as his sweatshirt. He's slightly overweight in a way that's attractive. He goes on to explain how he is starting to see how he has gotten himself here. He's also starting to see the value of doing things for himself.

"I mean, if you feed me, it isn't what I want to eat. If you clothe me, it isn't the clothing I want to wear. If you give me shelter, it isn't in the shelter I want."

Here's another clean-shaven, well-spoken person on the streets. I have to stop myself from thinking 'but that guy doesn't look homeless' because I've come to realize such commentary is useless here.

The man shares with Dawn that the drugs and alcohol cause him to not take responsibility for himself: "I can see what I've been doing to get myself here." He falls silent with a pensive look on his face. Dawn has been listening patiently. Now she speaks up.

"Did you see the movie 'Ray'?"

He says he did.

She asks him if he remembers why Ray Charles used heroin as she leads him to say that Ray felt guilty and that's why he used drugs—to escape his guilt. I can see the light bulb going on above his head. Drugs aren't the only issue. There is probably something behind his own behavior, something underneath it.

Finally she says, "You had a good reason for doing those drugs and you will discover it."

He leaves with a look on his face like it's all coalescing for him.

Dawn looks up at me, still lingering in the room.

"Isn't that cool!" she says in her New York speech. "I just love watching them 'get it'! It is one of the greatest things ever!"

I can tell this sort of experience is one of the biggest thrills in her life. Seeing my chance to talk, I comment on how good she is at facilitating change in others. But Dawn immediately reminds me that it's a group effort, that it's not the movie workshop alone. That man's shifts are the combination—the addition and multiplication—of many efforts by many people and from many different angles, and, of course, she says—his willingness to look inside. When a client 'gets is,' I can tell she has a sense of pride in them, not in herself.

Dawn makes me consider that people often don't think about what they really want and further they have good reasons for doing stupid things.

AMY, ST. JOSEPH THE WORKER:
Monday, February 2, 2009, 9:30 a.m.

St. Joseph The Worker is located within the LDRC, behind and to the left of its large center lobby. The office door and front wall is made of glass. Everyone can see right into it.

I let the receptionist know I am there to meet with Amy and sit in the small, four-person-max waiting area. I read a sign painted on the wall in large, green letters: "No one can go back and make a brand new start. Anyone can start from now and make a brand new beginning." The words "back" and "beginning" are in blue font for emphasis. A thick red arrow borders the entire sign as if to suggest movement, a coming around and moving forward.

Amy Caffarrello, St. Joseph the Worker's young director, greets me with a smile, two rows of white teeth, then escorts me back to her office to talk. On our way, we walk through a large room with tables and chairs nicely arranged for clients working on resumes and other projects. I explain to Amy my ever-changing project and my continual ignorance as to what goes on here and, in that vein, ask for her thoughts.

"In a nutshell, we help people get and keep jobs," she says of St. Joseph the Worker. "We're all about employment. A key to our success is we're all about sustainable employment. Because of this, we can only help a small number. We want to help people completely make a permanent change in their lives. We want them to work full-time, to their capacity. Not everyone can work 40 hours per week. We try and steer clients away from industries that aren't full-time work, like telemarketing or seasonal work. We prefer jobs that offer opportunity for growth."

Amy says she's has been in her current position for three years. When talking, she stops often to ponder which direction she wants to head and exactly what to say. It's not as if she is incapable of moving faster, but instead has a deep respect for the complexity of the situation here and the importance of anything she says about it.

Next, Amy explains a troublesome trend. They have seen a "surge in numbers," a "50 percent increase since last year," in the number of clients applying for help. She's clearly frustrated by this: "There are only so many new people we can help. If we're not careful and take on too much, we could create a bottleneck, diluting our effectiveness."

St. Joseph the Worker was founded in 1988 by the Notre Dame Holy Cross Order of Priests and Brothers, Amy tells me, the same order that founded the André House, a soup kitchen located across from the campus. The director of André House at the time was Michael Baxter. He, with the support of other community members, started St. Joseph in response to the requests from individuals who were receiving free evening meals from André House. They expressed that there were no resources to help homeless people get jobs.

St. Joseph the Worker is 100 percent privately funded.

"I'm glad it's that way because the government is unreliable for funding," Amy tells me.

St. Joseph provides basic office supplies, fax machines, clothing, transportation, training, a mailing address and a telephone number. "You need a place to call you back at if you got the job," Amy points out, "and you need an address to put on your resumes and job applications."

"We are a Catholic agency, but we don't do any type of proselytizing," she specifies. Instead of preaching, St. Joseph the Worker focuses on developing the values of social justice, human rights and dignity through their programming. "We operate on a premise of building people up," Amy continues. "If you don't do that, forget it. Being homeless, you expect to be told no and be disrespected. We really engage people. Homeless people are our customers. We work for them. We have high standards around here . . . We don't get people jobs, or place people into jobs. We teach them how to get jobs."

St. Joseph screens people very carefully for drug and mental problems, Amy says. Overall, about 35 percent are employable.

It is obvious that this sharp, trim, bright-eyed woman has a strong business background. This must be perfect for the Job Readiness Workshops they provide here, all taught by volunteers who are themselves employers.

"A lot of it is about putting on your game face," Amy elaborates. "Grooming, presentation, clean cut, organized, giving them organizational tools, resume, practice interviews, mock interviews, performing well. The other thing we do is pay for food handler's cards, certifications, clothing and tools for the trade."

Amy tells me that about 50 percent of the clients her organization works with have been incarcerated. St. Joseph's talks to them about how to explain this to an employer—in short, "own it and move on."

"This issue of sex offenders has come up several times recently," I interrupt. "Any comments?"

She says that although there aren't as many job options for convicted sex offenders, in her opinion those who work the hardest can still find employment.

"The Department of Corrections needs to take some responsibility for these people because when they get out, there are restrictions on where they work and where they live," Amy says. "If you are on a bus and a minor gets on a bus, you have to get off the bus. That makes it hard to go to an interview. If you do get a job, a Probation Officer shows up on your work site, and they are not very discreet."

Amy, a fast talker, catches her breath before continuing to talk about what happens after the prison system releases someone. "AZ Department of Corrections just releases people to the streets without putting any planning into where they will go. And talk about destroying a person—I mean everything. To know that you are part of this group that everyone hates. We have stories about people who have gone on interviews and have been told to get out."

Later, Amy and I discuss her concerns about the overall image of homeless people as drug addicts and criminals. "The fastest-growing group [of homeless] is families," she says. "They just have more resources and are homeless for a shorter period of time. There are family shelters and programs. It's being more effectively dealt with. But the people that are dealing with the most serious problems are staying on the street the longest. So that's who you see and what you think of when you think of homeless."

"Don't get me wrong," she insists. "Drugs and SMI (Serious Mental Illness) are a big part of it. But there are a lot of people who just don't have social skills so they continue to get pushed aside or overlooked. Even people who didn't have a MI (Mental Illness), because the streets are so traumatic, it could cause this."

I wonder does mental illness lead to homelessness or does homelessness lead to mental illness? Either way, the conversation has put a sad tint to Amy's face.

"People really prey on homeless people," she suggests. "If you are a pusher, you really want to get homeless people." Amy explains that trading sex for survival is not unusual on the streets for women and men; the young are especially vulnerable.

"But it is amazing how resilient people are and what people are grateful for," Amy adds, her face lightening up a bit. "This job has definitely taken the fun out of complaining in my life."

Tell me about it, I think to myself. "So why do you do it, Amy?" I ask.

"I think it's very important for people to give back," she responds. "When people have been at the bottom, they stop chasing that thing we all seem to be chasing. I think people value just having self-respect and valuing others. Just sharing love and peace is what it's all about.

"Anyone here, it's not because of the pay or the benefits," she laughs. "They want to make the world a better place."

At the end of our interview, Amy ties this idea back to the St. Joseph the Worker: Instilling "the dignity of work" in LDRC clients.

"It doesn't matter if you sweep floors as long as you feel good about it," Amy says. "Work is good. We tell people to first think about what do they like doing, what do they enjoy? If you like your work, you will stay and it will be sustainable. One of the job searching strategies is to think of what type of place would you like to work at and then call them up see if they are hiring or go volunteer there. We stay in the background. We try to teach and empower you to get a job. The dignity of work."

What is the meaning of life?

What's the meaning of life? I think it's really to um . . . learn how to be a true source of love. Pretty much.

What are your thoughts about society and/or societies in general?
I think that . . . if we can find a way to teach all individual people the value in living up to their own truth, you know, self-purpose, then communities are going to evolve because of individuals.

Who are you?
Gosh . . . Aaaa . . . I am . . . I'm everybody!

Amy makes me consider just how important are the other things we get from a job besides money—mainly, self-esteem.

COMPUTER CLASS, LDRC: Monday, February 2, 2009, 11:00 a.m.

I leave my interview with Amy and sit in the LDRC lobby to finalize my notes. Before I've started, however, I see John walking by and remember meeting him my first day at the Human Services Campus. John is a client who volunteers as teacher of computer courses. That seems a bit unusual to me. I ask him if he minds me sitting in on his class, and he seems more than enthused.

John has a thick head of white hair and a grey mustache. He wears his slacks belted above his waist with a T-shirt and tennis shoes and glasses. He looks a bit like Einstein, or a university professor, depending on what kind of university or college you went to. At the university I attended (well, flunked out of), he's just missing the corduroy sports coat.

The glasses shield a pair of kind, twinkling eyes that complement a gentle and quivery voice. His lips are shaped as though he might have dentures. He's a geek, through and through.

John explains to me that the computer lab, which has eight stations, is open some days for job searches and/or classes. Today he'll teach a basics course called Computer Navigation. John teaches other skills, too, everything from typing to advanced applications usage. This professorial client is also in charge of the LDRC newsletter.

He shows me a copy, and I read the newsletter as John's students take a test. It isn't just to inform the community at large about The Human Services Campus. It is a newsletter for the community at The Human Services Campus.

One article really catches my attention: "Waiting and Watching." Someone named "Matt Judah, Alumni" wrote it. Here is the article:

I spend a lot of time waiting. Forty minutes a day standing in food lines. Thirty minutes to an hour after lunch waiting to get into the Lodestar Day Resource Center. I have waited over and hour to use a bathroom. I wait for showers, a sink or faucet to brush my teeth, and patiently wait in line each evening to check into my homeless shelter. I am writing this as I wait to do laundry. It is seven-thirty in the morning. I have a bag of dirty clothes and I must wait until 10 o'clock and then hope to get a laundry ticket. That's another two and half hours. Thank God that I can write. The pad that I'm writing on was a gift. The pen was given to me as well. I'm lucky. I'm sitting here looking at a woman sleeping on a bench. She is bundled in three blankets and her head is resting on a ratty old pillow. On the ground in front of her, all her possessions are laid out. A dented and stained green plastic box sits on the cracked asphalt. On top of the box is a clear plastic shopping bag, containing what appears to be wadded up clothes. On the ground next to the box, a shredded black bag that once may have been a backpack, is leaking paper, envelopes, and crumpled yellow pages that may be torn from a phone book. Cradled in the collection of fabric and paper, sits a Styrofoam cup partly filled with cold coffee. Next to the remnants of bag sit a pair of pink house slippers. They are dusty and well used, but there are still little shiny ribbon bows decorating the tops. They sit, pointing outwards, waiting at the edge of her wooden bed for instant use. There is a blue ladies Schwinn bike in front of her possessions. The bike provides a barrier between her and the world. The old fashioned cruiser is in amazingly good condition, with hand brakes, reflectors, and a rear rack. Somehow all of her things must fit on the bike. As she gently coughs and half-rolls, she snuggles deeper into her nest. I think that she will sleep throughout the morning. The outdoor life at night is hard on homeless women. By the gray tufts of hair poking out of her blanket, I am guessing she is older. Local predators find these women easy picking. They are often frail, disoriented, and easy to corner. Addicts don't care that she may be someone's mother or grandmother. They need a fix and something as nice as that bike may be traded for a few hours of pleasure. It pays to stay awake and moving at night. Daylight brings out other people and a degree of security, allowing an opportunity to sleep. She coughs again and suddenly sits up and scans her surroundings. A sip of cold coffee, a bite of something taken from her bag, and she slips back under her covers. Phoenix nights are cooling off and her nest looks warm and comfortable. Soft snoring is now drifting out from her cocoon. I will watch out for her as I wait. At least, for a time, I'll be doing something productive.

I finish reading the newsletter as students finish their tests. John collects them and begins his lecture on computer viruses. John explains how a firewall works, and the importance of virus protection. He teaches like a university professor, too: very smart, but a bit dry. And he loves explaining not just the hows, but the whys. John explains how to do a virus scan of your computer, but he can't help but get excited when a question allows him to explain in detail how viruses work and how firewalls work to prevent them. One of the students turns to me and tells me he learns something here everyday.

It doesn't make sense to me. John is homeless and lives on campus right now, but he's teaching a class, working on something every day. If I didn't know, I would assume he was a staff member.

I ask John at the end of class if I can interview him. He's a very shy man, but agrees to meet in two weeks. We chat for a while, building rapport and a foundation to build on when we meet next. And, when we do meet again, the conversation picks up right where we left it.

John says he is on medical leave as a DPS (Department of Public Safety) officer—a state trooper, to be specific—because of a heart attack. He does not want to claim disability because once he does, he will no longer be able to work as a DPS officer. John also tells me he has a Ph.D. in computer science, a Master's in accounting, and a minor in meteorology.

I think John sees the wheels turning in my head, trying to rationalize this man's intellect with his current situation, so he gets into details.

While with the Nebraska sheriff's department, John says he "shot and killed a fella. It was justified. He came at me with a shotgun. I was cleared in 24 hours. He was on drugs."

John explains that the family tried to sue, but the suit was dropped and they later wrote him a letter of apology. After the shooting, John went before the review board and they asked him, "If you had to go through this again, could you?" John wasn't able to tell them for sure that he would be able to shoot someone again if necessary. He was put on administrative leave for a month, but returned to work.

One night, he says he stopped a car and the people inside were "getting fidgety." John realized that he would always be dealing with situations that might require him to shoot someone. He called his supervisor and resigned.

"That was the stupidest thing I've ever done," he says now.

John finally adds a critical missing fact about the "fella" he shot.

"See, he was nine [years old]," he says. "The family couldn't believe it, but he had a shotgun and was on drugs."

After resigning, the county was willing to re-train John as long as it was not more than three years. He got his Ph.D. in four years and three months. "I paid for the last 15 months," he says. "It was a seven-year course."

After earning his Ph.D., John says he worked for the University of South Dakota as professor of computer science for three years. There, he met his future wife, Heather, in a class he was interning at. It seemed strange to me that John was both a professor and in intern, but I decided early on not to worry about discrepancies in people's stories. I didn't want to get lost in trying to verify the "truth." It's not important if what a person tells you is the truth, but instead why they are telling you the story to begin with. She was going to school to become a surgical scrub nurse. They were married about a year later.

Heather came home one day and told John she got a job in Phoenix, Arizona. They agreed to move, as his professor gig was up at the end of semester. DPS hired John in 2000, three weeks after moving, and it seemed like his life was on the rebound.

One night, at 1:00 a.m., John's captain, a chaplain, and some deputies knocked on his door. He knew something was wrong because Heather was supposed to be home two hours before.

Heather was had been killed in a car accident. They later asked John, "Do you want one or two caskets?" John did not know that his wife was 12 weeks pregnant.

A client who has a bone to pick with John about the use of the computer room interrupts us. Neither handles the argument well. John is easily flustered anyway, and quite bothered by his small amount of authority being questioned.

John is an articulate man and I believe his story, but the small argument I witness shows there is also something mentally unstable about him. John can't deal with conflict—something I would expect a former police officer to be used to—and he's very guilt-ridden and understandably sad.

This ends my interview with John for now. Talk about a cliffhanger . . .

John, and Matt Judah's newsletter story, makes me consider how important our stories are to us, true or not.

NANCY, THE NEW ARID CLUB:
Tuesday, February 3, 2009, 2:00 p.m.

I ride with my windows down today, enjoying the perfect weather. I drive onto the campus, passing the New Arid Club on my right and a smiling man to my left. His is a new face. I smile back. He smiles even bigger than before. What is it that keeps a man open to a world such as this? He looks like he had been through some rough times. His appearance speaks volumes. Everything on him looks weathered, worn and old, except for that smile, fresh, new and alive.

I get out of my vehicle and head diagonally across the grass to the New Arid Club. It is the first time I ever walked on the campus lawn, but I feel like walking amongst the people sitting, standing and laying there. The grass is perfect, and I don't mean in that "nature is perfect!" sort of way. I mean it is perfectly mowed and while heavily used, there are no bald spots or yellow patches. I bend over to pluck a blade and discover how unobservant I have been all this time. The grass is fake. It is basically football turf, Astroturf, fake. I laugh at myself. What else have I missed around here that's right under my feet?

As I near the edge of the grassy field, I see the guy in the bright red Mickey Mouse sweatshirt from Dawn's movie workshop speaking with two other guys. He's hard to miss, with the matching red tennis shoes and all. I apologize for interrupting their conversation and explain who I am, what I am up to and that I would love to interview him. He seems to me to be a man on the edge of change. He's a partly cloudy sky or a partly sunny day.

Tony, as he introduces himself, is totally open to speaking with me. I am starting to see a trend. Those who "get it," who want to use this place to change their situation, seem to be all about sharing "it."

"OK, let's do it today," Tony says. I explain it will have to wait a couple of weeks. Of course I blame it on being "busy." Being busy does make us home less often, I think to myself.

There is a tall wrought iron gate around the red brick building known as the New Arid Club. It's meant to create a bit of separation for those who are trying to stay clean, dry, "arid," from those who may not be.

The gate is open, perhaps symbolically, as it is everyday. I walk through the large white door with its nine small, homey windows, and descend down 12 steps (yes as in 12-step program) to the lower level hallway. To the left is what looks like a meeting room, where I assume AA meetings are held.

At the other end of the hallway is a small recreation room, what appears to be sleeping quarters for two or three staff, and a storage room with lockers. I arrive in front of a man stationed at a desk, as if guarding the end of the hallway. I explain my business and he directs me past him to Nancy's office.

As I walk in, Nancy is on the phone telling someone to "be careful about the arrogant factor," explaining that arrogance is just a step away from relapsing. I watch her for a minute. She's quite fun just to watch, fiery and animated. Her blonde hair is shoulder length and straight, and she's dressed business-casually.

Nancy introduces me, while still on the phone, to a young man in the room who is working on some project for her on his laptop. I chat up the young man, David, and he reluctantly explains that he has taken a vow of poverty for five years. Further discussion reveals that he's well educated and socialized. He does not have to be here. He chooses to be here. David will accept food or clothing but says, "I do not accept money whether it's from a job or any other source."

I ask him why he chose to do this. He laughs and says, "Spiritual malady I guess. I'm an alcoholic and even though I don't drink, I discovered that I just transferred my addictions to money and material gain. So I decided to do like a five year mini-experience."

Five years hardly sounds "mini" to me. I find David fascinating. He's like an urban monk.

When Nancy ends her phone call, I immediately ask her about the other rooms in the facility. She explains the locker room is only for clients who are actively in the program. New Arid Club charges a small fee for their use because "it's all about responsibility and taking ownership." She also explains that the gatekeeper to her office is not there for safety or security but just to limit the traffic that gets through to Nancy.

The New Arid Club started as an idea with just three people and no money, Nancy says. By September 2005, they started operating in this current location.

"Nancy, you told me a while ago in passing that you 'get' addicts," I begin.

"It's through my brokenness that I've learned these lessons," she replies. "One of my characteristics . . . sometimes it's a flaw, is that I have to analyze everything." Nancy's title is Community Development Director of LDRC, "but my real title is Transformation Agent," she contends.

As Nancy explains all this, she has already handled two clients who came into her office without skipping a beat. It must be a combination of brilliance and way too much coffee.

An acupuncturist enters the room and is now putting needles in Nancy's ears. He is doing volunteer work here and the acupuncture is supposed to help with addictions, although I think Nancy is doing it for general health reasons. The office is starting to feel like a small circus and Nancy seems to thrive in this atmosphere.

All I can do is keep asking questions. "Jessica says you've done a lot here on Campus, not just the New Arid Club."

"Everything I have created on Campus has been successful, but almost too successful, in that it creates work for other people. At least that's what they tell me." Nancy is actually quite overwhelmed with her workload and when I probe she explains that she feels a bit guilty about creating more work for others, because they are all overwhelmed too. She's driven, like Dawn. And Nancy's work obviously takes time. Two more people have already come and gone. Nancy has briefly counseled them, warning one and congratulating another.

"How do you cure addiction?" I ask, trying to work my interview back into this menagerie.

"It's holistic," Nancy says. "You can't just fix one area. It's about life giving. It's about finding something to replace the horror of addiction with something that's life giving and positive.

"When you think about being sober, I used to think you had to be like your parents and you had to love God and drink buttermilk," She continues, somewhat cynically. "It's about us getting to heaven and not about everybody else." She takes a long pause; her face saddens. "I've seen a lot of people die."

"I once overheard you saying that you never believed in a higher power until you saw this place come together," I say. "But isn't the 12-step program based on a higher power? And don't you participate in that?"

David, still in the room, chimes in: "And she's married to an atheist minister. He believes that God is mythology."

Nancy confirms that she really is married to a minister. "He knows too much," she says. "He has too much of an education."

From what I can gather from Nancy's comments, her husband does question the existence of a traditional god. But he definitely believes in social justice, in the rights and dignity of people. He runs a nonprofit center down the street for elderly homeless people—The Justa Center. I wonder what dinner at their house is like?

"Nancy, you seem to have a real duality. You talk as though you don't believe in God but you have a strong sense of faith and you're married to a minister?" I have no idea what the guy at the desk does, because people are still coming in and out and she answers me while talking with them, too.

"Let's say the energy here is different now and it keeps building," she says. "Positive or negative, it grows. But I wouldn't say the energy is positive or negative. Even though there are things happening to me that are miracles. I don't know who you are or what you are, but I know you wouldn't punish for not knowing, so I'm praying to whoever is out there. And great things started happing in my life."

David keeps typing, the acupuncturist is still here putting needles in Nancy's ear, people keep cycling in and out of the office, and both her cell phone and her desk phone ring constantly. And Nancy continues talking to me. At times, she is literally having three conversations at once.

This office is a circus, but somehow, it's working.

Nancy answers the phone again. This time it's her husband, something about their cats. She hangs up, answers another person's question, tells yet another that she will get back with them. The flood continues as another man enters and shares some personal challenges with Nancy. She responds quite sternly, telling him, among other things: "You're in denial!" Nancy switches from being compassionate to stern and back again, but she does not do so willy-nilly. With each person she helps, there seems to be a process of gauging where they are at and what they need.

After the last client leaves, Nancy explains that one of the things she fears the most for others is when they get too comfortable with their sobriety and think their addiction problem is gone. She says this is when they usually relapse, using herself as an example.

"When I was first sober, I started having this high anxiety," she explains. "I went to my counselor and he said 'it's OK. You're just not used to feeling joy. I wasn't used to being happy.'"

Nancy continues to jump from subject to subject and back again. She is not scattered in the least, she just connects everything. And she processes as she goes along. It might be obnoxious except for the fact that she is so genuine and probably doesn't give a damn if she is obnoxious.

Switching gears again, Nancy says she's getting her Master's degree right now, but that life on the school campus seems sterile and unreal to her. People's priorities seem out of place; she doesn't understand why saving human life is not first on everyone's list.

Another ex-client interrupts us again. Nancy asks him if she can share his story with me. She laughs and cries as she tells about his ups and downs. He was an outrageous drunk to say the least, including many run-ins with law enforcement.

"When you get thrown out of a homeless shelter for drinking, one that you got into in the first place because of drinking, then you know you've hit bottom," the man adds to her rendition.

He thanks Nancy, gives her a hug and leaves. This man's life is completely different today than it was a year ago. He has gainful employment, good relationships and a nice place to live. As he is walking out the door Nancy reminds him to come to a meeting soon.

After he leaves, Nancy confides that she's worried about him for similar reasons to other clients who feel they've fully recovered.

"There are . . . people [who] don't think they need AA, because they feel on top of the world and they think that they will always remember how they feel," she elaborates. "Twelve steps is part of transforming your whole life. And it's hard to swallow. So you fail many times. It's about being honest and open and doing the stuff that's hard. Most people don't want to work the whole program. But you need to work the whole program. So I tell them, 'We love you. When you mess up, come back.'"

Nancy continues to talk about how tricky addiction is and how it can be driven even when one is not using or especially when one is not using. "I think it's about the obsession," she says. "When you concentrate on the problem, it gets bigger. When you concentrate on the symptoms, they get bigger. So people are concentrating on the wrong things."

That is partially why they have recovering addicts sponsor other addicts. They need to focus on something beside themselves.

Suddenly, Nancy turns cynical: "It's really cool to do charity. There are people all over the world who do charity and serve the poor slobs. They are doing it for themselves to make themselves feel better. If they really cared they would live the difference, but instead it's all about them."

She explains their approach at LDRC is different. They are doing the work for others, not themselves, and whether or not anyone else knows how much work they put into their charitable deeds. "That's integrity, when you do the right thing when no one is looking," Nancy concludes.

People keep coming in and out. The phones keep ringing and David is still quietly working away on his laptop. I feel like I had better get to my questions.

What is the meaning of life?

Jeez!... you should... David is contemplating this... he is in existential angst.

You remain humble and teachable and the answers will come if you pay attention. It's all about paying attention and lessons. It's just about doing your best for the earth and for your brothers and sisters.

You know, when I got sober I was 25 and I thought my first 25 years was about taking and if I try and make up for it, if I at least try and make the Earth even. I'm all about helping individuals, but I'm also about teaching them that they can help others too. AA didn't want anything from me. Their only motive was that I help other people. Unmotivated, positive behavior self-perpetuates. I used to never do anything I didn't want to do and I wasn't happy. I now do lots of stuff I don't want to do and I'm happy.

What are your thoughts about society and/or societies in general?

We are very impressionable people; we are very fragile; we are influenced by a lot of things. It's just like gangs. Gangs fascinate me. It's part of their reality that they are going to get killed when they are young. You get people alone and you can reason with them a bit, but once you are in that gang, forget it. And these gated communities have this belief system and everyone around them has that belief system.

So society is just... it's just really selfish... I just want to live in a society where the motives are clean and that's why I love AA, although there are problems in AA, but at least you have the honesty, open-mindedness, willingness." Another pause. *"So we just need to make a society that is a community, and gains momentum. The momentum is the hard part. When it gains momentum then everyone wants to hop on the bandwagon, but when it's not popular . . . It's hard to be unpopular unless you are very strong, but everyone is so fragile.*

Who are you?

These are such interesting questions. Who am I? I'm a miracle. So are you!

You know, I feel sometimes if I believed in any of that nonsense of religion, I am like the chosen one. And it sounds grandiose and I don't mean it that way. I think we are all the chosen ones. But that I have always had ideals, where anything is possible. When I got sober I was like, let's change the world! And everyone else was like, lets get a job and have a family. And I was like, we just survived this horrible near death experience and let's get busy! I think the low bottom ones, the over achiever of the bottoms, just living through all that pain makes you grateful to be alive. And I'm not saying we don't get down, but we have support. And that attracts the outside community and it builds.

Nancy makes me consider the dangers of arrogance, one being that we argue about spiritual truths instead of just rolling up our sleeves and helping.

The Twelve Steps leading up from the basement and out of the
New Arid Club . . . and addiction. Photo by: Steven Sable.

THE INMOST CAVE

ME, HOMELESS FOR A DAY: Monday, February 9, 2009, 10:00 a.m.

I WAKE UP IN MY WARM, cozy bed and don't want to get out. That's nothing new. My bed is the most luxurious thing I own. Its womb-like effects are intoxicating. Besides, Mondays and Tuesday are my days off. I typically spend them investigating the Human Services Campus, doing things with my kids, or just puttering around the house.

But not this time. I had decided to take David's advice and do an immersion. I will spend this next 40 or so hours being homeless.

God knows why, but I'm uncertain. All I know is my experiment will be just that—an experiment. One cannot experience being homeless unless they *truly* are. I will soon leave my house with only a duffle bag. But I will still own a home (for now . . .) and a car, and have a job to return to on Wednesday. I still have a network of friends, a few of whom are aware of my route and have instructions to come look for me if I don't return by 10 p.m. Tuesday. I have safety nets. I have connections. I have favors that can be called in. I know many people who are just a phone call away and who would do almost anything for me.

So I know my experiment is not in any way to be an accurate measure of what life on the streets is like, but I hope it will give me some insights I can gain no other way. My goal is still to really know what homelessness means, to feel it.

For the journey, I take only what will fit in the bag: a roll of toilet paper; a sleeping bag; two layers of clothing; one notebook; two pens; a book to read; matches; two cheap rain ponchos; a pocket watch (given to me by my kids, the word "Dad" engraved on it); and seven dollars in cash to walk the half-marathon's distance to the Human Services Campus, live there for a day, and walk back.

I will be traveling without identification, cell phone, credit or debit cards. I have had a cell phone for so long that I don't know anyone's number by heart. So for about 36 hours I will be cut off from my safety network. I will have no access to money or friends. I will have no proof of who I am. I will be nameless. And I hope that being over 13 miles from home on foot will make me feel at least a bit homeless.

There has been a cold spell in Phoenix and the temperature will be less than 50 degrees today. It rained all last night, and from the looks of things through my bedroom window, today it might do the same. Who knows what the night will bring?

And what do homeless persons in other parts of the country do in February where many places are lucky to experience highs of 17 degrees today? I can't even imagine. That's part of the problem. I can't even imagine.

I don't shower or eat breakfast. It's enough that I am leaving a well fortified home and in good spirits and good health. My life thus far has been one without hunger and without basic human needs for shelter and friendship ever being denied. I have never done without, not even for a brief moment in time.

I chose to walk to the shelter because I knew driving would produce nothing but an account of what it was like to sleep outside in the cold and use a Porta Potty that 300 other persons were using. Not pleasant, but not homeless either. When you know your car is 100 yards away and it can take you home in 30 minutes, it's just an uncomfortable slumber party.

By the time I get to the HSC, I will be four or five hours from my home. To me, this sounds at least a bit like being homeless—the feeling that you can't reverse your situation.

I kept a journal of my immersion, which is included below. This is homelessness as I experienced it, word-for-word:

10:30 a.m.

I'm wearing old but clean jeans, short sleeved T-shirt, baseball cap and tennis shoes. I have a small duffle with a jacket, two $1 rain ponchos, a sleeping bag, some toilet paper, my notebook, a book and two pens. I say goodbye to my house, my bed and my laptop. I start my journey . . .

11:10 a.m.

I am now roughly a mile from my home, further from it on foot than ever before. How strange . . . I have lived in that home for 13 years and have never walked more than a mile away from it.

11:30 a.m.

It's sprinkling, but not enough to put on a rain poncho. I can't wait too long because if I get wet and cold, hypothermia becomes a legitimate concern. It's a bit strange to me to be all of a sudden thinking about my walk in the city like a hike in the forest.

I have already passed over 50 little businesses from antique shops to rubber stamps made in a day; from to aerial mapping to x-ray laboratory services.

Thunder all of a sudden—the boom surrounds me. It's time to stop writing notes and move on. I don't want to walk the rest of the way in a true downpour.

11:50 a.m.

I pass a billboard that says:

> EASY STREET
> CASINO ARIZONA
> SHORTCUT TO THE GOOD LIFE

As I'm reading it a man passes me carrying a trash bag full of cans, presumably to recycle them. Sometimes life is so poetic. He soon veers off at a place called ABCO Recycling and Document Destruction Services. I wonder if that's his short cut to the good life. Seems a lot more practical than gambling. I stop in and a nice man tells me that they pay 30 cents a pound for aluminum cans. The gentleman before me had 12 pounds in his large bag and made $3.60.

12:10 p.m.

There are lots of people now walking out and about in this new part of town. This is a poorer part of town than the one where I live. My neighborhood is very middle class.

I don't think many of these people are homeless. They look more like they are merely car-less. Many of them are walking to perform tasks like carrying grocery bags home from the grocery store and laundry to and from a laundromat. I forgot how much I take driving for granted. I drive everywhere.

12:30 p.m.

It's still drizzling on and off and I have to pee. I turn left on 7th Avenue and all the people on foot disappear as nice houses reappear. It's all residential on this part of 7th Avenue and I am going to have to find a restroom.

12:50 p.m.

I pass many beautiful homes of all different types. This is an older, very well developed part of town. The diversity in architecture is impressive—unlike the outskirts of town where planned communities have houses that all look the same. This area rarely has two houses next to each other with the same style of architecture. There are modern, angular looking homes and southwestern adobe homes . . . Spanish style, American colonial, Santa Barbara style.

1:00 p.m.

I veer down an ally to pee before I wet myself. It's funny how nervous I am about being caught. It's against the law and I have overheard homeless persons on campus talking about having outstanding tickets for public urination. Not to mention that public urination can be deemed a sex offence.

I pass a house that has a three level tree house in a tree on the front lawn. There is lumber on the second level, suggesting still further additions. Maybe a fourth level? This tree house is nicer than some homes I've seen. My kids would love to play in this tree house. I would love to play in it.

I pass manicured dark green lawns, each seeded with winter rye. Where there is desert landscaping it is clean and the gravel shows lines from being raked. I pass a beautiful tree with bright, tiny pastel purple flowers numbering in the thousands. The tree has dark bark. It's wiry and old looking like a coat hanger whose main purpose is to display the coat. It's amazing how much you see on foot.

1:20 p.m.

At Glendale and 7th Avenue things start to change from residential to the outskirts of midtown. First the churches start to reappear, then small businesses, and then office parks and quaint small apartment complexes.

The wind is blowing hard but my clothing keeps me warm. Glad my mother taught me about layering, one of the most important fashion and survival techniques known to man. My hands are cold. It's hard to write when your hands are cold and a bit swollen from walking.

1:40 p.m.

Damn, how many churches are there on this street? I've passed at least five in the past 20 minutes. If they opened their doors, they could shelter all the homeless down here.

2:00 p.m.

At 7th Avenue and Missouri I see and old-fashioned ice-cream parlor, locally owned restaurants serving Japanese, Mexican, Italian foods, and, there is a Starbucks in addition to Long Wong's Pizza and Wings. They all look good. I must be getting hungry. I'm getting a blister on my right foot. Maybe I should have worn better shoes, but I assume the homeless don't have a closet of shoes to select from each day. My back is starting to hurt a bit. It has been good for some time now. I had almost forgotten about it since its miraculous healing. And my legs are tired. None of it's bad, but it's been a while since I've walked for three hours.

2:25 p.m.

At Campbell and 7th Avenue, Bunta Bistro offers a taste of West African cuisine along with beer and cocktails. Now food is sounding really good. I'm hungry. And I really want a drink. I don't know if I would be considered a heavy drinker but I usually have a beer or two at the end of the day and now one sounds good. I'm board and tired and it sounds nice to relax. And that's the thing that's stopping me. Yes, I know I only have $7, but I am seriously thinking about buying some beer, which sounds crazy, but I actually want to nurture myself. The only thing that's really stopping me is I have to walk for possibly two more hours—who knows—and I don't want to do that with a buzz. It will just make it seem harder.

I see a smoke shop and go into buy some loose tobacco. Yes, I smoke occasionally too, but truly occasionally. I am starting to think about how bored I might be tonight. Being bored is my issue—that's when all my stuff comes up. When I'm bored is when I start to over-question the direction of my life. It's when I want affirmation that I'm on the right path and the silence of boredom only echoes back my call of: "Will someone, anyone, please tell me I am on the right path, that I am good, that I am loved?"

I ask for a bag of tobacco. Loose tobacco, the kind you roll yourself is much cheaper than a pack of cigarettes and definitely cheaper than two packs, which is what you get out of one pouch. I ask for a brand I have never tried because they are out of my favorite.

The clerk says, "Absolutely, can I see an ID?"

I thought more about my ID as a way to prove who I am, maybe for some emergency help or something. I'm 39 years old. I didn't think about needing my ID for purchasing tobacco. Thank God I didn't try to buy liquor, although the irony is that I haven't been carded for that in a decade.

"I don't have my ID but . . . I'm 40 years old."

"I know you're old enough, but I'm just doing my job, and it's the law."

I never argue these sorts of things. He is just doing his job, but I start arguing with him. OK . . . pleading with him.

"It's not up to me. I have to slide your ID through this machine every time I ring up an order. Sorry man."

I catch myself, apologize, give up and leave.

Remembering the irony of not being carded in recent memory for liquor, I try to buy tobacco at a liquor store down the way. As I suspected they didn't card me, but they did charge me more than the tobacco shop would have, $4.25. And yes this leaves me with $2.75 in my pocket and no I'm not making this up to make a point. And yes I have been a responsible person all my life. I pay everything on time and have outstanding credit.

So why did I do it? Well for one thing I know that they will most likely feed me for free tonight. I don't really need money for food. It's no fun to drink on the streets regardless of what you might think about homeless people. Drinking is great in front of my big screen TV while sitting in my recliner, but not when I'm cold and wet, sitting on the concrete.

But the real reason is that boredom thing. I don't want to sit all night and feel those feelings. I am already wondering why I am spending my weekend doing this. I mean what am I really going to learn? I'm not homeless. And I'm not some saint walking all this way to sleep one night at a shelter, only to then walk home. I mean what's this going to prove? Is writing a book really important? And why did my ex-girl friend leave? And did I make a mistake quitting my job? Question after question. This is what goes on in my head at times like this, especially when I don't have distracting comforts, like the company of a beautiful woman, good friends, great food, TV and a comfy chair.

I have walked four hours from home and already have a new appreciation for why someone might drink a bit too much when living on the streets—or do drugs. It sucks having nothing and feeling like you don't have options.

For now these thoughts and feelings bother me more than my hunger. That's the simple truth. It occurs to me that we think of homelessness in terms of lack of money, employment and shelter. But maybe we should think about the homeless in terms of *their* thoughts and feelings because that's what is bothering me the most right now.

As for the $2.75 left, for the first time in my life I am really wishing I had more money. When I left the house I didn't think it would matter for two days. In the past, I've wished for more money, but now, for the first time I really feel it. This walk would be a fun exploration with $100 and an ID.

2:45 p.m.

I walk on and my thoughts drift to how to make money. I could beg, but I have too much pride. And . . . I can't think of any other clever ideas, except for going home and back to work on Wednesday.

3:00 p.m.

I can see skyscrapers to my left, way off in the distance. It's a good sign that I am getting near to downtown and thus to the Human Services Campus. I could use some human services right now. I already want to go home. I want comfort. I want companionship. This isn't much fun even though I am getting to see and notice a lot of things I would have never taken the time to see and notice. I still want a drink. But now I am much closer to the shelter, and possibly dinner, than I am to my home. The thought of turning around and walking four hours back home doesn't sound so great. I would like to sit down and rest a bit but I have done so throughout my entire trip to take these notes. I sit down anyway on the curb. The concrete actually feels good on my ass. My feet and back thank me.

3:15 p.m.

This entire time I have been walking into traffic on the left hand side of the streets. I have basically only been looking to my left because there is more than enough to hold my attention on just one side of the street (the vividness and variations of businesses, houses, people, plants, signs); there's a lot to see when you slow down. I also want new scenery when I walk back home, which I will acquire by walking home on the other side of the street. Sounds strange, but it's a damn long walk.

It's time to go. I'm close, but who knows how close at this pace and I don't want to miss dinner. I don't remember when they serve it for sure or even exactly where it is.

3:40 p.m.

It occurs to me that much of this segment of my walk has been filled with thoughts about my ex-girlfriend and why she ended the relationship. It's a popular question of mine that I must like to ponder when I'm bored because I do it so damn often. It all ties into the equation of loneliness equals boredom equals unpleasant questions with lack of validation for my choices and myself. I want to get to the shelter because this project and the people there have consistently chased away these meaningless sorts of questions.

They were getting better for the past few months, since the start of this project. In fact the back and the money thing just became not such a big deal. But now, on this walk, I have too much time on my hands. Time with nothing to do is a vast canvas—one that if you unwisely choose to throw your brains and heart up against will gladly display them in a mangled mass of sprawling thoughts and feelings. Ah . . . but is it art?

3:50 p.m.

I see very familiar scenery now. I am approaching the freeway exit that I normally take onto 7th Avenue. The rest of the way I have driven many times. And it's starting to work. Maybe I'm just tired and hungry so my pathetic ramblings take a lower priority, but I also think it's the magical cure of the campus. My thinking starts to change. I'm starting to feel grateful even for this very moment instead of searching for what is wrong with it. I see people again on the streets, people from the streets, people with real problems. I don't feel better in comparison; it just helps me prioritize my life and my bullshit or as Clarence would say, it keeps my heart in the right place. How quickly things change. Maybe the realness overrides the delusions of my mind? But for the moment I feel at peace, content, even with my other wants. Walking sure gives you time to think.

4:00 p.m.

I just made myself laugh. I just noticed I was talking to myself . . . out loud. It makes people look at you funny—that's when I noticed. At least I was saying nice things to myself. But regardless: five hours without company and I'm talking out loud to myself in public.

4:10 p.m.

I'm at Washington and 7th Avenue and I'm close. Thank God! I wait at the crosswalk so I can head up to 12th Avenue. I wait with three women who have just left work for the day and are crossing the street to catch the bus on the other side. They distance themselves from me a bit. They're a bit standoffish. I'm not used to this. I'm handsome and clean cut. I have a kind face and I'm used to smiling at women and having them smile back. I try it. I smile at all three of them. No one smiles back. I feel kind of emasculated all of a sudden. I realize that I look like I have no job, no money and I'm not that attractive in these clothes. Apparently I'm not all that when I don't fit in. I had always just assumed it was my good looks and charm that got me smiles and courtesies in return, but not that much has changed and now I'm getting nothing in return. I want to tell them, "Hey I'm not a bum. I'm important. I'm interesting. I'm a writer working on an important project." It strikes me as such a strong reaction for a 'homed' guy who is undercover homeless for one lousy night. But my ego is pissed or scared. It's hard to tell the difference. So much for the change in attitude.

4:25 p.m.

I arrive at the LDRC five minutes before they close. Which is perfect because what I need to do here will only take about two minutes. I need to pee again. I'm quite happy that I get to do this simple thing, even in their overused bathrooms. No one inside recognizes me even though I recognize quite a few of them. That's weird. I just didn't shave or shower, threw on some old clothes and a baseball cap. That and the bag—the bag that says I'm carrying my life on my shoulders.

I leave the building, passing by a homeless woman who does return my smile and I ask her if the line forming to the east by the André House is indeed the food line. Of course I don't say it that way.

She tells me it is and that they serve from 5:30 to 6:30 but to get in line now. So I do. And I'm waiting. I've been waiting to get here all day and now I'm waiting here. Waiting is definitely a big aspect of being homeless.

I'm not even 100 yards from the LDRC and just across the street from the HSC, but it feels different over here. Some people are getting angry with others for cutting in line. There are people not in line, just hanging out, sitting on the sidewalk across the street, watching us and drinking. It doesn't feel optimistic here like it does inside the LDRC. There are a couple hundred people in line now and it wraps around the corner of the building. A drug dealer drives by in his pimped out ride reminding me that we are in the "zone." My mind starts to quiet down, but not due to a sense of serenity. My mind quiets as the culture shock sets in and I have to shut out unnecessary thoughts in order to pay attention to my surroundings. It may sound dramatic but in a very short period of time I have gone into survival mode. I'm not scared. But I'm out of my element and know I need to stay aware of what's going on around me. This is no place to look unaware or like a victim.

4:50 p.m.

Gary, a tall lanky man with messy red hair and freckles everywhere; a man with tiny, sad eyes sunken way into his head asks me in a slow broken voice what I'm writing. I tell him, "I like to take notes. It helps me think." He, in contrast to some of my concerns about our general location and what probably amounts to a very small percentage of the persons out here, is very kind and obviously glad that I am too. He wants to have a conversation with me but he's tentative and careful not to impose. He starts slow but as I encourage him with polite responses he engages me more and more. He is happy just to have someone listen. There are two guys behind him who are rolling their eyes at some of his comments. Gary has some unusual ideas about politics, but hey who doesn't? He pauses a lot, sometimes forgetting where he's at with an idea. When I remind him, he apologizes, one time saying, "Sorry, my minds been in a fog since I came to this place." I tell him that's all right and understandable. I can already relate. My mind is quieting down into that same fog, a fog that causes you to forget other things and just stay on alert, but it's not a heightened feeling. It's a deadening feeling.

I see Tony in his classic read shoes and a red sweatshirt, not the Mickey Mouse one again but this red shoes and red sweatshirt is like a trademark of his. He is selling cigarettes to people waiting in line, very enterprising, .25 cents apiece. And there are takers. I should have thought of that earlier. Maybe his red shoes and red sweatshirts are a trademark.

Another guy passes by who is selling cell phones. By his manner and discretion, I assume they are hot. Tony is yelling about the cigarettes from the street; this guy is asking each person quietly one by one.

Gary continues to talk. He figures he just has to make it through this week. He has a job now and he gets his first paycheck this Friday. When I ask him how he likes his job he lights up and says, "I like it . . . and they like me." He has a goofy, lovable manner about him. And I'm well aware that many people like the guys behind him, would label him a bit off or dimwitted. I probably would too if I wasn't so happy just to have someone nice to talk to. Funny how that works—in a humbling sort of way.

A guy comes down the line to hand us tickets (handmade tickets with ascending numbers) to somehow verify our place in line.

5:37 p.m.

When the line starts moving, it moves quickly. We round the corner and are soon at an outdoor waiting area where there are four rows of very long benches, each seating 40 people. Gary and I sit and wait as they rotate through the benches, releasing one group at a time to enter the André House building.

5:50 p.m.

Once inside, Father Eric takes tickets while smiling and saying hi to each one of us. He welcomes each individual in as though it were his home. It's nice to be welcomed. It means a lot after you've felt unwelcome. Behind him there are 10 more smiling people serving food in two teams of five. It's very friendly and very efficient. I get the works, which is chicken with noodles and white sauce sort of thing, stuffing, bread with butter and a cupcake. Yes it's a super high carb diet but it's hot, fresh and it smells good. And again it's nice to be served by people who seem happy to see me. It means a lot to me, which is strange because I would have thought that it wouldn't be that big a deal. I guess when you get welcoming smiles all the time you start to take them for granted. Just six hours without and I really miss them.

After we get our institutional style trays of food, four very nice people also with big smiles serve us tea or coffee, sweetened or not, cream or not, or of course you can have water. The hot tea is great because I've been cold all day outside.

The eating area has eight tables that seat 24 persons apiece. I've got to interview the priest who runs this place because I'm guessing they process at least 1,000 meals a night here.

I sit next to Gary. He is putting his cupcake in a plastic bag, explaining to me that he will eat it tomorrow at work for lunch. It makes me realize that he doesn't have any money and free meals aren't any good to people who are at work. I offer him mine. He's quite taken back. "Are you sure?" he asks in a cartoonish sort of way and as wide-eyed as his tiny sunken eyes will allow. I assure him that I don't want it, which requires no acting on my part. I hate sweets—especially pink cupcakes.

While my pleasant exchange with timid Gary on my left is going on, the guy to my right lets a huge bite of stuffing fall out of his mouth, landing not in his tray but onto the table. His eyes look crazy drunk and his slurred speech confirms this fact. "This stuffing sucks!" At least I think that's what he said. The original gesture required no verbal edification. I break eye contact with him because he is looking for trouble. He is trouble. And he is way more than a little drunk.

I quickly finish my food and said good-bye to Gary. I tell him I will see him later. I don't know why I say that because I may never see him again. He makes me think that kindness is highly underrated. I really like Gary. Just before I leave, the gentleman to my right gets up with the help of the table and a chair for support. I notice he has either sat in a puddle or soiled himself. I literally don't know how he was going to navigate his way out of the André House.

He stumbles away from me for a moment and I make my break before he starts stumbling back. Who knows which direction he will end up going? I know eventually it will be down.

I give a teenage volunteer my tray at a window where he is spraying each one off and placing them into large dishwasher racks. The size of this operation is truly astounding. I thank him. He pauses for a moment, "You're welcome." What kind of 14-year-old kid volunteers to do dishes?

I pass a young lady at the door on the way out who is operating a book exchange of sorts. I want to ask her for details but some client is giving her what I can tell is a never-ending speech on God know what, so I leave. That is, I wait to leave as another obviously drunk client, this time a woman, refuses help down the back stairs and thus has to navigate the eight steps to the outside. I must note that she and the other gentleman are far from the norm; they just stand out.

6:00 p.m.

Finally outside, I can't believe they served me and I ate that fast. I have time to make the NA (Narcotics Anonymous) meeting at the New Arid Club and I want to go for two reasons. One is Nancy wanted me to go, just to see what they do. Two is that it's already pretty damn cold out here and it's starting to rain again.

I walk through the homey white door and down the half flight of stairs. Flacco, one of the client residents of the New Arid Club greets me and everyone else at the meeting room door. The room is long and narrow. It feels like a small chapel. There are rows three chairs deep on each side off the room, all facing the front, which has a slightly raised stage.

There are 20 people present and someone comments that it's a small group tonight. The facilitator explains that each NA group, just like each AA group is anonymous and in no way connected to any other. There is no hierarchy and no political or religious affiliations. There is no funding for any group from the parent organization because there is no parent organization. Each group is a unique entity and a personality in and of itself.

And this group is obviously no exception. This is not a well-pressed Scottsdale AA meeting. This is Narcotics Anonymous from the gutter. Many people in the room look like they literally live on the streets. They are dirty, haggard, bruised and battered.

Various people get up and speak on today's topic of How We Stay Clean Today. The first guy is very charismatic and clever. "I was a dopeless hopefiend," he begins. Each succeeding persons says something that sticks in my head.

A guy gets up who looks a little out of place. He is extremely well groomed. I assume he might be one of the few addicts who attend these meetings but are not homeless. Will states that he is 11 days sober. What helps him is listening to the people talk in the room.

"It's the same familiar faces that draw me back, those faces. My family and friends have no idea what an addict goes through. I have renewed faith." Will passes the baton, so to speak, by calling on another person in the room and thanks him for his past insights and says they have really helped.

A gentleman in a broad-rimmed hat with a large white mustache goes up to the front of the room, stepping up six inches on the raised front portion of the classroom. There is a podium but he stands in front of it.

"You are my fellow spirit travelers." He smirks. "I no longer live my life worrying about what you think about what I think about what you think I'm thinking about." He says this in a very animated tone as he gestures to himself, then to the audience, then back to himself, then back again to the audience, and finally back to himself again. Everyone laughs, especially me. I do that. "I try to thank God for everything instead of saying 'God damn' to everything." This guy is a great speaker. I can see why Will likes him.

The meeting ends with a prayer, which seems appropriate to me even though I'm not a religious man. This was the best church service I have ever attended. I feel connected to something greater than myself and inspired. It was a sad, happy, funny, depressing, alive sort of experience.

7:15 p.m.

I walk out into the cold, wet night. It is about 40 degrees, which isn't that bad; raining now, not hard, but consistently. Forty degrees gets pretty cold if you get wet and you have to be that way all night.

I head north down the sidewalk and across the street to the long line forming for the Outreach Shelter that runs along the fence surrounding the parking lot of the building. Of course this is a parking lot that never has cars in it. When the building is full, they park people out here. This is level zero, unless you count the street, which is in the negatives. The Outreach Shelter indoor area sleeps about 250 persons and the outdoor, gated parking lot could sleep even more. The line is already a block long. On a night like tonight everyone hopes to get a space inside.

I see Will from the NA meeting. I get behind him in line and strike up a conversation. He has a very soft and gentle manner of speaking, a bit effeminate. I think he might be gay. Yes it is because he is immaculately groomed, very nicely mannered, and has a feminine sort of voice. I couldn't care less. Right away he seems like one of the nicest most normal men I have ever met. It quickly becomes obvious that he is very well educated, which is evident from his vocabulary and how clearly he states ideas and links them together. And his social skills are truly better than almost anyone I have ever known. What is this guy doing here? I know he said he had only been sober 11 days, but he looks like he hasn't had a drink in his life.

He discovers through our conversation that it is my first night here and explains that I will probably get a space inside. "They give preferential treatment to first-timers." Many of the people who sleep in the Outreach Shelter are what they call overnighters. They aren't interested in getting into the main CASS building and the CASS program. They aren't interested in getting off the street or at least not interested in getting off the street the way the system wants them too. So they are the last to be sheltered indoors.

Will is very interested in getting off the streets. He is on the list to eventually get into the main CASS building as soon as a bed opens up. He explains that could take a week or it could take months. He has been through the system once before and so they did not give him preferential treatment. Once before? It just doesn't make sense.

There are three police officers standing outside the door of the shelter. CASS pays them for security and it's quite necessary. Overnighters can be a rougher group in general than those who are working their program to change their situation. That is not to say that there are not a lot of nice persons around, but we look like a motley crew of roughly 400 people.

As the line progresses I get to the door. It leads into a small room that I presume will eventually lead into a great big room. I explain, as Will told me to, that this is my first time ever. They stop me to fill out an application in this waiting room as I watch Will move ahead and out of sight into the shelter's main Outreach building.

They ask if I have an ID. "No, my wallet was stolen." This was the second lie I told since the start of my journey and probably would not be the last. I assume they were harmless enough. I need to play the part.

While my interview progresses, a fight breaks out in the room next door. The police are there in seconds. They find a knife. Someone is arrested and another person is thrown out. It's going to be an exciting night. My interview continues.

They ask for my name, Social Security number, age and if I am a veteran. I am truthful about all that. They then ask me a series of questions about if I am an addict, ex-con, etc., which I also answer honestly. I was only prepared to tell little white lies, not anything fraudulent.

Will was right. They escort me into the large room that sleeps about 250 persons. They give me one of the last mats on the floor and show me where the two dilapidated bathrooms are. I look around for Will and realize he is not there and is one of the many who are now being escorted in from the front door and out through the back door.

I ponder for a moment as I look around at the room with cots along the walls and mats covering every inch of available floor space. It is going to be a cold night for anyone outside, but I have a rain poncho and a sleeping bag. Further I came from a warm house, fueled by a good life and will return to such. It will be an even colder night for someone who is run down, depleted from life on the street. There is no telling how run down one can get before they don't get up. And with all my feelings, and as dramatic as I make this all seem, it's one night, it's 36 hours for me.

I ask the guy at the door what would happen if I give up my mat—wondering if they'd give it to someone else. He says "Yes, but you don't want to do that. You will be outside." I'm not being a saint. It just isn't right. What is one night outside going to do, kill me? No. But it might literally kill someone else. I realize how grave all this actually is. Sure one night of bad weather is nothing if you are properly prepared, if it's one night. It's so weird to be in the middle of a great big city and to have to think about things as if you are backpacking in the mountains.

I walk out the back door. I walked out into the rain, into the cold, into a sea of mostly men. There is a cover above part of the parking lot but it is a sun cover to protect people from the summer rays. It is not waterproof in the slightest. I look down at the ground. It is soaked and there are large puddles forming everywhere. My sleeping bag will be of little use because it will instantly get wet. I will most likely have to stand the whole night to stay dry or squat. And while I have layers of clothing on, I am starting to get cold. I was counting on that sleeping bag to stay warm. Still I will be all right. I will wrap up in it somehow and if worse comes to worse I can start walking home and be there in five hours. We are allowed to leave here anytime; we just can't get back in tonight if we do.

I look around and only about half of the people around me are as well prepared as me. A few better, most worse. How are they all going to make it through the night? I'm shocked that I don't hear about homeless deaths every morning on the news. Maybe they just aren't newsworthy.

As I look around at my wet bedfellows, some are wrapped in plastic grocery bags, some in newspaper, some in full rain gear, I spot Will. And I am glad to say the least. No one wants to be alone, especially out here. This might have been another motive of mine for giving up my bed inside. I'm used to being alone at home, but out here I am really craving a friend.

"Hey, didn't they give you a bed inside?"

"They did. I gave it up. I'm not going to be here long and it just didn't seem right."

"That was really nice of you, really nice. So you have some things lined up for yourself soon?"

"Yeah, this is temporary . . . I hope."

"Great! Good! You don't seem like the typical guys I'm used to seeing down here."

"Neither do you, Will."

"Oh, I don't know about that, but thanks. Either way I'm here. And I got myself here."

I handed my second poncho to Will. "I think you might need this."

"Oh no, I couldn't take that from you."

"Will, I can't use two at once."

He laughs, "OK, thanks. Thanks a lot!"

We stand there as I try to roll a cigarette in the rain, which I'm proud and embarrassed to say I'm pretty good at. The minute I roll it someone asks if they can buy it from me. I just give it to them. I roll another and am able to light it before being propositioned again. I can tell that while Will doesn't mind, he definitely doesn't smoke. I'm now very glad I had bought this tobacco, because I have nothing better to do than to dance with the cancer devil all night. And it really doesn't seem to matter at the moment. I know it seems shortsighted but cancer is not an immediate concern out here. This is my first night and I have been outside for less than 30 minutes. I wonder how much concern these other guys have for their general health after days, weeks, months or years out here?

Will, myself, and hundreds of others out in the parking lot get some good news. We are led over to the LDRC. The powers that be in CASS opened the lobby of the place I know so well to let us sleep in there for the night. Some of the other clients tell me that they often do this when the weather is bad.

There are too many people from the streets to be accommodated inside CASS. This is the overflow shelter. When it is full, people sleep in the parking lot behind this gate. Photo by: Steven Sable.

8:15 p.m.

I lay out my sleeping bag next to Will. I offer to open it all the way just so he won't have to sleep directly on the tile floor. "No, Mike, I'm happy just to be inside. This is great. Really great." Will leaves for a moment and returns with toilet paper from the bathroom. He then proceeds to wipe down the entire area of the floor he will be sleeping on. He takes off his shoes and replaces them with flip-flops he has pulled from his bag, a bag that has everything meticulously folded and organized. When Will takes off his jacket he finds a chair to hang it on to dry. He hangs it as though he cares that it keeps its shape. He then takes off his sweatshirt and folds it neatly, actually smoothing it out with each fold. He reluctantly places it on the floor. It is to be his pillow.

"You know one thing about being homeless is you often go days without showering. I'm a bit embarrassed to admit it, but you do." He says with disgust.

Will proceeds to tell me that some nights at 10:00 p.m. they announce that you can go over to the main building at CASS to shower but he is often asleep by then. "I hate the . . . no hate is not a good word. I dislike the showers over there. They have those little mister nozzles for saving water. No matter how hot you have them, by the time the mist hits you it's cold. And you are only supposed to take a 10 minute shower, but it takes an hour to get all the soap off with those misters."

Will goes on educating me as to where the good showers are in town. He often takes the bus down to ASU (Arizona State University) where he pretends that he is a student and uses their showers. As he talks about the showers at ASU it sounds like someone reading from a travel brochure about a tropical island paradise.

While Will and I are talking there is a lot of action in the room, which is now a giant sardine can of bodies. I cannot see a square inch of the tile floor in the lobby of LDRC. Blankets, bodies and sleeping bags cover it all. Most of the action is being created by five or 10 people, out of the 250 or so in here.

There is a guy behind me who has been standing and talking in one long, never repeating sentence. I mean the sentence has no periods in it. He is hard to understand because he talks fast and mumbles. I am listening to Will, taking notes, which I lie to him, is a cathartic thing for me, and at the same time I am trying to make out what this guy is saying or if there is a subject of some kind to this never ending sentence. All I can ascertain is that this tall, skinny, dirty, wiry haired man is talking about many subjects. He somehow strings them all together in a way that goes kind of like this: 'that's why the homosexuals are the way they are, because Bush's wife is in bed with the devil, which is why the judge didn't listen and threw the book at me and if it were the good book he would have seen as all shall see, but the satellites are controlling our minds so you must be careful, careful and good for even the schizophrenics know the truth that . . .'

And he's been going on like this for roughly 30 minutes.

Will continues to tell me other useful bits of information after his course on showers. He tells me about the bag and tag, a place on campus where you can leave your belongings in a big bag for the day, so you don't have to carry them with you. There are two clothespins on the bag, each with the same number. You take one as proof that it's your bag. It's like a hatcheck for the homeless. They lock all of the bags up for the day in a big, gated area to the east of the LDRC. The only problem is they don't keep the bags overnight, so if you don't pick your stuff up by 8 p.m. they throw it away.

Will has a dilemma to solve in a few days because there is a big job fair he wants to go to and he doesn't want to bring all his possessions with him. "If you show up with all this stuff you look, well, you know, homeless and I already have to tell them I'm a felon."

"You're a felon?"

"Yes. I'm a class two felon. I served a year in prison. I got out then, but violated my probation for being at a girl's house I was dating instead of at CASS, which is where my probation officer told me to be. When I went before the judge I just asked him to put me away for the full five months so I could buy down my probation."

"What? Buy down your probation?"

"Yes, you can do that. I would have only done a few days for what I did, but I could tell it was just going to be one thing after another with me and this probation officer, so I asked the judge to let me serve my full sentence which eliminated my probation. Now I'm just on parole."

"What's the difference?"

"Oh, it's huge. On parole I just check in once a month and can pretty much do anything I want, as long as it's not illegal. But on probation I have to do everything they say and it's like being on house arrest, which is fine if your house isn't CASS."

9:15 p.m.

They shut off some of the main lights, but there is still more than enough light to read and write. And much more than most people could sleep with. The poor guy behind me is still rambling on but now doing it on his knees with the palms of his hands together as if in prayer. And while the subjects repeat, they have a new seeming twist each time, so after an hour I still can't say that this is a script. Instead it seems to be an on going conversation that focuses around this man's main themes, which seem to be: courts, lawyers, prisons, politicians, morality, the Bible, homosexuals, women, conspiracy theories, satellites, aliens, gods and devils. You know, the usual Hollywood movie themes.

The sad thing is there is an umbrella theme starting to emerge in this man's personal dialog. He wants very badly to be good. He does not just seem to be kneeling, but to be repenting.

I pity him and then for some reason wonder how much of my own self-torment has been self-pity. This place always makes me think, question everything, and open up. Those lonely feelings are starting up again. Loneliness is my favorite self-pity subject.

9:30 p.m.

One of the staff members at CASS, a girl that some of the other guys refer to as Charlotte, yells out to ask if anyone wants to go to shower at CASS tonight. Charlotte is the perfect one to make this announcement because she has been yelling most of the night, mostly telling troublemakers to shut up or she's going to "throw you out myself!"

There are almost no takers for the showers, which Will explains probably has more to do with the weather than anything. "No one wants to go out into the cold to take a cold shower, to go back out in the cold to come back here."

Will then discusses how he wouldn't use the bathrooms here to go "number two." I agree with him, but it does remind me that I need to pee. So I get up and go to the bathroom. The LDRC does a pretty good job keeping their restrooms clean, but they still always smell like urine. They are just too heavily used. There is a guy in his shorts huddled in a corner wearing nothing else and having some argument with himself. He is very distressed and very sad. I smile at him, but he doesn't even seem to see me. The staff tried to get him to come out earlier, but to no avail and they were kind enough and smart enough to leave him here. He's full of fear but the idea of leaving the bathroom seems to scare him even more.

As I return to my place next to Will, Charlotte is making good on her promise and is literally throwing someone out for being disruptive.

10:00 p.m.

Will, apparently prompted by my recent tour of the facilities, proceeds to tell me all the good places near to here for going "number two." I find it quite amusing that the Superior Court Building ranks high in his book of clean restrooms and apparently has free phones for local calls if it appears that you are a student in their law library. And of course there's always ASU, not to mention a satellite campus of ASU. He also explains that the New Arid Club has very clean restrooms because they maintain them so well and keep the stalls locked so that not just anyone can go in there. The New Arid Club is open to everyone, but you can't hang out in there if you're not in the program.

10:30 p.m.

"Will, can I ask you something and by no means do you have to answer. It just doesn't seem like you belong here. What did you do time for?"

"No one belongs here, Mike. But I don't mind you asking. I've thought about it a lot. You have a lot of time to think about things in the DOC."

"The DOC?"

"The Department of Corrections. I call it that because it sounds better than prison. I actually have a degree in marketing and worked for quite a few years in that field, but it was never my thing. My last job was as a manager at a restaurant. I was there for 10 years. And we used to drink after work. And sometimes at work—during work. And the drinking might have tied into all this. That's why I go to the meetings."

"You said you were clean for 11 days but you've just been out of the DOC for 11 days. Did you drink while incarcerated?"

"No, I just don't count that time. I couldn't drink, so it doesn't seem fair to count that time. Well, we hired this new cook and every day he would say something rude about my wife. And I would tell him politely, please don't speak about my wife that way. I love my wife. Well, one night, after about a week of this, he said something and I picked up a rocks glass, you know those glasses with the thick bottom, and I smashed it against the side of his head."

Will explains that he thinks his drinking and some repressed issues had a lot to do with his explosive behavior, because he's not a violent man by nature. He's seems as gentle as a lamb to me. Will didn't fight the charge because, "I was at fault, Mike. I hit the guy just once, but I hurt him pretty badly." For that he got a felony two aggravated assault charge. To add insult to injury, no pun intended, Will's wife divorced him while he was in prison and he of course lost his job. This part of his story is all too common out here.

Somewhere during all this the guy behind me has laid down. But he only sleeps for about five minutes at a time and when he wakes, he stands or kneels and he starts up the same never—ending sentence that, now after hours have gone, by seems to keep repeating. Or, it could just be the themes that repeat. Anyway, he sometimes falls back a sleep after another five minutes of rambling. He seems truly tormented. It's as if his chanting wards off some evil for him. Will looks at him every so often with deep empathy but avoids eye contact.

11:00 p.m.

I roll two smokes and wish I had something a whole lot stronger although this is the last place I want to be disoriented in. The police just came in to arrest a client for stealing from another client. What the hell he was stealing I don't know. In some sort of cosmic counterbalance, an Hispanic man who speaks no English offers Will one of his blankets so he does not have to sleep on the floor. I tell him in Spanish that my friend says thank you. Will seems quite impressed with the kindness of the gentleman and my ability to speak Spanish, which I fail to tell him, is a farce. I lived in New Mexico long enough to fake the basics.

I get up to go outside to have a smoke. On the way out, a big black man with braided hair asks, in a Jamaican accent for a cigarette. I give him one. We go outside together and light up. He starts to make fun of another large black man for having an afro hairstyle, explaining that this is not the '80s anymore and he is not Michael Jackson. He is dancing like Michael Jackson while explaining all this and he is getting in the guy's face. And by the way, the Jamaican accent is gone. He was apparently trying to be funny when he asked for a cigarette as he is right now, but his humor has turned a bit rough.

They exchange some words and I'm thinking things are about to get physical. I take a subtle step back, because I would prefer to avoid any stray blows, when all of a sudden this small voice speaks up from a bundle of blankets in a wheelchair. He tells Mr. Fake Jamaican Accent Man to cut it out; he has gone too far. And it's weird. It's like a switch goes off in the guy's head. He listens to our wheelchair sage and he stops. Then the sage tells him to go inside and he does just that. Had this not happened I am sure, because of the stance of the two men and the words exchanged, that there would've been yet another fight tonight.

The instigator was a bit off. I can't be quite sure, but he didn't seem to understand when his joking became an attack and yet he was at least partially aware that he was pissing this other guy off. The guy he was making fun of now leaves too. I am alone with the tiny, black wheelchair sage. He seemed almost half asleep, but I have to ask him, "I don't mean to bother you, but can I ask you something?"

Speaking from inside a mass of blankets that surround him. "Yeah man, what?"

"That guy was getting all agro and you told him to stop and he just stopped. Why did he listen to you?"

"'Cause the cat knows he's fucking crazy as shit. He knows, he don't listen to me, something bad's going to happen. But he don't know that on his own."

This really makes me think about how crippling mental illness can be. This 80-pound homeless guy with more blankets than body in a wheelchair seems less helpless than a 220-pound man.

The door opens and another guy in shorts and a t-shirt with a blanket wrapped around him steps out and says he's leaving before Charlotte calls the cops on him. And he "didn't do nuthin'."

The voice from the blankets speaks up again, "If you didn't do shit then you ain't got to worry about shit."

Apparently the guy did do shit because he left in a shitload of a hurry, and none too soon. I walk back into the building and the cops are coming in right behind me. These poor guys never get a break—the cops that is. Charlotte explains that the guy left but she asks them to check on a woman who is excessively drunk and passed out. The woman's been giving Charlotte trouble all night because she wanted to sleep with her husband and they keep men and women separated. The woman did finally fall asleep where she was supposed to but it turns out that the man they arrested earlier was her husband, well actually her boyfriend. I know . . . it's a bit like a soap opera.

It takes the officer at least 10 minutes to wake her and when he tells her that they arrested her boyfriend she seems upset at first but the officer kindly tells her that it might be best for her to leave everyone alone and sleep it off for now. She seems to get the message and he seems satisfied that she is not a current endangerment to herself or others.

11:50 p.m.

There are vending machines in the LDRC lobby, which I have always found to be strange appliances in a homeless services center. But all of a sudden it's starting to make sense to me. While I'm not that hungry, I really want some sort of nurturing. Comfort food is in order. I buy a Diet Dr. Pepper for $1.25 and Fritos for .75 cents. And yes I know what you are thinking and I am thinking it too, but even if I had not been going home tomorrow I might have done the same thing. I'm not trying to be melodramatic, but you walk 13 miles from everything you know without any lifeline to anything or anyone, sleep on the floor with 250 disturbed and hurting people, and see if you don't want some salty corn chips, followed by the refreshing bite that only a caffeinated diet soda can provide.

Will laughs at me when I return. He's really amused. He's not laughing at me because of wasting my money, he's laughing at my poor health choices. He opens his backpack to reveal fresh fruit he purchased earlier in the day. He also has some multivitamins. Don't ask me. Will is a kind, gentle, well-educated, neatnik, health nut, who just got out of prison.

"I know Will, but I wanted some comfort food."

He laughs again. "I know just how you feel. I've got a can of Cheez Whiz. Do you want to put it on your Fritos?" For some reason we both find this extremely amusing and something we ponder for a few moments even though we don't go through with it.

Charlotte is threatening another person with dismissal into the cold. Will says, "You know, that woman is a real bitch." He's right in the sense that I haven't heard her say one thing all night without yelling. He continues, "And you know the really sad thing about it?" He pauses. "I think she's really hot." We both find this too to be down right hilarious. He's got great comedic timing. Will explains that there's something about a woman in charge. He's very respectful when he talks about women. I mean this guy just got out of prison and he has not once mentioned sex. He has talked, however, about how he misses the company of women, but he really means company. And I was whining about why I'm not with my ex-girlfriend. Geesh.

"So, Will, sounds like you are caught in Charlotte's web or should I say Willll-bur?" We laugh again and then he stops abruptly, "Hey, he was the pig." And continues to laugh all the more.

Then all of a sudden Will gets kind of serious and thanks me just for having someone to talk to, to hang out with. "Good friends and company are hard to find anywhere, especially here."

12:45 a.m.

I can't sleep. The room is a symphony of snoring and coughing, lots of coughing, not to mention that the floor is, well, tile and my sleeping bag doesn't seem to reduce any of its tile like effects. Whatever side of my body I am lying on goes numb after a while and I have to switch positions. Because of my back condition, my legs go numb if I lie on my back on a tile floor for too long. On my sides, my arms do the same. I even try my stomach, which is one of my favorites, but not the same without pillows and a mattress. And of course the sweet tormented SMI man is still waking every five minutes to mouth a few more verses before drifting back to sleep. And every few times of cycling through this he gets up to stand or kneel for a more formal delivery of his dissertation on heaven, hell, politics, anal sex and aliens. I must be loosing it too, because I'm starting to see how they're all related.

5:00 a.m.

Charlotte, in the melodious delivery of a drill sergeant tells us it's time to "get up and get out!"

Will says he doesn't know why they always kick everyone out so early. "There is nowhere to go. You can't even look for a job this early." He tells me to take my time rolling up my sleeping bag because they won't actually kick us out till 5:30.

I take 20 minutes to do two minutes of work while I watch Will go through his morning routine. He takes a multivitamin, puts on some deodorant, puts lotion on his hands because they "get dry and chapped from the weather." He folds and presses everything. He puts away his flip-flops and puts on his socks and shoes; clean socks by the way. He must do his laundry somewhere, but I don't ask about that.

Since we still have ten minutes I roll two smokes. The rambling paranoid schizophrenic from behind me asks in the first clear complete sentence he has spoken in the past eight hours, if he can buy one from me for a quarter. I give him the cigarette. And I am pleased to find out that he changes to some new sentence about honorable men like myself being rare and . . . and . . . then I lose him again, but it sounds good. It's full of words like noble and honorable. And he's incredibly happy with the cigarette. I go to the bathroom and on the way out I see him once more and he thanks me again. If I had known this eight hours ago I would have been giving the poor guy cigarettes all night.

I wait for Will outside. It's cold, really cold. This is stupid, really stupid. Will meets up with me and tells me that I don't have to hang out with him. He says it as though I am doing him a favor. I explain that I want to hang out with him. We get lucky and a guy hands us a flyer about a Christian halfway house very near by that is handing out bagels, coffee and according to Will, ". . . lukewarm oatmeal. By hey, it fills you up and who am I to complain?" Will does not complain about anything; in fact he censors himself from using strong language, which apparently to him are four letter words like "hate."

We walk in the cold towards the halfway house, avoiding puddles left from the rain. To my sadness we pass the tortured rambling man. He is on his knees, in a puddle, a deep puddle, praying.

I will never again think of homeless people as being lazy or lacking remorse for any of their mistakes. Will is most definitely remorseful and willing to work hard to reintegrate with society. As for the lost soul on his knees, there is no doubt he is remorseful and he works nonstop in the saddest, most unproductive way.

We arrive at the halfway house just a block from the main campus. Some very nice people hand us coffee, a bagel and a tray of lukewarm oatmeal. We stand on the street holding our coffee to warm our hands enough so that we can eat the bagel and oatmeal, while listening to Christian inspirational music. The music is the full extent of any proselytizing. I must say, the soft sell for God is much more effective than the people who come to my door twice a year trying to save me from hell. Down here, hot coffee and a bagel really do save you from hell.

6:05 a.m.

Will points out to me that the New Arid Club will be opening soon at 6:15 for their 6:30 AA meeting.

We go, if only to warm up and drink more coffee. Remembering that AA meetings are completely funded from within each particular AA group I leave my final .75 cents for their coffee fund. When you don't have anything and you have to give up everything, including your favorite substance, then coffee becomes pretty important. It is probably the best expenditure I made the entire trip or for who knows how long.

The meeting is run similarly, but this time by Nancy who recognizes me part way through and is happy to see me. While I am very impressed with Nancy I have no attraction to her and yet a warm smile coming from an understanding woman somehow changes everything. It is just nice to see a pretty smiling face, smiling in my direction.

Various people talk again on the topic of New Beginnings. Some of the memorable speeches come from people I've already met and learned from on my journey.

Nancy says, "We have beautiful scars, scars that allow you to help others. And it's not all about you anymore. So if you are sitting there feeling ashamed of your past, don't! because that doesn't work. That doesn't help you or anyone else. Surrendering isn't giving up; it's moving to the winning team. It's all about humility and acceptance."

Here, from my notes, are several other comments from this group:

"If you want to change you have to be willing. In order to get my higher power working, I had to take action. I didn't know it would work or how it would work, but I did it and it did work."

"I can leave here now but I choose to stay because this is where I got sober. This is where I choose to serve."

"I'm going to work my program as intensely as I pursued that hit of crack."

Finally, Running Deer says, "I was too busy worrying about things outside of me. But I couldn't change that stuff until I changed me."

After Running Deer finishes Nancy says in a very joyful and yet solemn and tearful tone, "I just want to say, Running Deer was a mess, a mess. I didn't think he was going to make it. It's a miracle he is here today. A real miracle."

We end the meeting with a prayer and everyone says, "Keep coming back! The program works if you work it!"

8:00 a.m.

I give my sleeping bag to Will. He reluctantly takes it. Out here, it is like giving a guy your horse. I tell him that I can't explain, but I don't need it tonight and I will explain when I see him next. He doesn't ask any questions. There is a real respect for privacy on the streets. And Will of course is respectful anyway. "I'll take good care of it an' give it back to you when I see you next."

9:00 a.m.

I go back to the LDRC, which is now open for the day. Laura, a beautiful young staff member recognizes me and smiled as I move past her in the crowd. I sit down to work on my notes.

I think about staying to attend some of the classes offered here other than the movie workshop, but there are none today that I am interested in. The classes/activities today are: Health Screening, Beginning Computer, GED and Choir Practice. I am interested in the Choir Practice because it sounds so unexpected, just like the movie workshops used to, but I can't sing and it is at 4 p.m. If I leave after that, I won't be home until after midnight and my family and roommate would be very worried.

I've learned a lot on this very small, very controlled journey. I know that if I stay additional nights I would probably learn more because my experiment would become less and less controlled and confined. The longer I stay, the less of an experiment it would be. But I will never know what it is like to be homeless as long as I have a home, a job and a strong support network.

What I learned, or maybe I should say, what I tasted, was a tiny bit of the emotional reality of being homeless. The wet and the cold are important realities too, but they aren't what being homeless is all about. I have been wet and cold when on a backpacking trip and felt completely different. Here, I tasted despair, loneliness and the need for comfort. I tasted invisibility, emasculation and public distain. I experienced a lack of options and a sort of disconnectedness that seems key to understanding homelessness. All that in 24 hours.

10:30 a.m.

I decide that while this is a sad, overwhelming and complex dilemma I really want to understand, this place does not need one more suffering person. It's time to walk home.

It's cold and very windy, but there is not a cloud in the sky. It's ironic but I don't want to leave. This is the only home I have right now and I must traverse the distance between it and my actual home being in the state of homelessness.

I sit down on a bench on the HSC lawn to roll a final smoke, which takes quite a bit of skill in this wind. I put the pouch of tobacco away and eventually manage to light it. I sit here, just watching the sea of infinite human variety around me swell and recess as people try to stay warm while greeting others, talking, moving in and out of view or just sitting by themselves. It is a beautiful, natural ever-changing ocean of humanity.

I commence my walk home on the opposite side of the street. I will take fewer notes because they would be redundant and because I want to get home. I figure that the note taking I did on the way to LDRC added significantly to the time it took to walk here. There was a time in my life that I could have run this distance in two hours instead of walking it in six hours.

11:30 a.m.

The blister on my right foot breaks, causing me to limp. It's going to be a long walk home. But I feel more at peace with myself. I'm not complaining about it. My mind is not churning and arguing with itself.

1:43 p.m.

I have lots of foot pain now and not so much from the blister but from trying to walk on my foot in a way that will not hurt my blister. It's like I sprained my foot. But I'm still doing OK.

2:47 p.m.

My foot is hurting more and I'm really limping along. It occurs to me that the pain doesn't make me feel 'woe is me.' The pain makes all my other feelings shut down. I'm not thinking about much except about getting to a place where I can rest, which is obviously my house.

3:45 p.m.

I pass two 9-year-old kids who are drinking soda pop and standing out in front of their apartment. They wave. I smile and wave back. One of them asks me, "Hey, are you a hobo?" I'm tired, I'm dirty and I'm dragging my right foot behind me. I look the part for sure. "No," I answer—in self-defense. What should I care what two kids think? But apparently I do care. Why did I feel the need to break character? Is it because I'm back in my old neighborhood and it hurts my pride or something? The homeless must bear incredible shame.

4:30 p.m.

I arrive at my house. It took me six hours to limp home. I remember that I don't have keys and have to break in through the dog door in back. It's big, but I'm bigger. I have to swim through like a fish with both arms above my head. As I rise to the surface of my house through the dog door, I have emerged from my immersion, which was more like a submersion.

I limp back to my bedroom to lie down. On my pillow is the following note from my roommate who is also one of my best friends:

> Mike,
> Hi sweetheart, hoping you are home before me tonight. Went to the store, been thinking of you. I bought eggs, cheese, bacon, fruit—being oranges for your vitamin C from all the cold and rain. Bagels and cream cheese. Help yourself. Wanted you to have great Wed. morning welcome-back-home breakfast. Tell me all about it when you get a chance. I love you,
>
> > Jenny
> > B.F.F.

My experience served merely to highlight how ignorant I still am about homelessness and how much I still have to learn. Maybe what really makes homeless people homeless is that they don't have a friend like Jenny.

ORDEALS

JON, COMPUTER CLASS, LDRC:
Monday, February 16, 2009, 9:00 a.m.

I'M REALLY EXCITED TO INTERVIEW Jon again. Even though I claimed I was not out to get stories, his sounded so interesting, so outrageous and yet plausible. How can there be a man who used to be a police officer, has a doctorate degree and now volunteers at the homeless shelter where he lives?

I arrive at the computer lab right on time. It's locked. One of Jon's students tells me that Jon was "mad about some politics around here" and disappeared. They thought he might have gotten a job and left. But nobody knows.

But the student's partial explanation makes sense. He didn't handle a confrontation well the day I met him, and Jessica once told me that many clients do just disappear. The reasons are many and often unknown: They get a job, get out and never look back; they get arrested; they move on to avoid getting arrested; they die. As for Jon, I may never know.

Jon taught me that tomorrow is always uncertain so one must seize the moment.

TONY, CLIENT, LDRC: Monday, February 16, 2009, 10 a.m.

I decide to do what I always do around here when I don't know what to do: Go to an AA meeting. I am fascinated by the way they work. There are two levels to them—at least two levels. There is the surface 12-step program, which I'm sure is anything but surface for those who wholeheartedly participate in it. Then there is the practicing of relationship and community skills, which the program necessitates. Learning to get along with yourself and others is a lot of what occurs in those meetings. The meetings are not always pretty. They are often raw, painful, challenging, but so are relationships. And to learn to deal with them without escaping is what it's all about.

As I look around the room at this motley crew it occurs to me that this place has had a snowball effect on me. I used to accept without judgment the weirdness of these people. Now they don't seem so weird. I am the one who is weird. I am the one who comes from a mindset that when anyone doesn't look, sound, and act normal, there is a problem. I thought I was the normal guy trying to learn to accept these abnormal people, but was I? We marvel at the diversity of nature, but when we see it in man we fear it or distain it. I have lived in a world where we pare down diversity and individuality to the point where it's abnormal to be an individual. How often do I really talk, walk, dress, act and even think like I really *want* to? These people in the room have a lot of problems, but acting like they think I think they should is not one of them. That's my problem.

It turns out to be a great stroke of luck that I'm here because one of the guys to get up and talk is Tony, with his red sneakers, sweatshirt and all. Though his appearance is unchanged, the man sounds much clearer than he did when I spoke with him a week or so ago and he is much clearer than the first time I met him in Dawn's movie workshop.

Tony is a great public speaker. It's not in his clear crisp speech, because he doesn't have that. It's his presence. He's very animated. "My life used to be like this," he says, then spins round and round like a dog chasing its tail. "And sometimes it was faster," he speeds up the spin, "and some times slower." He slows down. "But always round and round."

He stops. "And when you stop, you're a bit dizzy. That's where I'm at today."

Tony continues on, briefly making a point that he cannot fix anything outside of himself; he can only fix what is inside. He then eloquently thanks some of the other speakers previous to him that had points he felt were meaningful. He says to one guy, "Thanks for talking about your life, which was my life." His whole speech has this inside/outside theme.

Many other people speak and what I get out of it is that addictions are mental or emotional traps that often catch the smartest and most sensitive people. And the worse they feel about their mistakes, the more it drives the cycle.

At the end of the meeting, I ask Tony if he remembers me.

"Yeah. The book guy."

"I really want to interview you if you're still interested."

"Yeah."

"Well what are you doing today?"

"Hanging out here. Working over at St. Vinnie's later."

With that, I whisk him over to LDRC where Ryan gives me a key to a cubicle in the Magellan Health Services of Arizona offices. It is becoming my own private interview space.

I explain to Tony about my book project and that I don't want to direct the interview in any particular way. I don't necessarily want his entire life story. I just want the reader to know about him as a person.

"Where do I start?" he states, as though I've given him too broad a range to work with.

"Well, I loved the speech you just gave at the New Arid Club. When you spun around like that it conveyed more than a thousand words could have."

"It's about coming out of that spin with sanity," Tony begins. "It's about recapturing my goals before I did. I'm getting older, teeth falling out, eyes getting bad. And that's not the way it started off. I was the youngest of seven kids. Father worked; mom raised the kids. I was the last one to leave the house so to speak. Mother was a practicing alcoholic and gambler. Brothers gangbanged and had guns in the house. My two sisters left the house early on. When my dad left, the house was in an uproar. Mom got drunk. Gang members came over. My brother was the leader of a gang in south L.A. He was my hero. He had respect, a low rider, girls. But I had a sister who was a JW [Jehovah's Witness] and was trying to pull me away from my brothers. It was like a tug-of-war on the inside of me. I wanted to be in a gang, but I wanted my sister's approval. I wanted her approval because she was more of a mother to me than my mother. We did fun stuff together. I felt like my mother abandoned me for the alcohol and the horse racing. So when we hung out together with her two kids, that felt like my real family.

"It was two different lives. I felt mixed up," Tony continues. I just let him keep talking. His life story is amazing—and telling. What follows is that life story, verbatim.

"I went to my brother's house at the age of 13 and smoked some weed with him and his wife. And then I started smoking weed. I used to love sports, elementary, junior high, high school. Every school I went to I played basketball on. Dr. J and Magic Johnson were my favorite role models. My dad was somewhat of a role model too because, when he stayed home on the weekend, he would fix cars and they would line up down the street.

People would pay him. Sometimes we would do things as a family like go to the swap mart. But for the most part I missed my dad because he got home at 1:00 a.m. So there was a missing of that male role model growing up. There was no hanging out and him telling me things that dads tell their kids. What was being told to me was how to be a gang member. I was a wannabe gang member.

"So now I'm 15 and I'm drinking and smoking weed. In 1984, I went to a party and drank too much. I threw up on a girl I was dancing with. This guy picked me up and slammed me inside the party and then outside. I tried to get on a bike and ride five blocks to my mother's house. Five days later I woke up from a coma. I went through an intersection and got hit by a car. I had a bike pedal in the back of my head. I say this because it was a changing event in my life. I lost my teeth and think about it every time I brush my teeth. From that day forward, I drank like it was water. I felt like I was missing my teeth and now I looked all messed up. I felt like people were looking at me like I was not a cool basketball player.

"I left high school and went into Job Corps, Reno Nevada. I got my GED and took automotive repair. Job Corps helped me to see that the world didn't revolve around South Central L.A. I played basketball and baseball, did GED, automotive repair and working at McDonald's on the weekend. I had a nice girlfriend. Things were looking good. I wanted to go into the military, but I scored real low on the math part [of the GED]. I could have retaken the test, but said to hell with it. Job Corps placed me at a gas station back in south central L.A. and I worked two weeks, got my first paycheck, and never went back to work. I didn't like how hard it was for me to get the grease from underneath my fingernails. I was still trying to be the Don Juan in my head. I wanted to be hip, slick and cool like my brothers. I remember that.

"After that I went to California Conservation Corps in Sacramento. I went to a four-week course with intense physical training. It's like a fire preparation class. I graduated with high honors. So they placed me in San Fran [from] 1988 to 1990. We worked with helping the state of California to restore its natural resources. We would clean up floods, build parks, erosion control, fire fighting, fire prevention, fence building. I once fought a fire once for 17 hours. It made me feel like what I was doing was helping me save people's property. It made me feel good. I was still drinking on the weekends but I was making a contribution.

"That pattern repeats. I drank and lost my job; got angry and hit a wall. I joined L.A. Conservation Corps, but now I was drinking more, smoking crack with marijuana in it, which is called primos. I'm not maturing into a man. I'm missing days after paydays. And now taking drugs at work.

"One day I was called into the office and they let me go. He asked me if I had any problems at home. I was referred to a rehab center, 90-day inpatient. It was like being at Camp Snoopy in the mountains. It was nice. I had never seen anything like it in my life. I never wanted to leave.

"Then I worked at Studio City California and worked at the Village Barbeque in an upper class neighborhood. I'm a chef's assistant. I started off as a dishwasher, but they kept moving me up. They eventually gave me the keys.

"I went to downtown L.A. one night and got drunk. I found a prostitute. She took my keys because I didn't pay her what she wanted. So I lost that job. I returned home, but the family had grown apart even more.

"1996. My father passed. I didn't even know he was dead. I woke up in a detox and someone told me there that my father was dead. When I got out, I went to the liquor store. So until September 2000, I would drink and do drugs. I would work two weeks, get a paycheck, quit.

"I was born September 10, 1967, and I got picked up September 10, 2000, by a program called Back to Life, based in Arizona. They told me they had a place to live, with a job, no drugs and would help me save my money. And it worked pretty good for the first nine months. I stayed clean. They kinda lied to me in the first six months. I only got $5 a week. But they told me that I needed to focus on the inside of me and not material goods. And they were right. So they took care of all my needs. I completed the program and they placed me on a job where I got paid hourly wages, Arizona Precision Metal. It was a good job. I was making slot machines. I had my own little section. I played music. The people were friendly. We all worked together to make those slot machines.

"Something came back as being built improperly. So there were a lot of layoffs. Not me, but here was another emotional situation coming. I was doing two jobs for the price of one. I asked for more money. When I didn't get it, I quit. From that point on I found you never quit a job unless you have another one. From that day on it was day labor. I couldn't pay the rent at the program so I went to the liquor store and ended up at CASS for the first time.

"Later I went to a place called the Streets of Joy Ministry, 12th and Indian School. I've always been drawn to that since my sister, but I'm still not being responsible to myself and God. It was an in-house discipleship. It wasn't a drug program, but there were people like that. I was able to stay there. A guy asked me if I wanted a job because he saw me cleaning up around there. I always clean up, because they taught me in the Conservation Core, if it isn't biodegradable, throw it away, get it off the ground." He thinks for a second, nods, "I wish I would have applied that to drugs. So I got a job at AZ Flood Control. All of my past training in California Conservation [Corps] came into play. Probably the best job I ever had.

"I got put in an unsafe working conditions. I disagreed with my supervisor about standing on a dumpster. He told me to go sit in the truck and I told him I could do better and I walked out of my last job at AZ Flood Control.

"That was four years ago, so for the last four years, I've done day labor and wandered from job to job, drinking and doing drugs—to come to the conclusion that job is where I belong. But I can't have that job unless I change, because I'm going to meet another person like him down the road.

Tony finally arrives at the latest chapter of this amazing story, where he's standing today.

"It's not life that needs to change, it's my perception about life," he says. "Not the situation I'm in now. Not blaming CASS or The LDRC or the Overflow for the situation I'm in, the situation I put myself in. It ain't nobody's fault but my own. It's my reactions to situations that need to change; it's not the situations. It's my old conclusion that the problem is on the outside of me.

"What I have learned now is that I am capable of looking at it from a different angle. Rather than saying there is someone else to blame, I need to look at how I set this up. I can look at taking some different actions. At the age of 40 I have learned that I can take different actions and get different reactions. There is no one to blame and no one is at fault. I just need to take responsibility for myself. If I don't like standing in line for food, I do something about it. I can't say I don't like it and do nothing about it. It's kinda contradicting of me. If I don't like sleeping on the ground, stop using drugs and alcohol, get a job, and pay some rent."

Tony says the New Arid Club has been the safe haven he needs to look at life from a different angle. He gets to hear from people who are in the same situation as him, and what's more important, who are taking action to change their situation.

"Do you remember the first time we saw each other?" I ask him.

"Yeah. I love that movie workshop," Tony replies. "That actually has been the motivating factor for me to take some action. That, and the staff at

LDRC, especially Jayne, Nancy and Jessica. They have been the motivation for me to get off my rusty dusty and take some action. They believed in me when I've been in fear. They've supported me. They saw something in me. They've actually been kinda hard on me, but I understand the motive of them telling me it's time to move. They helped me to see I'm going in a circle, with my hands out. I now volunteer at Saint Vinnie's eight to 10 hours a day and it's helped me to see that I can give back to this community.

"All my life, alcohol has been a comforter for any emotions I can't handle. I didn't mature emotionally. I don't do to well with them. Even to this day."

Simply asking Tony to tell his life story was more productive than I could have possibly imagined for this interview. Still, I ask him the big three questions.

What is the meaning of life?

Well I find the meaning of life is what I put into it; it is probably going to be the same of what I get out of it. If I put negativity into life, then negativity is what I get out of it. If I put positive love into it, then that's what I get out of it. That's what I think the meaning of life is.

What are your thoughts about society and/or societies in general?

People in general . . . we love in others what we love in ourselves. We despise in others what we cannot see in ourselves. That's it. If you don't like something in me, it's probably because it's something in you. If I don't like something in you, it's probably because it's something in me. That's how I feel about society.

Who are you?

I am spirit trying to become a person, ever evolving into a different person each day. That's who I am.

He laughs, as though he just figured this out and likes the way he put it. I ask if there's anything else he wants to tell the world, and he responds in classic Tony fashion.

"No. That's cool."

Tony makes me consider that we don't have to be healed to help others, and further, helping might be the perfect healing.

JESSICA, LDRC: Monday, February 16, 2009, 1 p.m.

Jessica greets me in typical fashion: unguarded, open, warm. She's wearing a long flowing blouse that moves about her like fairy wings, flapping without effort or form. As she settles into her chair behind her desk, Jessica asks how my immersion went.

I explain how I felt lonely and wanted to nurture myself just three hours into my walk.

"Well yes, us people with resources can be kind of needy," she replies, simply.

I'd never thought about it that way. Chewing this over, I ask Jessica what she feels was the best thing that happened this week. She begins to talk about the "cardboard campaign" the center took part in for Homeless Awareness Week.

"Staff and volunteers wrote on cardboard. Things like 'My favorite color is purple,' 'I like dogs, do you?' but nothing to do with homelessness," she says. "Then we walked around downtown and just held our signs and noticed that people looked away. They must have just seen 'person with a sign.' So we started to say hi to people and they looked shocked. There were some of them who almost laughed as though they were laughing at themselves, like they caught themselves."

"I can see how this was enlightening, but how did it raise awareness?" I ask, ever the skeptic. Jessica replies that they handed out cards to raise awareness, but didn't ask anything from anyone during the campaign.

"We just wanted to jar people a little bit, in a friendly way," she says.

I think yeah, but does that really make a difference? Then I realize this place has jarred me in a friendly way, and it has definitely made a difference.

"What was the worst thing that happened last week?" I ask.

"Well, we may have some budget cuts and the problem is, where do I cut? Some of the people I'm paying could be homeless for the first time or again."

Over half of Jessica's staff is composed of clients or ex-clients. She ensures that her philosophies reflect in all of her practices. If the LDRC's job is to end homelessness, then the homeless get the jobs.

"Jessica, I wanted to interview Jon from the computer class but someone said he left because of politics. What does that mean?"

"I think there is more going on with Jon, some sort of guilt or mental illness," she says. "I think we use that word 'politics' to mean, like, some sort of bizarre social construct . . . I don't even know what 'politics' means."

Jessica pauses, choosing her next words tactfully. "Nancy has an anti-rule rule: Let's think about what we need to do to correct this without making a rule. That's what a lot of politics is about—rule making as a solution. A rule is not a solution. A rule is like a Band-Aid. Rules make more problems."

She pauses again with a deep look of conjuring on her face.

"As I have gotten older, rules seem less and less relevant because I'm not sure what rules I've followed. I think the way I get things done is slightly manipulative, because I make them think I am following the rules, but I'm not; not that I'm exactly breaking them either." She laughs. "When I was younger my mom would ask me to clean my room and I would say 'OK' but wouldn't always clean my room."

Jessica makes me consider that rules get in the way of relationships.

HECTOR & PETER, MAGELLAN HEALTH SERVICES OF ARIZONA, INC.: Tuesday, February 17, 2009, 6 p.m.

Tonight I'm going on an outreach drive with Hector and Peter—who Hector lovingly refers to as Pedro.

The object of such an outreach is to expand the visibility of the HSC. Hector and Pedro are caseworkers for the mentally ill. My temporary office is a cubicle in their permanent office. They go on these outreach rides around the downtown area to meet and form relationships with individuals who might be labeled as Seriously Mentally Ill (SMIs) in hopes that one day they will get them to come into their office so they can get them whatever professional help is needed: mental, medical, housing, etc.

As we ride around in Peter's SUV, Hector tells me that his job, as he sees it, is really to ensure the rights of SMI individuals. He cannot force someone into treatment, nor does he want to. "You have to want to participate in order to get better," he says.

The outreach is an opportunity to understand people and meet their individual needs, Hector explains to me. The label of SMI doesn't say anything about the person. "Everyone out here, they're all different and unique." Hector and Pedro can't reach them if they don't know and understand them.

We spend an hour or more just driving around and talking to various people. I am amazed at how many people they both know. Hector says if they are lucky—real lucky—they might get someone to come into their office after meeting with him or her five times on the street. Those labeled as SMIs have lots of obstacles to seeking, receiving and utilizing help; a big one being that they may not even realize they need it. Hector believes they need their dignity first and foremost. He and Pedro are just there to build relationships and inform them of their rights and what might be available to them.

Some of the people we meet are chronically homeless, a term designated for when someone is on the streets more than a year. We meet people who have been on the streets for over 10 years. As Hector puts it, "At this point, they don't know any different." He elaborates that by this he means that they can't fathom things being any different than life on the streets. It's hard to make good choices about things when you can't comprehend that choices exist. (There's that choice thing again, I think.) Hector and Pedro's job is to introduce choices to those who think they have none.

As we continue to drive around, stopping every few minutes to say hi to someone in hopes of building a relationship or following up on their progress, Pedro tells me of the various people he has met over the years. He had a client who was a young surgeon, with the documentation to prove it, who developed paranoid schizophrenia and lost his job. Another paranoid schizophrenic client with a Ph.D. from Harvard had forgotten she had Social Security for over a year. They helped her to get her back pay and other assistance. When Pedro asked her what she was going to do with the money, she said, buy a laptop so she could get on the Internet. Her mind was still brilliant and she was happiest when she was plugged in and could research the infinite wealth of information available on the Internet.

We stop to check on some people Hector has never seen before. They come up to Hector's side of the car and ask him something in Spanish. Hector laughs and tells them no. He talks with them for a while, asking them if they need anything or if they have been to the Human Services Campus before. They have, but prefer to live and sleep out here. As we drive away I ask Hector if I heard correctly: They were asking him for drugs? He laughs and says yes. They thought he was a dealer. He kind of looks like a dealer (whatever that means.) And this might be an advantage. It's not uncommon for SMI individuals to be wary of the HSC—or any organization, for that matter.

A few miles from campus, we meet a woman at a park that I have seen before at the LDRC. Hector, who in his own words is a "chubby, bald, tattooed, Chicano," gets out of the car to speak with her. He instantly switches from his extreme street style to that of a polished gentleman and

I can tell she appreciates it. Hector asks if she is hooked up to services and discovers the woman does not have housing, but has some income from Social Security. He and Pedro give her a ride back to the Human Services Campus because she wants to spend the night there, even though she will not sleep in the shelter itself. She wants to sleep outside the New Arid Club: "The guys are real nice there. They'll keep an eye on me."

Pedro is a kind, soft fellow with a thick white-yellow mustache. He gives the woman his card and asks her to come and see him the next day so they can get her some housing and medical services. Pedro has a deal with a nearby apartment complex for very cheap housing. It's not a subsidized program; just an apartment complex that has a 40 percent vacancy problem and is willing to do whatever it takes to fill those rooms.

I ask Pedro if she will come to see him tomorrow.

"Probably not, but after a few more interactions she might," he says.

The outreach guys drop me off at my car after a couple of hours of driving around. I tell Hector I can't wait to sit down with him next week to chat.

"Yeah, man, there's a lot going on out here," he replies. "It's tribal out here and the problem is these people have been enabled and codependent for so long they don't know any different."

**Hector makes me consider that relationships
have to start with dignity.**

JESSICA, LDRC: Monday, February 23, 2009, 10:00 a.m.

Jessica left me a message, saying she had to cancel our regular weekly meeting. She also told me I would have to cancel all of my interviews. The campus was closed for the day.

The campus is never closed. I don't even know what that means. What I do know is that Jessica sounded lost, foggy and sad. Having spoken with her so many times in person, I can picture her face just based on the sound of her voice. The vision of it now is painful to entertain.

Two hours later, Jessica phones me again. She explains that one of the clients shot and killed a CASS staff member named Kevin. While she did not know Kevin, the sound of devastation in her voice, the sound of loss of life, is tremendous. It takes her quite some time to relay this information to me; her words and facts are dripping through the phone like tears.

I too feel like crying, like some great rift had been torn in the universe. I never would have had this reaction in the past. People die all the time. But I feel different now about community. One of my fellow humans, a man I never met and will now never meet, died through violence today.

Jessica must be scared, but I can only assume she is devastated more than anything. What is the most disconnected, uncooperative, incomprehensible thing that someone can do? Remove someone else from the community—permanently. And her life is based on including everyone into the community.

If we think we can ignore the problems of sad, confused and lost people in our society, we are mistaken. And if it were not for the Human Services Campus, that killing might have taken place in my neighborhood. But the point is, it is my neighborhood.

We may be insulated, but we are never separated.

Jessica's delivery of bad news and the shooting cause me to consider the sanctity of life and the fact that everything is in our backyard.

HECTOR, MAGELLAN HEALTH SERVICES OF ARIZONA, INC.: Tuesday, February 24, 2009, 1 p.m.

I arrive on campus and see the presence of extra sheriff's officers. As I walk from my car toward LDRC, I can overhear conversations about the incident. Many of the clients are upset, stating that it could have been any one of them. I can feel fear thickening the air.

I say hi to Running Deer on the way in to the LDRC lobby. He knew Kevin and is very upset about the entire thing. He tells me that Kevin, who worked in the main CASS building, has a son who works in the Outreach Shelter. I ask Running Deer if things like this make him want to use again. He says they do, but he won't. And he seems pretty certain about this. It's hard for me to imagine how Running Deer manages staying clean during stressful times when I can't stick to a diet or a budget.

The Magellan Health Services offices are located on the far right wall of the LDRC lobby, behind glass doors. Ryan lets me in as he so often does when I have an interview to perform. But this time I pass the empty cubicle I always use, and pass three more to Hector's tiny office.

It is cluttered, full of books, pictures and various knick-knacks. He is wearing bright yellow baggy sweatpants. He really does look a bit like a drug dealer, a very short drug dealer. When I tell him this, he laughs. When Hector laughs, his whole body laughs with him. He tells me it's not unusual for people to ask him if he has anything for sale. He forgot that this actually happened when we were doing our outreach together.

Hector is rugged, stern, with a beard that is trimmed very close to his face in a Van Dyke with sideburns. And he's also bright and loving. But every ounce—or pound—of him is from the streets.

"So talk to me, Hector."

"I think what it is, is I've been doing this for 15 years and people is where my heart's at," he begins. "I think what I try to do is try to teach people how to be with people. Like Pedro. I try to teach Pedro how to step back from his reality and be in someone else's reality! It's a God given gift. That's what it is!"

I nod. And Hector continues in a rhythmic fashion, emphasizing every third or fourth sentence.

"See bro, from a bleeding heart perspective, sometimes you just feel sorry for people. Their instant reaction is to want to stop the bleeding, to just put a Band-Aid on it. But they haven't observed the wound! Sometimes they don't realize that you are just looking at the outside of the cut. The Band-Aid, because they haven't done the proper observations of the wound, gets bloody, wet and falls off. My belief in people is to teach and inspire people to clean up and observe their own wounds! To do it with them. To look at the wound with them and to help them decide for themselves what to do! Then to advise them where to go."

I nod again noticing that Hector not only emphasizes every third or fourth sentence with his voice but also by leaning forward, closer to me while delivering it, before falling backwards in his chair for the reclining delivery of the next three sentences. I also notice the warmth in Hector's smile, all the more noticeable due to the sternness of his delivery at times, when he talks about outreach. This man is very hard and soft all at once.

"You got here a cluster of providers who grew up on the streets," Hector says. "That's our life! For some reason, that's who people really tap into, because we can actually say we've been there. I love people.

"I guess, bro, you have to see people through my eyes to see the potential of what can change," leaning back in his chair.

Hector then talks passionately at length about disenfranchised communities he's worked with in the past and how he helped them to organize so they could overcome adversity. "I've seen so much, bro. I'm just talking about the greatness of what people's beliefs can do. They can move mountains!" he says, putting oomph into that third sentence.

I nod again, just listening for now. This guy doesn't need any prompting or directing.

"So we move forward to what I do now. But rather than me doing everything for our clients, I try and get our clients to do for themselves! In the last year, we have gotten 20 SMI, chronically homeless out of their situation. These are the hard-core cases! We have seen the success of what they have done. They are more engaged with their services because of the work we have done here. And what is going on is we are trying to apply that to working with the other agencies to achieve our goal. We have different sources and approaches but the same goal. We've had a lot of success over the year. It's been cool." Hector leans back again, smiles and nods as if he's remembering.

Hector switches directions, thinking aloud about yesterday's shooting, as if he knows it is on my mind, and everyone else's on campus. "I don't think the gentlemen who did this thing had a message, but clearly people try to take a message from it," Hector says. "My thing is, if we show fear, they are going to know it; they are going to smell it. We have to move forward! I grew up very Chicano, very gang oriented. So for me it was all about my *familia*. When I grew up all Chicanos were my family, so I had to have an enemy. But I realized nobody wins [that way]. I realized that the only things that matter are love, happiness, and my kids."

"I used to carry around so much anger. Everything I do in my life now is to represent my parents, my kids and my wife in a positive way. I think, had you met me five years ago, you would have thought this guy is a hardcore thug and he is never going to change." Hector laughs now, shaking his head. "I think God has given me the compassion to see outside myself."

"Hector, you laugh a lot. I like it."

"Honestly one of the things I've learned, the secret to being a success in this work, is laughing your ass off, laughing your ass off! If you can't laugh . . ." Hector punctuates the moment by laughing his wholehearted, whole bodied laugh.

Hector holds up a client complaint form that was just delivered to him by Ryan. Clients can complain about staff and it is formally documented. This is done so repetitive complaints can be identified and dealt with, but it is also done for another reason that Hector discuses.

"Bro, anytime you can get a client to fight for their own self, that's a good thing! You know when people fight for themselves and advocate for themselves that's a good thing. Especially SMI people! They fall into a sort of hole where they don't feel they have the right to fight. We are all equal! There are two things I can guarantee you in life, death and taxes and with taxes who gives a shit!" Hector laughs again.

At this point, Hector shares with me some of his personal stories—and not the flattering ones. These are tales of broken relationships, sexual abuse, substance abuse . . . He concludes, "I've destroyed myself, but I always return to give back!" Hector says. "I remember doing things that I wasn't proud of, but if I do mistakes in a community, I try to make amends by giving back to that community and I learn from that community. Even my ex-wife taught me things. One of the greatest things that came from that [his divorce] is it got me talking to my dad again. I called him and told him that I didn't want to live anymore. I lost my kids, job, wife; and I wanted to die. I was losing control and the only control I could get back was to take my life. And my dad said, '*Mi hijo*, I've always been proud of you. You don't want to do this. I just want you to know that the only reason these things are happening to you in your life is because you have lost your faith! We haven't lost our faith in you.'

"I've had my battles. I still have them today, but I'm just more mindful and I don't want to end up back where I was."

"Anything else you want to tell me, Hector?"

"That's it in a nutshell, bro," Hector says. "I'm just another person in this world trying to make small, little changes in people. Some times they listen; sometimes they roll their eyes."

Hector pauses and thinks for a moment. "My philosophy has changed a little recently. I always wanted to save everyone, but now, it's one person at a time and I'm not moving on until you are taken care of. When it comes to a person's needs, don't be quick to move forward until that person has been transitioned to move forward! They may not be ready. You might need to move back a bit, brother."

What is the meaning of life?

I'm only 33. I don't think I've discovered that yet. I can tell you that life don't mean nothing if you don't take care of your responsibilities and have a heart full of love. And not necessarily in that order. Sometimes your responsibility is to give love. I don't think my life would mean anything if I didn't have my wife and my kids right now.

What are your thoughts about society and/or societies in general?

I think society has a long way to go in regards to true love, companionate love. I think when we can stop viewing humanity with a price tag; when we can stop selling God, Jesus and religion, stop pimping them! Then I think we can just accept that our role in this world is to help other people.

Who are you?

I think I said it earlier, bro. I'm just another guy trying to make a little dent in the world to make someone else's quality of life a bit more comfortable. I think the world is always looking for heroes. My heroes . . . there's a line from a movie defining raza. Raza *are people out there working with pride and dignity. That's* raza. *I think we are always out looking for heroes and my heroes are the people out here just trying to survive with pride and dignity and in order to help them we have to meet them with that dignity. I hope whatever work I do will inspire one person to help just one more person. I really believe if each of us helped just one person then that would provide us with a domino effect in life.*

"Do you want to tell me anything else, anything at all?" I ask.

We talk about God, family, and football for a while more before officially ending the interview. Hector thanks me for my time. He explains that he needed to talk things out after the shooting and that me, just listening, helped him reaffirm his goals and direction. As I leave, he seems lightened, refreshed.

**Hector makes me consider that true helping
is helping others to help themselves.**

LAURA, LDRC: Tuesday, February 24, 2009, 3:30 p.m.

I meet up with Laura in the back office hallway of LDRC. She is setting up a display of musical instruments in a shopping cart with a tie-dyed picture behind them, so she can take a picture for a flyer she is making.

Laura is perpetually wearing jeans, Converse tennis shoes, a T-shirt, and maybe a scarf or hat. She's very 'college student.'

Today there is green paint on her fingers from some recent project. That's another thing—there's always paint on Laura. I once asked her what her official title was and she told me, "Program Coordinator and Queen of Painted Projects."

Today is typical in that she says hello to me, but keeps focused on what she's working on. Laura, 21, is very self-motivated and always doing something. She is mellow, yet driven and independent, never waiting for the approval or disapproval of those she meets. Also, Laura never talks to you about what she's doing, though I have never seen her not working.

You'd think Laura was simply lost in her own little productive world, except that she authentically greets everyone in her path and listens whole-heartedly to what they have to say, all the while unencumbered by the need for acknowledgement.

She is so not me.

We go to the LDRC staff lounge to hold our interview. I want to get her out of her office setting so she might speak more freely. Laura is often at her desk when I come to interview Jessica, which is located in the room just outside of Jessica's office. Her workspace faces her co-worker Terry's desk. He was born years ahead of Laura and I'm surprised he is not bothered by the alternative rock music she is always playing. And Laura adds to the volume by singing along.

We enter the staff lounge and Laura plops herself down on one of the couches and lays out, practically from end to end, apparently not too concerned about appearing professional in this interview.

I explain to her that besides the three final questions, I try to avoid directing things so she should feel free to just talk.

"About what?" she asks.

"Anything; yourself, why you are here, your job, homelessness."

I wait. I can tell she is thinking because she is using her top lip to play with the ring that pierces her lower lip.

"Why am I here?" Laura asks herself. "Well, after college I was working at a deli and had been working there for five years. I was the night manager and was pretty much running the place."

"So you have a degree?"

"No I dropped out of college after one semester."

Laura does not follow up with details, but not as if she is hiding something. It is as if this book is not going to read itself. "Can you tell me about that?" I ask.

"I went for marketing communication and advertising and it just wasn't for me. All the classes were boring, too easy. I attended most of my classes drunk and still made As. It didn't seem OK to pay $16,000 [tuition] and do nothing."

She stops and as I wait. I look at her new haircut. Her hair had always been short but now it is angular and spiky at the ends. I expect her to continue but she does not.

"So, you were at the deli?"

"My goal was to get away from a small town. So after beating myself up for six months or so I was laying one night in a field with my friends and we were all talking about joining the Peace Corps. I looked online and found you needed a degree, so I was like, fuck! I was at a kegger the next night and a girl told me about AmeriCorps. I applied to every state outside of New England."

Again, Laura just stops when she feels everything necessary has been said.

"That's where you're from?" I prod.

"Oh, yeah. And I said the first one that comes back I'm taking it. So Phoenix came back. So I did all the interviews and even stopped smoking weed for three months."

"Laura, just to remind you this could all come out in print in a couple of years," I say. "Now I cannot use your last name, or . . ."

"You can use my last name. I don't care," she says, not defiantly but quite casually as though she has nothing to hide.

Again, silence. This girl just does not ramble on about herself. Everyone I have ever interviewed rambles on about himself or herself.

"Laura, I overheard the other day about you riding your bike to work. Is that because you are too broke to buy a car?" I say, just trying to get the ball rolling.

"I had a car but I broke it, so I ride my bike."

"And . . . how far do you ride to work?" I emphasize the question, trying to make fun of her for not carrying the conversation.

"Nine miles."

"Each way?"

"Yep, but only a couple days a week. I live with Ryan, so I carpool with him."

Ryan is a Client Coordinator at the front desk and he and Laura just recently became roommates.

"How long have you been working here?"

"I've been working here for about a year and a half."

"And do you like it?"

"I love it!"

"You seem very mature for a 21-year-old. Most 21-year-olds don't do this sort of work."

"Oh, I still live the 21-year-old life, just not intensely as when I was 19 and 20. But now it's calmed down a bit because of the need of people here for me to be 100 percent. For me to come into work with a hangover makes that pretty hard. So work sobered me up."

I laugh. I can't help it. Laura is so unapologetic. She's like some socially conscious, beer drinking, hard-working, hippie stoner.

Silence again. "So . . . now you're here and it beats the deli right?"

"Well, I loved the deli too," Laura says. "I loved connecting with the people, the regulars. It was kinda my escape."

"Does this place feel like an escape too?"

"At times it can feel like an escape," she says, cautious of her next words, "because I feel like I'm doing something that no one understands, like my friends and family. Except for my grandmother who gets it. Oh, and my other grandmother gets it too."

"What is it about—doing something that no one gets?" I ask.

"Because either it's going to get to the point where I start talking about it and they get so frustrated that they will come down here and see what's going on, or they do research on the Internet so they learn about it. I like to see their eyes get wide when they hear about what's going on at this place. And also, I just love to debate with people when they have stereotypes. I like to make people feel uncomfortable. I like to mess with them."

Laura begins to open up now, saying that she's always dreamed of doing something phenomenal with her life.

"I used to think it was sports, and one day I realized sports aren't phenomenal," she says. "Everyone plays sports and makes lots of money for it. So I tried grades and that got old after a while. Then one day I saw this kid who no one liked because he was different. I picked him up because he needed a ride and a friend of mine said, after we dropped him off, 'why did you do that?' And I realized it had something to do with what I wanted to do. I wanted to break down stereotypes. I told my friend that he [the person she picked up] just expresses himself a bit different than everyone else. I like getting people to accept that people express themselves differently, dress differently, appear differently, think differently, act differently, talk differently."

"And . . . why is that important?" I ask again, trying to keep her talking.

"It's important because I feel that because of all the stereotypes and judgments, that we don't have any sense of community, so people are even afraid to go to their neighbor and say hey do you want to have a barbeque? The amount of fear is just incredible!"

"Laura, I don't know if you're aware of this, but you don't talk about yourself much. I have to prod you to get you to discuss yourself."

"I'm not very good about talking about myself," she admits. "I can talk about issues. I'm good about talking about issues . . . I can tell you stories."

"Why are you not good about talking about yourself?"

"Because I have always been irritated by those who do and I don't want to be a hypocrite. 'I'm so good at this. I'm so good at that.'" Laura explains that it especially bugs her when people play the victim, or put themselves on a pedestal: "And I'm like, 'do you know what's going on in the world?' I guess it depends on what they are talking about and if they are intelligent."

"I will say this: I am sick at Wii Bowling," Laura offers in conclusion. ["Sick" means "good" according to the online Urban Dictionary . . . popular slang.]

Good enough for me. I move on, asking about the art class she teaches on Saturday mornings. I ask if I can attend one week and Laura agrees.

She also organizes volleyball tournaments in the afternoons. "Saturday is the perfect day. All the agencies are closed. It is the perfect day to engage, to go out and talk to people, to ask them, 'what are you doing today, what are you doing on this fine Saturday?' To get them into the art class."

"And you have a booth for First Fridays to sell the client's artwork?" First Friday is an art walk that is held the first Friday of every month in downtown Phoenix, where local artists can show and sell their art on the streets alongside the art galleries.

She answers with a nod.

"And you once told me, if the client's art sells they get to keep the money, but if it sells for a lot you might ask for a small donation to help with art supplies."

"Yeah, it just depends."

Shockingly she follows up, unprompted.

"We went on a field trip last Saturday, which was exciting."

Then, silence.

"And . . . tell me about it?" I plead.

"Well I was hoping we would get more than four other people to come with me, but some people don't like to leave. They get comfortable. But we got two mentally ill people to come with me. One is a lady who only likes me some days and another guy who doesn't talk to anyone and when he talks to me, it's very brief, unless I am sitting down next to him in a closed space.

"So the fair was for autistic kids. I asked the angry woman if she did any crafts and she said she didn't want to take away from the kids."

"This is the grumpy lady?" I ask.

"Yes, grumpypants lady."

"And you liked that?"

"Yes."

"Because . . . she considered others?"

"Yes." Laura continues describing the silliness of that day, saying that the goal was to make the clients less grumpy in general, not necessarily more serious about art in particular.

"I think some people get so caught up in their artwork that they forget that they are doing it for fun, for enjoyment, for release," she says. "I think if people get to the end of their project and no smile has come across her face, then they need to continue until it does."

Laura puts out a monthly calendar of classes and events held at LDRC and on the Human Services Campus. A typical month might have one or many classes with the following titles: Job Readiness, Life Skills, Computer, Visit a Nurse, Beginner's Computer, GED, Choir Practice, Art, Open Lab, Creative Writing, Chess/Backgammon, Employment Coaching, even Tai Chi.

She had recently sent me some intriguing information about a new or expanded program called Rhythm of Life: Clients reach into their own creative source and transcend the obstacles of poverty to gain confidence, strength, self-esteem and experience joy. Rhythm of life utilizes art, writing, poetry, theatre, music and dance.

"Laura, I know Rhythm of Life is a transformational healing program via the creative arts. I kind of know what that means or the potential after attending some of the movie workshops, but can you talk about the program a bit?"

"It's not just a program; it's how I live my life, whether it's how I work, how I play sports, or whether it's me saying hi to people as I walk through the day room and maybe saying, 'Hi sunshine.' So art just got encompassed into that."

"'Moving in harmony with our inner self,'" I say, quoting the pamphlet. "What does that mean to you?"

"It means, ah . . . that with the way the world is, that people tend to lose touch with their inner being so they aren't truly connected to them, so they lose their way. I see it as like if you were walking down the street and you and your shadow aren't connected and for you and your shadow to be connected at you feet, you are in harmony with yourself."

"'Releasing the power of our being?'" I question her further on ideas from the brochure.

"So you become in harmony with yourself, you have your pulse. With that it's so powerful you have to release it to everyone. It's like when people ask me why I work here. It's like shaking up a soda bottle and releasing it. Everyone will hear about it and it sticks to them and they will remember why I work here."

"'Expressing the truth of our spirit?'"

"Being real. I'm not going to make things all fluffy and nice if they aren't. This is reality. Yesterday was reality," she says, referring to the fatal shooting yesterday with a caring but unburdened tone.

Laura is the only person I have met today who doesn't seem disheartened in the least by yesterday's shooting. And again, it isn't that she doesn't care. It's because she expects things to be messy and dangerous. That is no reason not to live.

Laura explains that she understands the fear some clients have of moving on to a better life, because she had that same feeling as she prepared to leave her hometown.

"It was scary, but the good scary," she says. "It was like the same feeling I had when I decided to hop in my car and drive 3,000 miles from my family. It was new, unknown. It was that same feeling that I had before I knew my purpose here."

"You seem to have a lot of confidence now."

"I think sports, mixed with AmeriCorps, really helped that confidence," Laura says, finally talking about herself at least a little bit. "I used to be real quiet. Then I just stopped caring what people thought. I decided that they are going to judge me even if I am quiet."

What is the meaning of life?

The meaning of life . . . the meaning of life is love, is family, is laughter. It is just . . . it is experiences: it's learning; it's making mistakes; it's being stupid; it's being young; it's being free. I'm a huge person on freedom. It's taking every risk you can, challenging your fears, trying a new food you have never tried before, meeting as many people as you can, coming to the understanding that everyone is connected. Travel, traveling for sure. Nature, being in it, laying in a field and looking at the clouds and making shapes out of those clouds. Although

Arizona doesn't have very good clouds for that, New Hampshire does. It's also heartbreak, crying. Just being balanced. That's it.

What are your thoughts about society and/or societies in general?

OK. Um . . . I think society is unfair, unforgiving, unjust . . . and all of that's because they are scared and they fear what they do not know, what they cannot change, what they cannot fathom or accept. And other societies outside the United States I don't know too much about. I like Montréal's way of living because it's free. It's cultured. It's fun. It's meeting and greeting people from different places. It's just great.

Who are you?

I am a traveling being. I am definitely sent from another planet to assist with this one. I am an odd species, I think. I have an old soul. I should have been born in the '60s. I am an artist, a jock and a mathematician. I'm a caregiver. I am a hopeless romantic. A sarcastic bitch. I'm a comedian. And I'm not very good with my emotions. You know, the more negative ones, like being sad or expressing why I might be sad or upset. I am amazing at handling my anger. I have developed and matured my patience for people. I'm random and predictable. I'm randomly predictable as some would say. Oh, and I'm a problem solver. I have to fix things. And I'm a Cancer, 21, and I'm female. That is me.

"Laura, is there anything else you would like to share with me, with readers?"

"I don't know. I'll call you one night when I'm drunk."

I laugh and know she might do just that.

Laura makes me consider that this world is my home and taking care of it should be fun.

Laura teaches yoga on the lawn of the Human Services Campus as part of the Rhythm of Life program. Photo by: Dawn Shires.

JESSICA, LDRC: Monday, March 2, 2009, 1 p.m.

Jessica called me and told me she was tired and was only going to work a half day, then go home and work from there. Instead of our weekly meeting, she asked if I wanted to meet her for lunch at a small café called the Paisley Violin.

I locate this café that is just blocks from the campus. Like many businesses in the area, it teems with character. It is an open, airy shack constructed with old, perhaps antique, pieces of used materials. I see a tin roof above me, concrete floors below, knick-knacks everywhere and a man playing the banjo while wearing tambourines on his knees.

The place is very Jessica. It feels like it should be located on a beach in Key West.

We decide to sit outside on the uneven patio against a palette of cars, men welding nearby and the smell of a single distant cigarette.

A week's time has done nothing noticeable in improving her feelings about the shooting. Jessica is concerned for her own safety and the safety of her staff. But worse, it's made her question how life works—if it works. Jessica says that she has always felt that the mentally ill could somehow sense her and her staff's good intentions and thus would not lash out at them. Kevin, the victim, was a nice man. This realization was enough to make her feel unsafe.

Worse still, the event seemed so unfair to her in a cosmic sense. "That a caregiver would be killed by a person he was caring for . . ." Jessica's faith that life, God the universe supports good acts and good people has been shaken. And while she probably doesn't recognize it herself yet, she has not had time to process much of this over the last week. She feels she's "had to be strong for others" instead.

Jessica takes much longer than usual to form her thoughts and then longer still to voice them. I just listen patiently. And I have little solace to offer. You cannot restore someone's faith. And Jessica seems lost without her faith.

Still sad, Jessica gives me a hug goodbye. I think that hugs are not things you just give or receive. They only work when you are giving and receiving at the same time. As we part ways I think she's not much better than she was before lunch. However, I am much better than I had been 90 minutes ago and all I had done was listen. I feel filled up inside.

Jessica makes me consider the necessity of faith.

MICHAEL, CLIENT, LDRC: Tuesday, March 3, 2009, 1 p.m.

Due to the shooting's aftermath, I didn't have any interviews set up for today, but decided to come down to the campus anyway and sit in the LDRC lobby to work on my notes and soak in the surroundings. Every time I do this, I overhear conversations and get a general feel for people and things down here. When you don't know exactly what you're looking for, you have to spend a lot of time looking.

I have been here less than an hour when a young black gentleman approaches me. He walks right up, out of a sea of people, and says with politeness, "Hello, sir." As he reaches out his hand to shake mine, the man does not lower his head to look me in the eye. It is as if he is standing at attention.

"Hello," I respond, feeling tentative.

He stands there in silence for a moment before I ask him his name. He tells me, "MICHAEL. LEE. DENNEY. NIEZ. Jr. THE FIRST."

I tell him I am writing a book and wonder if I might interview him.

"Yes sir. Let me acquire a chair."

When he returns I asked him his name again and he says it and spells it and explains that it is in all capital letters except for the r at the end of junior and then proceeds to explain that I need to add three periods and where they should go. He looks at my laptop to ensure I have gotten it right and approves.

Strangeness aside, the man is extremely polite and formal in the way he talks with me.

I tell him that anything he shares might be viewed by many others. This does not bother him in the least, but elicits some possible excitement—a faint smile. I explain that my name is Michael too and ask if it's OK to call him Michael. It is, and we proceed.

"So, tell me about yourself."

"I was born in Marion, Ohio, on the reservation and I'm 27 years old and from the time of six months old I was drafted due to selective service. I was honorably discharged at 27 years of age. I was adopted. I was horribly abused by the parent, being that of the mother. And otherwise, culturally understanding. I speak other languages: Irish, German, Egyptian, Oriental, Native American, purely and foremost. If I didn't say Irish, Irish. I speak Latin, all Arabic, even the Tamils in the original form.

"I have been to war in native and non-native American status."

"There is a book about me, *Golden Water*. It's a Native American status autobiography with a picture of me next to a judge, as a young man."

Michael continues on without prompting and he has a slight smile on his face at times. I obviously cannot say what generates that smile, but it seems as though he is pleased with himself. Maybe that he is talking about himself or maybe that he knows he has a tendency to exaggerate and is getting away with it.

"Otherwise I am culturally understanding and speak many languages." He repeats most of the languages listed above.

"I've graduated college and high school. In my past and in my teens, due to cultural misunderstandings, due to tribal issues, I have been lethally inclined. I have been incarcerated in prejudice assumption of ethneticity. I am somewhat reformed. I do work now as a law enforcement officer. I do have legal education: lawyers, priest exam, law enforcement, possibly more that I don't have knowledge of or memory of.

"Other than that, in my teenage years you might say I was emotionally deprived and socially deprived. In past relationships was ignorantly inclined of the other partner who was always female. I can be dominatingly prominent in terms of homosexuality and religion.

"I am outgoing and fun loving, as far as you know. Otherwise I am not a people person, especially other males. Except in business. Can be, uh, tortuously behaved under speech inclinement of other persons."

I notice that Michael has a habit of creating his own words. Of course, so did Shakespeare.

"Otherwise, family background from past to present. Father [gives me the name and spells it and it's similarly long like his] left Marion, Ohio under disrespect and our state birth providence due to lack of assumption in a reverse form of prejudice and left in 1992 in safety not just of himself but public.

"I have seen him here in Phoenix one time, in Sunnyslope [a neighborhood in Phoenix] and on the reservation. Mother, I do not talk to mother. I don't have much emotional attachment to my family because of abuse and DNA climate. Otherwise I have traveled not just under the military, but as a young boy or child under the age of two. I have not been to many states but I have been to New York, to Mexico, to Phoenix for the first time of memory, but otherwise my travels out of the country military and nonmilitary. I have been to Ireland, Egypt, China. I've have been to Thailand and China as far as two separate sites. I have been to historical sites. I have been . . . I have been to historical places such as sites where the Queen of England has been.

"Sherlock Holmes is in my blood line and William Wallace and William McCloud. In Ireland under Germany, the Schindler family has been proven by genetic testing. As far as here in the United States, I have been to Blair County, where the Blair witch trials took place, under historical bloodlines of the family."

Finally, I have to politely stop MICHAEL. I had not prompted him since, "tell me about yourself" and there is no end in sight. There is also much repetitious material I left out from the above excerpts. "Great MICHAEL. I think I have a lot about you here. Can I ask you a few questions?"

"Yes, sir."

"Where do you live?"

"I'm in a transitional stage. I just had a house rebuilt; remodeled from the ground up. It's down that way." He points north. "2141 W. Washington Street off of 19th and Van Buren. I'm also a Leo zodiac. Other than that I'm a chief medicine man. Blood proven. What else would you like to know?"

"Do you work now?"

"Yes. I do it because there is nothing else to do in my spare time. I feel that I am not occupying my time if I do not properly work. I am a Phoenix Police Officer multitasking. I am my own boss basically. I report, but I don't report, meaning as far as my patrol I report any criminal activity even in light of clairvoyant, psychic and climate of hereditary, genetic; naturally of mental status."

I ran this last line back by him just to make sure I got it right and he confirms that this is what he said. And no, I don't know what the hell it means, but I love the sound of it.

"What are you doing here today?"

"Medical check up as far . . . as far as my blood sugar. I'm considered nimphomaticism." Again, I verify this word with him. "It's a sexual inclement hereditary disorder. Otherwise hyper and hypoglycemic diabetic A1, type one. Otherwise than that I am hypermanically energetic."

A man from Southwest Behavioral Services walks up and gives him a bag with something in it. I don't ask. It may have been medication. I decide it's time to ask the final three questions.

What is the meaning of life?

The meaning of life is to basically . . . the key is love, understanding, forgiveness, and acceptance, and the fact of responsibility under behavior and mental wanting to do. It is religious, moral standard of belief. Besides truth and honesty.

What are your thoughts about society and/or societies in general?

As far as society goes there is a lot of intolerance on as far as the citizens aspect, as far as behaviors they have chosen to do. Lack of moral standards; both under religious aspects and normalcy or cultures, other a lack of respect. Otherwise than that, not for all on that behalf of accusal, included, otherwise than that there is lack of emotional understanding and deprival amongst the younger generation, let alone the adults in this present time of age and the lack of education needed in order to help those understand. There is a lot of assumption of prejudice even under marital and legal otherwise status. Again not including all on that behalf of accusal. A lack of honesty.

Who are you?

As far as a person of who I am, a person-based naturalist of wanting to live life on life's terms, know the educational factors in and religion factors in; knowing the true promises of the American dream factors in. Not wanting to be anything than what I am. Otherwise than that I am a very emotionally expective person. I'm very understandingly, educationally and not educationally. Hold on; let me put it like this. I will give you a briefer version. I am emotionally carefreewilled [You've got to love that word, and I verified that it was one word.] and loving person with the fact of love and truth and honesty, not only under religion and belief; also a very willing person. As far as relationships I am very attachable under emotional inclement of relationships do to past painful relationships of my past. Other than that very loving caring. Feline behaved. Torturous living as far as inclinement of speech. Meaning if it is said of me or asked of me, I live it and live it under military standards. You may want to do it future term, but on your own way. As they say, actions speak louder than words. You can say it, but can you do it? It's like saying you can drive a car . . .

It is 4:30 now and I'm saved by the bell, so to speak. They shut down LDRC for the night at this time and are asking us to leave. I use this as an opportunity to ask MICHAEL if we can stop there, because he seems to be headed on another ramble.

He finishes his explanation about the car and ends by telling me, "I am albino and ethnetically, non-colored prejudiced, meaning I don't care about the color of anyone's skin. Other than that, willing to stand up for what's right, not just under religions but legal. As far as physical I am not abusive. I do not believe in putting my hands on a woman or a man, unless I have to fight for my protection of my wife or my family. I am dominantly dominating. Very Neanderthalicly stubborn. As far as materialistically, I like to get things on my own. I am very proud of my culture."

I tell MICHAEL I hope we will see each other again. He is a very nice man and pleasant to talk to even though I rarely understood what he was saying. He did not look Native American to me but anything is possible (though he definitely did not look albino).

I go to the address he gave me for his house. There is a beautiful home but a different last name on the mailbox.

I search for his book on the Internet, but find no mention of it.

As with all my interviews, the truth in this case does not matter. It was MICHAEL's truth. That's enough. My own has changed so much in the past few months; who am I to judge?

MICHAEL showed me how differently the mentally ill can see life. But isn't that the case for all of us?

ART CLASS, LDRC: Saturday, March 7, 2009, 9 a.m.

I feel completely different coming to campus this Saturday. I don't feel that low-grade depression for the first time in what seems like forever. I didn't even realize what a weight I must have been carrying. I think my interview with MICHAEL had something to do with it. Somehow, he helped me to see that my fears are just my stories and my stories are just as delusional as his are. It doesn't matter if they're true anyway; it matters why we chose to tell them or worse, to believe them.

To MICHAEL's credit, he has the intelligence to shape his stories to his liking. It's humbling to be helped by the mentally ill.

I arrive at the campus a little late, enter the class and see that I haven't missed a thing. The class is being held in the movie room. All the lights are up and long tables are in place of the rows of chairs I am used to. There are only five students present and Laura is not here. There is a student facilitator in her stead. Toma is a short man with a goatee and a black-and-white Yankees baseball cap worn backwards. He wears army fatigue-style Bermuda shorts with tennis shoes and a sweatshirt jacket patterned with skulls and crossbones. He is helping the others to get their supplies while playing alternative rock music—Laura's favorite.

The room is quiet; students are painting and drawing. There are no directions given, just supplies. I watch them work. Some of their work is impressive. There is some talent in the room. I can't understand why some of them could not support themselves with their artwork. The students who lack artistic talent seem to enjoy what they are doing as much, if not more than the others. These paintings and drawings range from simple landscapes, to Japanese anime, to portraits.

There is one student sitting across from me who does not paint—a young man in a slightly wrinkled suit that is too large for him, with no tie. He has short dreadlocks and an ever persistent, warm smile. He is just sitting, looking at the people and the art, smiling all the while. He has a very stylish look, even in a suit that doesn't fit him. I think the smile helps.

Laura walks in and starts writing on the board:

> Creative Block?
> Take 2-3 shapes and create a landscape scene using just those shapes.
> Pick 3-5 objects, places or people that are normally not seen together and place them in a picture together, ex. Snowman, a cactus, car tire, art supplies and a lamp.
> Point perspective—place a dot on the center of the page and then draw 2 lines coming from it. From here you can create a picture of a sunset, a road, a hallway, etc.

I ask Laura about First Friday which was yesterday. I ask her if some of these talented people sell enough art to support themselves. She points to a half-finished picture leaning up against the wall, an incredible portrait of an Aztec warrior. "Like this one?" She says.

"Yeah. If they finish it."

"Why would they not finish their work?"

"Some people disappear. Some get housing. Some don't want to be here on the weekends if they don't have to be."

"So some of these people could support themselves on their artwork?"

"Yeah. If they had the energy."

"You mean if they applied themselves?"

"Yeah."

I ask if she feels that they often don't apply themselves because they are busy dealing with the necessities of life. For example, trying to get a job and find housing.

"Yes, that, and I think the stress of things."

My immersion showed me how emotionally stressful being homeless can be. True, there is no stress of fitting everything in such as cleaning, paying bills, yard work, car maintenance. But it is very emotionally stressful. You never fit in and you have none of the security that paying bills brings. And stress often comes from a feeling of being out of control. Homeless is the epitome of being out of control.

Laura sees art as a natural therapy, a conduit, something more than a hobby. Finishing art projects can lead to an attitude of wanting to follow through with other projects.

"I think it [helps] alleviate the stress," she says. "Art could be an outlet as opposed to drugs. A sober step, you know?"

As Laura and I talk, the class has more than doubled and has become quite animated. There are still people hard at work, in deep concentration. But now, two students are playing on a piano that sits against the far wall; a lively, impromptu duet. Alternative rock is still playing and somehow it blends well. Students move around the class, talking and sharing their work.

I'm shocked that they are all interested and supportive regardless of the quality. The most talented students in the room view some of the least talented student's work with great appreciation, seemingly for the fact that it's important to the person who made it. This is unusual to me. I can only assume that Laura had something to do with creating such an environment. And all the while, the guy in the suit just sits in front of me, smiling away.

I always thought of art in terms of quality until this very moment. I now see Laura's point. This class is fun and expressive, and that's enough.

Dawn walks in and asks if I might be going to the movie workshop today. I wasn't planning on it, but she tells me I might want to because they are having a meeting, at the request of the clients, about the shooting. The campus director, Arlene, will be there as well as many other directors, including Jessica.

Sounds interesting. I change my plans.

Laura's class makes me consider that art's greatest value is in the process toward the final product.

THE NEW ARID CLUB: Saturday, March 7, 2009, 11 a.m.

Now committed to being on campus until afternoon, I walk toward the New Arid Club to sit in on an AA meeting. It is a warm sunny day. The weather is perfect. I am walking slowly, not because the meeting doesn't start for 45 minutes, but because I don't have an agenda. It feels good not having an agenda.

I get to the building but can't go in because the women's meeting is not finished. It's explained to me that no men are allowed in the building during this time. It creates a sense of security for the women. I can't imagine what it's like to be a homeless woman. I was more than glad I was a strong, able-bodied man when I did my immersion.

A group of girls from a church youth group pass by and one of them gives me a sack lunch, which I take. I haven't eaten breakfast. People always want to feed the homeless. And of course, food and shelter are the first concern. On the Human Services Campus, everyone is fed yet there are many outside organizations who want to help, and not knowing what else to do, opt to feed this population. The campus agencies frown on street feeding because it doesn't address the client's real needs. It litters the streets. While it feels good to everyone for a brief minute, the act of giving people fish instead of teaching them to fish actually lowers self-esteem in the long run. It's not dignified to just hand out food to people who live on the streets when there is a cafeteria on campus. If you ask any staff member at LDRC they will tell you they focus on feeding the soul.

A girl in the group has her hand over her nose to avoid the smell out here. I don't notice the smell anymore. It smells, but doesn't every place? It just smells different down here.

As I eat the peanut butter and jelly sandwich, MICHAEL walks by me. We look at each other and he doesn't even pause. As far as I can tell he doesn't recognize me. But he makes me smile as he walks by, smiling to himself.

I watch a man in a dark green oversized sweater stare at a lamp pole while holding on to it. It looks like he is drunk and needs the pole for stability or friendship. I can't tell. It's fascinating. He does a sort of dance with it where he works his way around the pole as if he is looking for a place to get off. He lets go briefly from time to time in a seeming attempt to leave, then quickly grabs hold again as he seems to lose his balance. After many revolutions, he tries other approaches. He squats down but this does not make for an easy getaway. He tries various altitudes between standing and fully squatting, but all of these seem to present problems either in balance or mobility. The man does not merely cling to the pole, but also interacts with it. Finally he frees his hands and his unseen connection to the pole. I watch, expecting him to fall over but he doesn't. In fact, he is able to walk quite well. He's not drunk; he was truly having trouble leaving the pole.

After walking about five feet away, he looks back at the pole, pauses for a minute as though he might return and then instead shakes his head and crosses the street. It is sad, comical, mysterious and wonderful all at once.

The doors open as the women's meeting ends. I walk down the stairs, turn left down the hall and turn left again into the meeting room. Like in the other meetings, honesty is emphasized. It occurs to me how honest all the people are that I've met down here. And I don't mean honest in the traditional sense but more so in an expanded sense of 'it is what it is.'

They pass out chips for particular lengths of sobriety, from one day to 10 years. Each of the recipients is a mix of emotions—happy, sad, embarrassed. But I would not say that any of them are proud. Part of it seems to be that they have a hard time truly releasing the past, but more of it seems to be that they respect their vulnerability as humans and they know that pride is on the road to relapse.

A gentleman by the name of Jack stands up. He explains that he has been clean and sober for 32 years as of today. He got sober at the old Arid Club (it burned down at another downtown location and was ceremoniously replaced by the New Arid Club here on campus) and while he goes to regular meetings elsewhere, he came back to 'the original' to celebrate the anniversary of his sobriety at the New Arid Club. He took the day off work to do so. He felt it was that important.

"You have to stay spiritually connected to stay sober," Jack says. "AA is a simple program for complicated people. People make excuses, very complicated elaborate ones, but the fact is, if you don't drink, you won't get drunk."

After Jack finishes, a guy from Pittsburg says a few words. He is here on business, staying downtown. He came to this meeting because it was close to his hotel. He goes to meetings regularly whether he is in his hometown or traveling. He explains, "If I miss a meeting for a few days, I get irritable and my thinking starts changing." The incredible thing about AA for him is it is always a place of refuge. "As soon as I walked in here, I was home."

I never really understood what AA was or how it worked but this guy really summed it up for me. AA is home for people with the problem of alcoholism. It is a home where they can heal, be loved and be challenged to grow. Maybe that's why I like coming to these meetings. They accept everyone. Even though I am not an alcoholic, I feel at home here.

The people in the AA meeting today made me consider how *home* and *acceptance* are synonymous—or should be.

MOVIE WORKSHOP, LDRC: Saturday, March 7, 2009, 1:00 p.m.

Jessica is already here when I enter. The room feels different; there's no smell of popcorn. The popper is there, but apparently they are waiting until after the community meeting.

People file in as Dawn explains today's format. "OK, last week some people told me that they liked the open forum we had on Wednesday concerning the shooting, so we did it again. And I definitely didn't have all the answers. And someone said, 'We would like someone to listen.' And I said, 'Well, I'm listening.' But they said, 'We would like the higher ups to listen,' so . . ." Dawn continues to explain that she got the directors of many of the main agencies here to attend this week's movie workshop.

A client speaks up, asking a question many were probably wondering about: "Who has authority here?"

It is recommended that the panel first introduce themselves. They are: Arlene Pfeiff-Maraj, director of the Human Services Campus; Jessica Berg, director of the LDRC; Steve Carter, director of Nova Safe Haven and other Nova-related agencies; Steve Zabilski, in charge of St. Vincent's; Bill Black, CASS case manager and assistance supervisor for the Outreach Facility.

Arlene, a tall, slender businesswoman, explains that there are 15 independent agencies and five anchor agencies here on campus. She provides the clients with a literal answer to for every question.

"All [agencies] have a director and all have a board of directors," she says, her voice crisp and clear. "We are currently trying to figure out how to run this place [the HSC], which, by the way, doesn't exist anywhere else in the world. My role is to fundraise and to work with all of the directors and agencies to help us work together. There is no central authority and it is a cooperative model where all have to agree because there is no one single person at the top. It's a very innovative way of making decisions and we are very committed to that way."

"Different agencies have different boundaries and authorities," Bill chimes in. "If it's at night the police often have more authority than we do. So it's a give and take thing."

"So it's a learning process each day that goes by?" a client asks.

"Right," Arlene replies. "If you look at the Human Services Campus we are very new, young in our maturity."

"Who is the homeless representative?" another client asks. "Who represents what the homeless want, not what the staff wants?"

Dawn interjects: "Isn't that you guys? Isn't that your job?" As always, she's teaching to own what you want and work toward it.

Bill says he thinks the New Arid Club and Madison Street Veterans Association are examples of representatives. The veterans have already established responsibility and leadership in their lives, according to him. And when speaking to a representative from MSVA, Bill knows "there are 80 guys behind him."

It's a live history lesson for me. I feel like I'm witnessing in miniature form the reason for government of the people, by the people.

"I would like to know where our shelter connects to any of these organizations," a client ventures. "I'm in a woman's overflow shelter on Watkins [Street]. I don't know how it relates to me. What privileges would I have in these 15 organizations? I don't know what they are. I would just like to be informed about all the groups on the campus and how they relate to the women's overflow shelter."

Jessica gets up and writes on the board: PASS—Plan of Action Self-Sufficiency. "I think . . . I think everyone would agree with me when I say that we all want you to get out of here as quickly as possible," she says. "I mean, we want you to keep coming to the workshops and volunteering, but we want you to become self-sufficient. So when you come here next, ask for a PASS, which is a plan of action towards self-sufficiency." She explains that PASS, a booklet used for orientation, is about the all the agencies and how to use them to move forward.

Dawn points out that LDRC has an orientation for anyone who wants it. It is designed for those new to the campus so they might know the various services available to them and start to form a plan of action to get out of here. This really strikes me as unusual—an orientation for a homeless campus. This place is truly amazing.

Running Deer enters the discussion: "I understand that we need security, but it seems since Kevin's death more of the clients are being punished for one man's actions."

CASS tightened security after the shooting and searched for the missing gun by going through all the clients' possessions. Tensions, in general, are higher now.

"I liked Kevin a lot," Running Deer says. "In fact, if I was there, I probably would have killed the guy who did it. But, I get the impression that we are more considered inmates than human beings. I understand that there is a lot of fear here, but there are still clients who are trying to get on their feet. Some are just lazy and don't do nothing but lie around all day.

But I'm trying to get out of here. I'm going to school. I do my best to work with staff members because I know they are doing the best they can."

From here, Running Deer points out problems unique to those in wheelchairs. For example, the gate that separates LDRC from St. Vincent's and André House is often locked to prevent drug deals. This means Running Deer has to roll all the way around the buildings to get in food lines, which makes him arrive too late.

"There has to be a way where people can have access but everyone is still safe," he says. "I don't want to take this out on staff because I know things are rough and especially the way the economy is. I do my best to keep myself in check . . ." Running Deer goes on, and makes many good points, but perhaps too many. He does conclude with, "So I think if we had more meetings like this, then maybe we could work together better."

"There has been a trauma with the staff of CASS as well," Bill says, "and I will share this with you because I think you are feeling the vibrations. Some of the young staff said to me, 'I'm afraid to talk to clients now.' And I think the fact that we refer to each other as staff and clients is something I wrestle with, but I realize it's a reality of here."

Later, a discussion ensues about the gate Running Deer had mentioned. Every suggestion is different: The gate needs to be open for convenience of reaching André House and St. Vincent's. The gate needs to be closed for safety. Staff should man the gate and open it when necessary. Arlene responds that it costs money to staff the gate and that would mean taking funds from other places. "It's not that we're not listening. It's that we are learning how to respond."

More and more hands go up. People are really getting involved.

"You don't mind if I stand? I want to and it's my choice." It's Tony, who has this low-lying humor about him that I really like. "What I have noticed: Mr. [Bill] Black, who told you to give a damn about other peoples lives? Where did you get your training about how to speak to individuals with special needs? Why do we need a volunteer to help you do your job? Why do the staff get paid and the volunteers do it for free?"

Tony seems very confrontational at first, but he continues on to talk about the need for on the job training so that others might learn the people skills that Bill possesses. In the end, he's complimenting staff, in a way. I really like the way Tony speaks, though it requires a bit of patience to listen as his ideas unfold.

"Well, you made a lot of points," Bill says after Tony's long-winded performance. "Let me address one of them. I often wonder if . . . how the staff would change if they had to interview with you [the clients]? That would have a profound effect on the staff that would be hired. They would understand that they are working for you as well. So who [which clients?] would do those interviews? How do we pick them? Do we pick our favorites? No, you do."

Clients continue to raise small challenges at the community meeting. Some are very universal, but many don't affect enough people to be addressed in this group setting. Eventually, Dawn interjects again: "Should we continue or should we watch the movie? We can do either, but we have to make a choice."

"If it wasn't for the movies this [meeting] would have never happened," a client says. Jessica thanks Dawn for her movie workshops and for organizing the meeting.

Dawn, of course, sidesteps all the praise and asks if the community should do this once a month. Clients seem interested. Dawn tells them, with Jessica's approval, that they can provide a time and space at LDRC for such meetings.

Then she starts to pull herself out of the equation. Dawn is not about handholding. The clients can organize, elect a representative, decide on what the main issues are, and then present them to the people in charge. But Dawn's emphasis is on them making their own decisions about what is important. This part is critical, because many of the clients have opposing views about basic issues, like the safety gate—closed or open? Dawn is insuring that the clients first work out what is best for them as a group, come up with solutions and then present them to the persons in charge for implementation.

"This is so important . . . so that the people who make decisions can make informed decisions that aren't going to create further problems," Dawn concludes.

One client gets exactly what Dawn has been saying and says, "The staff of CASS represents them. We have to represent ourselves. Otherwise you come with problems and no solutions. They have enough confidence in you all to do that."

"It's your world, so tell us what you want to do," Jessica adds.

There are still hands up, and I can tell Dawn wants to hear from everyone, but the group already agreed to watch the movie. Arlene has to leave, and Dawn uses this as an opportunity to end the meeting.

This community caused me to consider that a government for the people has to be by the people and that is up to individuals—not 'the government.'

JESSICA, LDRC: Monday, March 9, 2009, 1:00 p.m.

We have quite a rapport by now, so I begin my chat with Jessica by talking about a book on meditation I finished reading last night. This is unusual for me because I hate meditation. I always fall into the trap of thinking I have to do it perfectly, which serves to do everything but quiet my mind.

Jessica says she can relate. "I think—consciously or unconsciously—it used to be one of my goals to be perfect. But no matter what I do, it's impossible to always do things right and make everybody happy. And it's hard to know if what I'm doing *is* right. In some ways I need really great anecdotal evidence for what we are doing [at LDRC]; there are so many pieces. It's hard to know if it's working."

As she talks, I realize how challenging it must be for Jessica to have a job that no one else has ever had, facing a challenge that no one else has yet navigated. It's also obvious that Jessica is struggling with fallout from the shooting. She still questions whether she is doing a good job, as if she was somehow responsible for the tragedy. In fact, a lot of the substance of our chat is Jessica processing these lingering feelings and doubts.

My conversation with Jessica today felt like a donation to LDRC. And again, it felt good. If the director is not taken care of, then the organization is not taken care of. And isn't that placing the cart before the horse?

Jessica makes me consider that perfection isn't all it's cracked up to be and caregivers need caregivers.

ARTHUR, CLIENT, LDRC: Tuesday, March 10, 2009, 1:00 p.m.

Terry, a staff member of LDRC who helps run the Madison Street Veterans Association (MSVA), bumps into me in the lobby and says he just met a good interview subject for me. Arthur, he tells me, just got out of prison and is new to the campus. Apparently he's a bit intense, but very interesting.

Perfect.

Arthur is lean, very fit, wound tight. Though his face is serene, his muscles look ready to spring into action at any moment, like some meditative martial artist.

Arthur takes a seat next to me in my cubicle in the Magellan office. He sits perpendicular to me. He looks directly forward, eyes softly fixated on some imaginary point in the distance. Those eyes are relaxed, but the gaze is uncompromising.

"So talk to me, Arthur."

"I've learned in my life, if you want real peace, you have to cultivate patience," he begins in a quiet, gentle voice. "For the first 30 years of my life I was a criminal; I was a drug addict. I lived by my own means. I was in prison twice. When I was in prison my second time, I was trying to be a gangster. I came to a crossroads in my life. I was thinking about homicide or suicide. I was thinking about spending the rest of my life in prison. But I decided to give God a chance. I told him to show Himself, and I had an awakening. He revealed something to me that I could not doubt."

Arthur, now 37 years old, says this faith took away his cravings for drugs, alcohol and cigarettes. He also began to smell a stench on himself that wouldn't go away even after a shower. So he dedicated himself to detoxifying and reading spiritual books in search of some truth.

"Even though I was raised Roman Catholic I didn't have the faith. All's I could see was the hypocrisy of it. It didn't work for me the way it was being taught to me . . ." Arthur turns, looks directly at me and says, ". . . the way it was being expressed to me!"

He stares forward again. "There was love behind it, but the love was superficial, was shallow, and I was told I had to accept it on blind faith and my spirit wasn't having that, no way whatsoever. The first book I actually connected to was *We're All Doing Time: A Guide to Getting Free*, by Bo Lozoff. That book became my companion in a sense because in the way it spoke a truth to me. It spoke my language," he says, again turning his gaze toward me in a way that captivates and terrifies.

I notice also how meticulously dressed Arthur is. He's just wearing jeans and a white long sleeved T-shirt with FAV (Foundation of Arizona Veterans) on it, but everything is spotless and looks pressed. He has a buzz haircut and bit of a receding hairline.

There is also a dog tag around his neck, which I ask him about. It is a "Stand Down dog tag" for homeless veterans in the state, he explains. Arthur tells me that he participates in the awareness group to make up "for poor conduct in the military when I enlisted as a kid and had no desire to be in the military."

As Arthur explains his interests in Hinduism, I notice he's also wearing a silver cross. Not very Hindu, I think. "Because all religions are ethically all the same," he says immediately, as if answering my thought.

"It is the covering that makes them different and the covering is the philosophical part. How one understands the truth is what is different in each religion. But love is the base. Understanding is how we color that base. Kind of like the rainbow. Each color represents a different understanding of the light, a different religion, a different understanding of love. The mind itself represents the prism because the light has to go through the mind, the love has to go through it intellectually and that's where the different philosophies come from and how we have different understandings of that love, light."

Arthur ends by saying he had five years in solitary confinement to think about all this, "to work on myself, on my cleansing, on my awakening."

I ask why he was in solitary confinement for his second stint in prison.

"Mainly because of the politics," Arthur says. "There was a lot of political racism involved. And being that I was once a racist myself, I didn't want to be around that." Arthur points his laser gaze at me again. "I would tell people what I thought. And I would get into fights. I once requested protective custody to protect myself and others because I would have to defend myself. It's not just the inmates; it's the officers too. Generally speaking the officers were decent, but there were some who were snakes and those were the ones I had to stand up to. After I woke up, I never lost a fight, even against bigger guys." He smiles calmly as he says this, looking off in the distance. And it is not a smile that he is pleased with his physical prowess. He sees this as another sign from God.

"You know it's very interesting, the environment in solitary can be taken two ways," Arthur continues. "It can become very self-centered and focused on the ego, or you can go beyond the ego and sacrifice yourself for the betterment of others. I sent out for other books, other places that would donate books to me. Most Hindu-based, some Christian, some Buddhist, and I have studied the Jewish faith as well. I made it my business to do my time without any appliances, without any TV or Walkman, which for most people in solitary is a necessity because if you are not working on yourself, you will lose your mind. Solitary can increase the hate and the loss of a person's mentality. Solitary confinement is not for the weak-minded, because people in solitary confinement don't know how to use their mind and the mind starts to sort of stagnate. It took a great deal of strength to overcome that, which I could not have done without the Lord's strength.

"You know that people like to say that prison is a place to change your life and rehabilitate"—a laser gaze again here—"but the fact is that it is very, very difficult to change your life in prison. The environment breeds hatred."

"So now that you are out, things are a bit easier?" I ask, Arthur still staring directly into me.

"I thought things would get easier for me but they have gotten much more difficult. Much more difficult. And for the most part, Mike . . ." his gaze now looks more steely than anything, ". . . I make no compromises with the world, whatsoever! It's either God's way or no way for me. And that's created a lot of difficulty." He laughs, looking forward and off to the distance again. "It always will."

"So you still struggle with this path?"

"The struggle is definitely within." He laughs. "There is great suffering."

"So didn't you go through greater suffering before you awoke?" I ask.

"I wasn't really alive the first 30 years of my life. Life doesn't really begin until you start struggling to live."

"To survive?" I ask.

"No, there is a difference between surviving and living. Living means you are living for a purpose. Life is a battlefield, and there is a great war going and it's an internal one . . . but that is the road to salvation. We must face all our fears. We must face all our fears if we want freedom. That is the road to freedom."

"So you are not thinking about getting to heaven, so to speak." I seek to clarify.

"No. Beyond it." He smiles and nods. "There is a place beyond heaven. Salvation is where you go beyond life and death, you go beyond good and evil, you go beyond all dualities. As long as there is a name, it's still dualistic in nature. Pleasure and pain are both a delusion; they are states of mind. Life is just a learning process to get rid of these dualities. Salvation is indifferent to pleasure and pain and success and failure are the same." Arthur pauses before completing his sutra. "Not unaware, but indifferent."

Arthur chooses the next topic, that of why he came to HSC after getting out of prison.

"So for five years I did yoga, writing, meditating, chanting," he says. "I got out of prison a totally different person. My family was, I guess, shocked and, I guess, misunderstood. The problem with me is that I keep it real, because that is how great my love is. I love your mom as much as my mom. We all must strive for that equal love. I would die for your mom as much as I would for my mom."

The conviction in Arthur's voice is so overwhelming that I believe him.

"I can't help but speak the truth as I understand it," he continues. "I don't allow how people see me to affect the way I speak to them. I don't mean any disrespect. But they don't understand that they are seeing a reflection of their own weaknesses. I love you, but I'm going to rebuke you. I see you drink and I'm going to tell you it's wrong. But they were like, 'I'm your mom and you need to respect me' and I was like, 'Well mom, you need to respect yourself.' What son would respect his mom drinking?"

"So what happened, Arthur?"

"My family basically said, 'We don't want you here no more, Arthur.'" He looks both sad and calm.

"So what did you do when you left home?" I ask.

"I stayed at a halfway house for a while and I worked for most of last year," Arthur says. "I did have to quit a job last year. There were people getting high on the job and we were roofers, so there was a major safety issue. When I told the boss, he praised me, but no one would work with me anymore because basically they were all using. So I've been out of work since December. It's very difficult to get a job—and especially housing—when you have a record. People don't know how to be flexible with the rules. People change. And they think they are hurting me by not giving me a chance but they are not giving themselves a chance."

Despite his intensity, a lot of what Arthur says about life and its subjective, reflective properties really makes sense to me. Next, he explains his two short-term goals or commitments while at HSC.

"One is being a caregiver to an individual who I met here who needs constant care. My job could be getting him into his own place and me being his caregiver. The other commitment I made to the Madison Street Veterans Association, which is to be there for the growth and the full, firm establishment of the organization."

"Those sound like very good goals," I offer.

"What comes out of you is bound to come back into you," is Arthur's reply to my compliment. "That is karma. So what is the intelligent thing to do? You want good things? Then give yourself to the world. Effort is everything. Put your whole mind, body and soul into it. Most people are very half-hearted about their endeavors, which is why they don't get very far," Arthur says with a nod and a half-smile. Again, he has a point.

"The mind is a doubter," Arthur says, fixing the laser gaze on my one last time. "Don't listen to the mind. Always follow the heart . . ." here, he points to his heart, ". . . even when the mind thinks it is unreasonable to do so. Even if the mind cannot see where it is going. And that is a leap of faith there. Those are our biggest times of growth. That's when we really grow inside.

What is the meaning of life?
Love.

What are your thoughts about society and/or societies in general?
Blind shepherds trying to lead blind sheep; both ending up in the ditch.

Who are you?
I can't say anything but love. I am love. That is who I am. I am a man of love.

"Is there anything you would like to say to me?" I ask.

"To you or to the book?"

"OK, to me and then to the book."

"Meditate more, only do it with very deep concentration," Arthur says. I am somewhat taken aback.

"Why did you tell me that? I never think about meditating, but I just considered it the other day."

"My heart just felt like telling you that," he says, smiling like a child. "Deep concentration begets depth and purity. Holiness is in degrees; the deeper you concentrate, the deeper you clean within."

"And to the book?" I ask.

"Anything you want in this world is based on sacrifice," Arthur says. "I sacrificed everything and that is why I can speak this way now. And my spirituality is more important now. Being spiritually blessed is more important than being mentally or physically blessed. I don't even care about being homeless. Arthur cares about being homeless."

I figured he was speaking to the difference between him and his ego.

He pauses for a minute. "Spirituality is a very lonely thing. It's just between you and your God. I mean even Jesus Christ felt that his last minutes on the cross. Everyone has got their own path. I always return people to themselves. That's what a good teacher does; he redirects people back to where God is, in themselves . . . and that is going beyond duality and that is salvation. As long as there is a worshiper and a worshiped, salvation has not happened yet. Salvation is to *be* God. And when I do that, I will realize that I was Him all along and just forgot. I am God, I forgot I was God, and now I realized I was God all along. That is the journey of life. But unfortunately the ego mind takes that in an egotistical way and wants to be God too."

Arthur thanks me for listening. He shakes my hand and solemnly leaves me with my mouth still hanging open.

**Arthur makes me consider that regardless of the
path, we need bravery and conviction.**

BRIAN & SEAN, PHOENIX POLICE DEPARTMENT:
Tuesday, March 10, 2009, 6 p.m.

There are well over 2 million persons incarcerated in the U.S. at this very moment. And it costs us an average of $67 per day, per prisoner to keep them that way. I find it interesting that we can house 2 million prisoners but can't house the roughly 650,000 men, women and children who are homeless right now.

The police officers on the Human Resources Campus seem to be working to help the cause here, even if America's incarceration epidemic is not. So I am particularly looking forward to my interviews with the two officers this evening.

I arrive outside the Outreach Shelter, the one I stayed at not too long ago, and meet Sergeant Freudenthal, a young, tall, fit officer with a buzz haircut. At first glance, he has the same stern look to him as the first time I met him.

After chatting for a while, he relaxes and there is a definite boyish innocence to his demeanor. I get the interview rolling with a simple, "What are you doing out here?"

But first, he introduces his partner, Lieutenant Connelly.

"He is the one who really got the ball rolling down here," Freudenthal says. "We used to come down here and arrest everybody and lock them up. But it was all misdemeanor, petty stuff. You'd put them in jail for maybe not even a night. You know, they would go in for their initial hearing and then be back out on the streets, before the end of your shift sometimes. It didn't seem to be really solving any problems at all.

"If you were out here five years ago, there were people everywhere," the sergeant continues. "It was really bad. The department realized—well, mostly Sean [Lieutenant Connelly]—that arresting everyone wasn't the way to solve the problem."

Instead, he explains, the solution seemed to be working with the HSC staff to connect people to services, in hopes of getting them off the streets for longer than a night in prison. As he talks, Brian's face has a gentle sadness that floats just beneath the surface. It's a confused, compassionate sort of look.

"Is that why we see less trouble on these streets now?"

Crime has come way down in this area in the past five years. By 50 percent, to be more precise. And still we need solutions. Roughly 3.5 million persons will most likely experience being homeless this year. More than 7 million persons are currently incarcerated, on probation or on parole. That's roughly 3 percent of the U.S. population.

"It came from us realizing the difference," Freudenthal replies. "And we have a training program that's been put together since on how to deal with these Seriously Mentally Ill (SMI) subjects. And that's helped. All the officers who work this area have to go to that training in order to work this location."

Moreover, officers work here both on—and off-duty, as security for CASS. If they didn't, Freudenthal says, more homeless would be sleeping on surrounding private property instead of CASS and the Outreach Shelter. This was a big part of the problem a few years ago. This new system of cooperation has made those sleeping outside safer and the surrounding neighborhood happier.

"There were outreach programs here but not many, if any, including the police," Freudenthal continues. "Some of the concerns, the initial concerns were that people felt like, 'Oh, you are going to force people into services.' But if you look at it, a lot of the people who need services, if they are at this point in their lives, don't realize it or they would have sought it already. At times it will turn around and we'll say, 'Hey, we have a misdemeanor warrant for your arrest. We can take you to jail right now, or you can go try and help yourself and we'll deal with the warrant later. You try and get yourself into some services and help yourself out right now.' And that's really seemed to make a big difference in connecting these people to services as opposed to just locking them up."

"So what are you doing out here?" I question him. "You could work another location. You have enough seniority."

"Yeah, this is actually a position that I applied for," Freudenthal replies. "It wasn't that I got stuck here. Honestly, Sean is a close friend of mine and I saw it through, you know, his eyes." In addition, Freudenthal had been working the surrounding precinct, so he was familiar with the types of charges pressed against the homeless and how broken the system was. "I believe in what they've done out here. I believe in the cause. I'm not out here to arrest and book everybody, because if I was, I'd be doing it all day long. I'm just trying to get them to help themselves and also to protect the neighborhood."

Goals around here should be long-term, the sergeant contends. The arrests, tickets and bookings are all short-term solutions and therefore the wrong thing to focus on.

"How would you define your job?" I'm compelled to ask in response to this idea.

"I'm not a social worker by any means," Freudenthal says. "I'm a police officer, true and blue. But by working together with the HSC and combining the two . . . I don't know how to describe it. It's just a combination. It's not just me having that mentality. It also took a lot for them in the HSC community to have the mentality to trust us. Before, they had always experienced us just coming in and booking their clients and taking them all to jail and not being, you know, so open-minded about homelessness."

Police and social workers—joined in an effort to ease, and even end, homelessness. I comment that this seems to embody the motto 'Protect and Serve,' and Freudenthal agrees. But he says budget cuts in the department are making it harder to continue with this system.

"It's going to be very interesting and very difficult to say whether we are going to have to go back to the option of booking them in jail, if we don't have any other options," he says.

"And that costs us money, too?" I ask.

"More!"

Dropping that issue for now, I ask the sergeant if this more compassionate interactive approach undermines his police authority at all.

"There is a need to balance it. We don't let everybody go," he says, laughing. "If anything comes down to safety, you know, if there was any kind of issue that could affect the safety of anyone, then obviously we have to step up and show that we are still here to arrest people. But now when I contact these people, it's not a confrontation. Respect is a two-way street. They show it towards me; I show it towards them. And they realize I'm not out here to throw everyone I can in jail. The contact I have with these people . . . it's just a better contact, as opposed to them being intimidated, you know, afraid of being arrested."

I ask Sergeant Freudenthal if he has anything else to share and he says no but the man I really should be talking to is Lieutenant Connolly.

I explain to him that I would like to ask him three final questions that I ask everyone. I feel a little apprehensive about asking a police officer my esoteric questions so I start with the second question: What are your thoughts about society and/or societies in general?

He thinks for a while and says, "What are the other two questions?"

I laugh. "What is the meaning of life?"

He pauses. "Alright, and the third?"

Who are you?

About me, about myself, you know, I was born and raised in a strict Catholic family in the south side of Chicago and um, I'm a firm believer in religion and God. However I don't see it in the same way that my family did and in the way I was raised. I see it in that there's good in all people. And I truly believe that life is just about being a good person and living your life responsibly and respectfully. I have three children and a family. I believe I was put here to raise a family, and to be a good person to other people. And am I that 100 percent of the time? Absolutely not, but I try to be as much as I can be. But I realize I can't do that all of the time. But I try.

What are your thoughts about society and/or societies in general?

You know, I think anybody who spends any amount of time at a homeless shelter here would have some pretty jaded thoughts about society, be it that you know when you see a guy playing basketball or football or baseball, making millions and millions of dollars, like Alex Rodriguez for example, to make two hundred and fifty million dollars playing baseball and then to cheat while doing so. I don't know. I've got different thoughts . . . like I said, it's jaded because of where I work and what I've seen over the years. And I realize I'm not somebody who is here to change the world. I am not here to keep everybody in Phoenix safe. I'm just here to do my part and, ah . . . I don't know. It's hard. I'm sorry I don't have much of an answer. I have kids that are raised in a wonderful area and the world in their eyes it is wonderful and then I come down here. And it's wonderful in my eyes when I am home and society is wonderful in my eyes when I'm at home, but then I come down here and realize that it's not so great anymore.

What is the meaning of life?

Honestly, I see that my life is to live it as a good person, respectful of others, and just try to be good to other people. And then, like I said before, I can't do it all of the time, but I try to do it as much as I can. But um . . . that's all I got.

Sgt. Freudenthal ends in an exasperated, slightly embarrassed, humble sort of way. There is a deep look of compassion and sorrow in his face, like a man still reconciling the blessings of his life with the lives of those he protects and serves.

Brian makes me consider that you don't have to have all the answers to try and find solutions to bridge the two worlds.

Lieutenant Sean Connolly is a fairly large, well-built man with a head as shiny as his shield. Despite the tough appearance his eyes, if anything, twinkle as he describes his nearly 16 years serving this community as an officer. "It's a privilege on a lot of levels, and the biggest reason is I've been able to see a progression," Connolly says. "I was down here in early '90s and, uh, everybody was winging it. We'd just had, in the decade prior, a dumping of people from mental institutions by a certain administration. As a society, we kind of created homelessness. And we didn't know how to manage that.

"So the city had to deal with it," he continues. "I mean, you have a huge population of people now living in parks. And so how do you handle that? There was not a lot of communication between the services. They were all vying for their own; they all have different missions. But those missions were connected. So what ends up happening is this whole neighborhood is littered with services for homeless, mentally ill, drug addicted, alcohol-addicted people. And you have a meandering group of mentally ill, drug addicted, alcohol-addicted people going from service to service for sustainability. North of here you have some tremendously challenged neighborhoods from gangs and drugs; to the south and to the west you have that also. And you had a population of 800 to 1,000, if you're a drug dealer, clients, persons who will purchase your product."

"Sounds like a catastrophe," is all I can say.

Connolly nods, eyes widening. He looks like someone you would most definitely not want to mess with. But he also has a warm, paternal glow about him and a jolly demeanor and delivery.

"At times, it was a catastrophe," he says. "And it was the place in the Valley to buy your crack cocaine in the street. And I can remember nights when here on Madison and Jackson [streets] where there were literally hundreds of people hanging out, smoking and bartering. And there are a couple of cops who were responsible for that neighborhood shelter here. And there was violence. There was rape, aggravated assaults and everything else that went along with all those quality of life problems."

He continues with his very animated and clear speaking voice that is a delight to listen to, despite the subject matter.

"If I'm a down-and-out, mentally ill person, can I tell you that if I walk by a car down town and it has an open window with a purse in it, that maybe I wouldn't take the purse because I need a meal and need some money? You know, I don't know if I would or not."

The lieutenant talks with candor and empathy, but also humor; even when the discussion is serious, like ours now; there's almost laughter behind his words, eyes and shining bald head.

"And I've been involved in dozens of crime suppression programs," he continues. "Under the Seventh Avenue Bridge, there were hundreds of people smoking crack at night on any given time. So we'd go round up people for a couple of weeks and do this and that and then uh, tout ourselves as 'mission accomplished.' And it would be quiet for a couple of weeks, then . . . it flared right back up!"

This improved once all the entities providing services to the homeless in this area came together and formed the Human Services Campus, he says. Though the two groups don't always agree, it's been an opportunity for police to work with a large social service organizations on this even larger neighborhood problem.

"But really, [at first] I just had the perspective of a beat cop," Connolly says, acknowledging that some of this 'large-scale solutions' talk is retrospect. "This was my beat. Then I was able to transition into a supervisory role, where I had a little more authority and control over a squad of guys. And we were able then to get some things rolling. So what we did was we sat down with Mark Holleran, David Bridge, all these entities, Jessica, Arlene, Jerry Castro, Father Bill, everybody. And the biggest thing I preached to them was, 'You need to be able to see through my lenses and I need to be able to see through your lenses.' And realize that we are on parallel courses but they cross every day, all day. The mission is the same. We're about community safety. We're about making this a safe environment for their clients."

Connolly says he and HSC leaders needed to work together at first, to create a mentality they could all share about what the HSC's purpose was.

"They ran this in the past as a 9 to 5 business operation," he says. "And the analogy I used was—and it's not about dehumanizing it, but it's an analogy that sticks in people's brains—If I'm the Phoenix Brick Company, I make bricks all day long. The byproduct of my brick making is sand. And at the end of the day, I take it and dump it into the street and then I call the

Phoenix Police Department and say, 'Hey, I need you to take care of that sand.' And so Mark [Holleran] looks at me and says, 'I think I get it.'"

The bargain, as Connolly describes it was this: The police remove the hardcore criminal elements from the neighborhood, and the HSC makes sure the rest stay safe, day and night. Together, they formed outreach teams to go out and engage people. With police no longer alone on the front lines of poverty, more and more homeless got connected with services and less of them were arrested. It was the longer-term, less costly fix everyone wanted.

"It took a year of outreach and partnership, but right now there is nobody under that 7th Avenue Bridge. And that's not because of the Police Department. It's because those outreach teams were in there nightly, reconnecting people. And once you took away the customers, [who] were the drug—and alcohol-addicted and mentally ill, the drug dealer is gone. Once you took away that, there is none of the fighting that leads to escalations that leads to stabbings. It's all linked. So it all went away once they started to proactively engaging people."

Connolly explains the partnership now between social services and cops is so successful that officers compete to work this beat.

"What's very important is to understand too is that all of the officers down here are hand-picked," the lieutenant says. "And when I tell people from other organizations, they say, 'Are you telling me that cops are testing to work with the homeless people?' Well, yes. There's also a lot of other things they [get to] do. They are also involved in some drug enforcement. They work the city projects. They're also bike-trained. They're part of our tactical response unit, to respond to civil unrest. So they get a lot of other benefits from being here at this position, but this is their primary mission."

Connolly says police officers on this beat also receive 40 hours of crisis prevention training, where they are taught to de-escalate tense situations, as well as training in recognizing mental illness. He admits that the campus can be a dangerous place where his cops may face "life-threatening scenarios." He says never has a police officer shot and killed a client on campus.

"And that's because we are taking the time to connect!" Connolly says, with audible exclamation points. "I've seen my guys be within that 21 feet span [of a knife-wielding person] where they would have been totally justified in using lethal force. But I'm standing here now as an officer who has a different mindset. I'm not just looking at the knife as a threat. That's a person. I'm ready to do my business; don't get me wrong. But my mindset is that I'm now dealing with a mentally ill person that might not be even hearing my commands, that has voices in their head. And I'm going to give this a few more seconds and use some of my skills and things that I've been taught to de-escalate the situation so I don't have to shoot the person. We do that on a daily basis down here."

This comment jogs a recent memory. I saw Sergeant Freudenthal do this just the day before with a very aggressive man who was holding a bottle. But he got him to calm down and directed him towards services instead of escorting him to jail.

"Now the last thing I'll say is that this is a never ending endeavor here," says Connolly. "I know some people, their philosophy is to end homelessness. And if that's your goal I say, hey shoot for the stars. But us in this business, it's how do you manage it? And that's my point. I will never say, 'Mission Accomplished.' [But] I'll tell you that this neighborhood statistically is not the crime spot in the city anymore. I'll tell you that statistically there is a lot less crime down here and it's a much safer environment."

The lieutenant is proud of the strides that have been made since the HSC opened; that much is clear not only in what he says, but how he says it. Still, Connolly has a bit of an outsider's perspective on this cluster of social services—and he's not afraid to raise what concerns he still has.

"Enabling is a big thing down here," he says. "They are getting better with it, but don't just give people meals so they can go out and get drunk and high again and do it every day. And I know the Catholic mission. I'm an Irish Catholic. There was an evolution, or teaching process, that went on at André House and St. Vincent's, because they were blind. Just to feed, feed, feed. That's our mission. And I said, 'Take a deep breath. Think about what you are doing related to just feed, feed, feed.' First of all, they're getting three meals a day down here, 8,000 calories. I've got obese homeless people down here. Uh, so let's think about that aspect of it. The second thing is that you then have a bombardment of other faith-based groups from around the valley who come out and randomly hand out food. And you are just perpetuating the ability to live out here and be an addict. You take that away and here's a human."

"It sounds like you've modified some of their ideas and they've modified some of yours," I observe.

"That's my point exactly," Connolly says. "Remember the beginning of the conversation when I talked about the lenses? I've got to see through their eyes and they've got to see through mine."

"You sound like you have compassion. Like you see through these people's [the client's] eyes as well."

"You have to or you can drive yourself crazy," Connolly says, his bald head gleaming under the streetlight. "I mean, if I work in this neighborhood for 16 years and I don't have the ability to laugh, I don't have the ability to uh, have compassion, and I take everything super literal and it's hard core and it's black and white . . . I would be probably walking into that door [he points to the Overflow Shelter] myself and be out of a job. You cannot from a mentally healthy aspect be a police officer in this environment and not have compassion. But still understand, I am the law and I'm going to do my business! There is a lot of compassion and a lot of de-escalation, but there are some days were we come out here and handle our business. And everybody sees that!"

After a while, Connolly returns to the issue of mental health and how it affects homelessness. On this issue, he's pragmatic, blunt, even harsh.

"I tell you though, the number one thing down here is mental illness. It's huge, mental illness and drug addiction. I'll bet my paycheck that it's over 70 percent of the people out here. But the guy who lost his job at Motorola, who's now homeless—very rare for me down here. And if they are here, they're not here very long. What the challenge is for CASS and the Police Department is to create an environment where, where we move life forward. 'cause there's some guys—and we all know them, those of us who are down here a lot—the same old faces that have been here for years. Granted, it's a pretty good gig for some of them. If I'm an addict, I can eat for free. All my check can then go for drugs. I got Circle Ks and liquor stores all around. And occasional drug dealer comes through. I've got connections."

"Can you clarify something for me?" I ask, hoping to capitalize on the lieutenant's honestly. "I've heard there is a monthly cycle of activity out here that happens when government support checks come in."

"And it's something somebody needs to speak to," Connolly obliges. "It's a tough issue for me on a lot of levels. But when the checks come in from the government, usually around the first two weeks of the month, when they are here for the first couple of weeks we see a lot less homeless people, and it's quieter. A lot of these guys will get those checks and go get a hotel room for a week or two and then party for those two weeks. And then they run out of money and come down here for the last two weeks. And that's a cycle. And we're all to blame for that, especially the government. If our welfare system is to just randomly give money to people and have no . . . my theory, Sean Connolly's, is to link it to something that creates sustainability and success. And some of these guys are truly disabled—don't get me wrong. But we are a massive country; we've got a ton of humanity. And what everybody does down here, I don't want to put any negative spin on it. I just hope this place has the ability to survive during these economic times."

Having pushed enough buttons for one interview, I wrap things up by asking this Man In Blue my three questions.

What is the meaning of life?

Per Monty Python? [He laughs.] Um, the meaning of life? For me, it is about family and my Irish heritage. So when I think of life I think of, although this is a different kind of profession and we have a second family here at work, it is a means to support my family. Life for me, the meaning of it ties directly into my family and I'm spiritual so I think the ability to do this job allows me to engage my family, take pride in my Irish heritage, and then enjoy the outdoors.

What are your thoughts about society and/or societies in general?

I'm a big believer in community, the power of community. We do community based policing. There are studies to indicate a tight-knit, efficient community is a healthier community. If you look at the Italian Rosati, that group of people who moved over and lived in Pennsylvania. They have incredibly low rates of heart disease and they eat horribly, they don't exercise and they drink, smoke and eat pastries. But they have this unbelievably strong sense of community. So I think we need to be more attuned to us as a community. And work on establishing those connections through community, because I think that would produce a lot of good things.

Who are you?

I am Sean Connolly. No, that was a joke. I think what people need to understand is I'm a human just like anybody else. And I think sometimes we put on this badge and this uniform and we have this presence and we drive around in our cars and we create a perception that we are less than human or we don't have feelings and we don't have emotions and we don't smile and touch and feel like everyone else. When I go to schools and talk to kids you get some of that. I'm a father. I'm a husband. And I'm an Irish guy who likes a good Guinness.

I ask Lieutenant Connolly if there is anything else he would like to tell me and he says no, wishing me luck with the book. He half-jokingly tells me to remember his role with Phoenix Police Department and to not print anything that might damage that for him. I tell him I won't and that I appreciate his trust. He says, "That's how we work out here. We do everything based on trust."

Sean causes me to consider the importance of seeing things through other people's eyes, which in and of itself is an attempt to reconnect.

A WEEK OFF: Monday, March 16, 2009

I have no other interviews set up for today or tomorrow. I decide to take the week off. My kids are on spring break and it will be an opportunity to spend valuable time with them and to catch up on the volume of notes I have already acquired. I want to read over them, because I am starting to lose sight of the forest for the trees. Each interview seems to come close to answering my original question, but also poses new considerations. It's all fascinating and inspiring and seems to be heading somewhere. But where that is, I still do not know.

I consider that family needs to be the core of any project.

REWARD

JULIA, CLIENT, LDRC: Monday, March 23, 2009, 1:00 p.m.

TODAY, I FEEL SO DIFFERENT than when I started this project. I know things now in my heart that I had known only in my head. This place is some sort of distillation of humanity, a condensation of learning.

I walk across the campus lawn and see a young girl, maybe 10 years old, sleeping in curled-up ball position on top of a suitcase with presumably her mother and father sleeping in the grass beside her. I've never seen a young child on campus; family services are provided elsewhere. In my open-to-all-that-life-has-to-offer state of mind, the moment strikes my heart deeply. I have 14-year-old twins and can't imagine doing an immersion with them, let alone truly being homeless with them.

It's tragic enough down here without being reminded of the children involved. My feelings of personal growth are quickly shunted by the inexplicable nature of this moment.

I move on to the doors of LDRC, bumping into a large man who immediately stops, turns and apologizes. I do the same. I am used to this. With so many people on this crowded campus, this happens almost every time I visit. Will was right; courtesy and respect are big things down here, much bigger than in the Ordinary World.

As I wait outside for the doors to open I spot MICHAEL (with the five names and three periods), sitting on the ground three feet from me. He is still unshaven, his t-shirt is very dirty, and he is wearing flannel pajama pants. This time he recognizes me, and launches right in. MICHAEL says that he has been "doubly blessed" today. He is not only here to get some medical services of "a mental and not mental nature," but also he had been awarded a music contract and will be famous soon.

MICHAEL speaks in the same manner as before and repeats his praise of God and his personal pride for his success. I congratulate him. He asks how my book is going and we chat for a bit before he excuses himself to go and find a smoke. I watch him walk away and rummage through the outdoor cement ashtrays for a cigarette butt. Despite his problems, there's something I really like about that guy. He may not be in touch with the same reality the rest of us are, but his reality is sure more creative, not to mention happier and more polite than most.

I sit in the lobby of LDRC, people-watching while working on my laptop. To my left a large woman sits sideways in her chair with her back towards me. She's rocking back and forth, back and forth. She seems a bit disturbed. But then all of a sudden she turns her head and looks down at me as I'm typing and comments, "You type pretty fast . . . for a man." We both laugh. She asks what I'm working on, and we discuss the book for a bit. As we do, the woman to the right of me jumps in to introduce herself.

"Julia Lynne Kleckner," she says, proving it by whipping out her state ID card, debit card, Social Security card, and voter ID card. Though a bit overzealous, Julia otherwise seems quite "normal," whatever that is. I ask her if she would like to be interviewed. She agrees, but as if inquisitive or curious.

We move into my cubicle behind the glass doors of Magellan and away from the sounds of all the people in the lobby of LDRC.

Julia looks tired and sad, yet full of fire.

I explain to her that anything she tells me could appear in print and she says, "That's fine. I have nothing to hide. You're the interviewer. So what do you want to know?"

"Just talk to me. I have a few questions at the end, but just tell me whatever."

She starts talking: "I've seen lots of things that were human and inhuman here, and that's on both sides of the fence. I have seen people be derogatory and inflammatory towards the staff. Course, I have seen staff be derogatory and inflammatory, but everybody has bad days. Just because someone looks slovenly that doesn't mean they don't deserve respect."

Julia continues in a scattered—but coherent—manner. "I was deemed SMI, but I have had that reclassified. I'm medicated now. Course, I was court ordered to take it."

I ask what she's doing down here: Is she getting services, shelter or both?

"I come down here because it's closer to my son," Julia says. "I have a place, but it's not good to be there right now. My friend and landlord [are] going through some things. Nothing illegal. It's just not good for me to be there right now. This place has changed since I was here on my b-day, 2002, but that was the old CASS, when it was at 1209 West Madison and ironically that's my birthday, 12/09/1966. There are a lot of things they do to help people down here. Don't get me wrong. I'm not one to spread negativity."

Truth is a big preoccupation with Julia. Her descriptions are dotted with exact dates and addresses. She tells me long tales of going through the court system and social services and again shows me all sorts of documentation to back up what she says.

"You look sad, Julia," I observe.

"My daughter was murdered in 2004," Julia replies. "She was 17 when she was murdered. I was in jail at the time and they wouldn't let me make a phone call or see her. It was June 8th, 2004 in Mountain Home, Idaho, 1475 West Frontage Home in my sister and brother-in-law's home. The headline read 'Bullets in Garcia.' And you can verify that. It's all in the newspaper."

At this point, I believe her and am surprised she doesn't carry documents to prove this too. "Garcia?"

"My first husband was Paul David Garcia. The guy [who killed her daughter, not her husband] had just done eight years in Walla Walla [State Penitentiary] for rape and was paroled early. He tried to rape my daughter. She fought back and he shot her with a nine-millimeter in the face and then three in the back as she ran out the front door. Kids in the neighborhood found her as they came home from school."

She starts to cry and I join her. Her worn but bright face smiles kindly at me, appreciating my dim understanding of her pain.

"It's OK now," She says, trying to pull herself together.

But I find myself screaming, unable to do the same. "No it's not OK Julia! It's not OK!"

And am I wrong? It's not OK for a parent to have to bury their child. And sometimes the best thing we can do for another is help them to cry. I just cannot *not* be involved anymore.

She nods in agreement, cries and smiles more. "You're right. It's not OK."

After a while, I ask Julia what she had been in jail for, and she says it was for a criminal damage conviction. "I went into a 7-11 store to ask for water and [the cashier] didn't give it to me. That's illegal in the state of Arizona in the summer. You have to give someone water if they ask for it. You have to. I even offered him a quarter, but he wouldn't give it to me. I threw him out of the 7-11, locked the door, told him to call the cops, destroyed the computer and pulled the hot dog machine off the counter. I got some chips, and a Slurpee, sat down and waited for the cops."

She pauses.

"It was not a good day for Julia." She laughs, shaking her head, but the sound is laced with sadness. And even in this story, Julia makes sure to prove the veracity of what she says. "I had a major panic attack. And that's public record. You can verify that. It's all on tape."

"What is your diagnosed mental illness?" I ask at this point.

"I have Post Traumatic Stress Disorder," Julia replies. "I had done 317 days when I found my daughter was murdered. Then they took me from Estrella to Perryville [prisons] for 17 more days to kill my number [serve out her sentence]. From there I went to a treatment center through Value Options."

Knowing that Value Options is a service provider with an office at LDRC I ask, "Treatment for drug addiction or mental illness?"

"Both. I wasn't rational. My daughter had just been murdered. I wasn't rational. I was on 300 milligrams of lithium, three times a day. But when your mind shuts down, when it's not capable of handing something, you're not right. There is nothing that can prepare you for a tragedy like that. I'm amazed I can walk and talk. She was a beautiful girl." Julia pauses, giving both of us time to reflect. "I hate that demon, but he was shot and killed himself two weeks later in a high-speed pursuit. So we don't have to worry about him," with a nod of the head. She explains, when the police pulled over the suspected murderer of her daughter, he took his own life.

"I have two other children," Julia continues. "My son Paul is 20. We kind of keep him sheltered from all this shit. He doesn't need to know the things people say about his mama. He's says he doesn't believe what people say about me and I tell him he doesn't need to worry about that shit. He's had closed heart surgery one time and open heart six times. He's in Gilbert (a suburb of Phoenix) now. His fight is to maintain health. They were 15 months apart," She concludes, saddened by every reminder of her daughter.

"My lastborn child [whom she had to give away at age three] was born out of wedlock. They [family] don't accept that neither. For peacefulness, I leave her name out of things. She just turned 10. She was adopted out when I was in prison. But I don't want to talk about her. She has a good life now. Her adoptive dad is a sheriff, so I know she's safe."

As she talks about family, I'm still bothered by something, and ask: "I still don't understand why you are here if you have a place to live."

"This is a safe place . . . for me to collect my thoughts," Julia says. "I have a home in Glendale with Harry but I can't be there right now. It's not a party home or a flophouse. I just can't be there right now. I'm not paranoid or schizophrenic. But at one point the truth will set you free. Do you think I'm crazy?"

"So far, no," I say, flashing a smile. And it's true, I don't. 'Crazy' would be way too strong a word for Julia. But she is challenged. "You seem upset, not crazy."

"I'm tired of being shit on. I'm tired of being looked at like a freak!" She cries a bit again. Julia does not look like a freak. In fact, she's slender and attractive, granted a bit worn by her life's condition.

"You get frustrated," she continues. Her voice is equally attractive yet sounds beat up. "If you are a woman out here, you don't want to look shiny. It draws too much attention to you. I just put on makeup now because I wanted to feel better about myself. You can take the worst person out here, shave them and bathe them and they look just like you."

In an attempt to pick herself up further she writes her name on a piece of paper in beautiful penmanship. She proudly states, "You can go to any penmanship in the world and Julia's penmanship cannot be duplicated. Penmanship says a lot about a person." She pauses. "I have Tourette [syndrome] too. I react to sound and noise. You know Tourette isn't just cussing. It's a form of autism . . . it's in the same family. It's electrical."

"Do you have other family here?" I ask.

"My father is buried in the Veterans National Cemetery in Cave Creek [Arizona] in the Legion of Honor section. My mother died January 2005."

"Wow. How did you deal with all that loss?"

"I blew a fuse when my daddy died" Julia says. "I was sad when my mother died." She pauses as her eyes grow sadder still. Slowly and quietly she says, "I don't like goodbyes . . . But it would have been nice to have the opportunity to say goodbye to my daughter."

Having no response to her last statement, I ask Julia the three questions.

What is the meaning of life?

The meaning of life is a continual learning process. From the moment we are born we are dying. That's just scientifically proven. Life is terminal. I'm blessed to have the opportunity to know that for every action there is a reaction. Positive and negative are a necessity and there is also grey area; call it gray matter; call it space piss. [She laughs.] Oh, and one more. Motivation without direction is chaos. And opinions are the mother of all mess-ups.

What are your thoughts about society and/or societies in general?
That's such a deep question. Society or societies in general . . . um . . . no opinion. That would be that grey area. That would be that space piss. It's just a classification.

Who are you?
I'm Julia. And that's it.

As Julia walked away she turned back and half smiled—a grey, space piss sort of smile.

Julia makes me realize that it's not OK!

RUNNING DEER, AUTOBIOGRAPHY:
Monday, March 30, 2009, 1:00 p.m.

I arrive at the Human Services Campus in very good spirits. Lately, everything seems to make sense to me. Actually everything just feels right—nothing makes sense. And for the first time in my life I'm not just OK with that—I'm happy about it. Life is way too complex for it to make sense. I feel very unsure and very alive.

Someone far away calls my name. I see Running Deer waving to me across the lawn. I walk over and squat down to talk to him. Running Deer had managed to get readmitted into CASS since our first interview, but he's very concerned about what the future will hold. Just as David Bridge had warned, Running Deer confirmed that he and all the other sex offenders will be kicked out as of June first, and this time for good.

The VA will provide subsidized housing if he can show proof of income, but Running Deer is still unable to find employment. All of his skills are in manual labor. Honestly, I'm not surprised he is having a hard time. Many of my well-educated friends are in the same predicament now due to the economy. I doubt anyone wants to hire a sex offender in a wheelchair.

On top of everything else, Running Deer is still not approved for disability benefits. His back might require surgery, but they are trying a series of shots first. Following the story with my eyes, I notice a tattoo on his left forearm for the first time: "Proud To Be Indian" it reads, with a peace pipe underneath it. I ask him, what about Native American benefits?

He explains that only those who are at least one-quarter Native American can receive benefits. Running Deer is only one-eighth Apache.

The good news is Running Deer has now been clean for four months. I know he's clean because he is clearer every time I speak with him. But I've never seen him this stressed. He's worried about being thrown out on the streets, and that leading him somehow back to jail. If it were me in his predicament, I would have been drinking like a fish by now.

He asks me if I'll read an autobiography he's working on and hands me six pages torn from a spiral notebook. He leaves and I sit down in the noisy lobby of LDRC, settling down into the silence of his pages.

The following is an exact reproduction of Running Deer's autobiography. It has not been changed for grammar, content, or any other reason. This is Running Deer's life story, as he wrote it:

This is my Storie 3-7-09

I was born in Feb. 19th 1961 in Fresno, CA in a town called Sanger, and the first thing I can remember growing up is watching my mother ironing clothing as a fire broke out behind the gas stove and as she ran past me in order for her to get out. She did get a man to come in and put it out, but no one even though of getting me out of there.

Now befor I go much further, I have to say that even though I can remember these things taking place, the Days, months, years I can't ever seem to, and even in alot of what I remember are mixed around and are not in order.

I well not menchen the real names of people in order to protect alot of them because I have forgiven them, but two people I talk about I will use their real names in hopes of a reaction from them.

now as I was saying. Going from the part about the fire, I can tell you that when it came to doing anything to protect my life my mother really could care less about. Growing up was a living hell for me because there was one person after another from my mother to almost anyone coming around me that abused me in one manner or another—sexually, fisicly, and mentaly. My mother was a person that when ever she was mad at me would bent me to the floor and then would start kicking me in my back, head, and stomic, she just didn't care. I even remember a time when it came time to cross the street when I was 22 months old she let me run right out infront of a car. I also remember a time I think I was five at this time she said that she couldn't control me any more and sent me to the Robbinson's foster home in CA. and you want to talk about living in hell, catch this my life in this foster care was this: I was pulled around by my hair, ears, nose, I was slapt around contantly. Locked in the attic at night, given on jar of baby food for breakfast and one for diner, wasn't aloud to watch TV, had to do all the house work, couldn't go out to play and brought down at night and they would put make-up and a dress on me and made me do all kinds of sick shit with the both of them and even the Bitch that they would have baby sit me would make me sit in the bathroom when she had to use it then would make me get down and clean her with my tonge. I ran away so meany times it wasn't funny. Most the time my mother would find me and every time I tried to tell her what these people were doing to me, she would just say that she didn't care, she didn't want to hear it and that I was going back. I never matter what took place with her or who's fault it was, I would be the one who got the heat for it every dam time.

There was these people "Let call them, D + LG" living in CA. on j, street who my mother had baby sitting us kids and this D-Lady was as bad as the Robbin's in every way other then the sexual stuff, but close to it, her husband LG was o.k. because he did not do any of these things to us, but! he did nothing to stop it. I ran away alot from there two and even in the sam time from one night late I must of be around 7 when we arived home and the front door was opend with no lights on some one had broken in to the house, my mother didn't know what to do, back then there was no thing like cell phones so she and my two sisters stood there scaird, so I went for the door to find out what was going on (not knowing if I would be killed or not) my mother making no move to stop me, so I go to the door and yelled that whoever was there had better leave or eals and then I turned on the lights, so even on came in and my mother had called the police.

Now I was sexualy abused in every way from the I guess from 3 to 9 when around my 10th birthday in '71 we moved to Oregon where my mother was bourn and that is when all the rage in my started coming out. I struck out any way I could to get even with my mother, Father, sister, and any one I could get even with. I started doing drugs, and running away from home more, breaking into home, and stilling cars. Skipping schools shoplifting and just striking out anyway I could. People were now finding any reason to lock my up to the point of making things up and lieing to get a conviction. I seems as every one I got around would play mine fuck games with me, I would get kicked out of school for things I had no part in. Every one that had a problem in life it was my fualt or they would come to me to get them out of it. I drop out of school at 16 and could care less if I ever seen school again, I hated people so bad I just wanted people and mostly my mother to pay for every thing ever done to me, but I was the one paying all the time. Then one day when I was 16 I came home from work and my mother gave me the news paper showing me and add that looked like a really god job opportunity, so I called and the answer was the Army Nati. Gaurds. I told my mother who it was and she said forget it that they wouldn't take me due to some past medical issues and I made a bet with her that if she would sign the papers that I would make it in. I told the Man that I wanted to join and they sent some one out with the papers to signe me up. I was on the plain on my 17th birthday for boot camp in '78. I really loved it, so I asked my drill Sargent how I could go regulair Army, so the called the Armery I to report to after boot camp and they told us that I would have to come back and go through the red tape and they would send me back. I get back after I got done with boot camp and my commanding officer Told me that I could not Swich because if I did the person that would get the credits for my inlestment would lose em and he told me to try again when we got back for our training in Washington. When we got back I asked again and got the same bullshit. My blatoon Sargent told me about them sending people into rugulare Service as a punishment for going Awall, so I stop going.

The Army never came after me and one night I put a man in the hospitle for hitting a woman, so I got arrested and taken to jail another bref moment when to cops abuse me stoled money out of my pockit there in Salem, OR. but any way the Army never came after me untill I got locked up, and all they did was have me signe a peace of paper saying that I would give up my class A's and uniforms or pay $300, and that I would be receiving my descharge papers sat dishourible discharge. 4 years down the road I ws telling a Man in the Army about what the army done to me and he said no that by law I was still in and the Army owes me for 4 years of back pay because I had never recieved my discharge paper, so I wrote the the Army and told them what I had found out, so they sent me my discharge papers say honrible discharge with reinlestment N/A, but no back pay and this was in '84. untill this day I have never recieved nt 4 years back pay the Army owed me. Then in '91 because I kicked this freak out of my home for disrespecting Blacks in my home, it started a bight between myself and my mother and when she had me thrown out of her home I retail against her by trying to bourn her shead down and took off for Mill City, OR and got hooked up in a church, and was working.

One day I got to thinking how stupped I was because I had worked so heard to stay out of prison, I felt that I needed to hold myself responsibile for my actions, so I had explained to my paster what had taken place between my family and my self and what I did, I told her that I was going to turn my self in for it. She wanted to talk to my mother and see if she couldn't get my mother to drop the issue so I wouldn't have to go back to prison, and my mother told her that if I came around the family ever again that she would do what ever she could to have me put away fro as long as she could. Then one day wating to go to work my mother calls me at the church and tells me that the family would like for me to come up for Thanksgiving dinner to Washington. She told me that every thing was fine that every one was wrong and there would be no problems.

So I hitched hiked up and everyone seemd fine there was no problems, my mother gave me a ride back to Mill City after we got back and com lat Jan. I get a Detective at my door talking about my Mother bringing Sex Charges against me. One for attempted Sodomy one against my nice Danilla, and sexual abuse one against my nice Shuvirie.

I told the Detictive that he would just go back and tell my mother I know what She's doing and once I prove it in a court then She will be going to prison.

I was told that its my right to take it to court, but I would not win no matter what I could prove because the courts would see that I was convicted no matter what and, thats exactly what they did.

My nice got on the stand and looked right at my mother and said that I did not do it that She was told to say that I did and the DA tryed to get it striken from the records and the jugde said no that they would keep it, but in the transcripts they changed alot of what was said and did in court that day. It was proven that I didn't committ these crimes, but they convicted me any ways and then the judge good whent into retirement right after words.

So you see, my life was not only fucked when I was bourn, but all the way through life by my Mother, Army, Government, and Society and an still getting fucked today.

I am forced by the law now to live at CASS a place where a man that is supposed to be free is treated everyday as if he's in prison, like a lowe life Scum bag that's a dreg of Society living in a concentration camp where very few of the Staff even treat you as if your humen in anyway.

See in the Great U.S. of A where men are supposed to be free and have rights, you really ant got Shit.

I hate life and whant my life to end and I regret to day I served in the Rmy or did anything good because what did it get me but screwed.

I am no disabled no place to live and still getting screwed by Government, Army, and Socity.

So Why Should I Want to go on.

See, back when when I was in old CASS, three jobs that came my way, I lost them because of CASS making me stay back to do chores and even now trying to get the help I need everyday to get to School is getting to where I am about to get kicked out because I can't get the means to get there. The help I'v gotten so far was mostly through L.J.

See CASS dose not want to help a person make it because they can care less. All CASS wants is to use their power to make homeless people jump through their hoops.

I am about to loos every thing because I just can't get the help.

I want out of here so bad and yet I have no way of getting out.

I think about what Dawn told me about the will and how we often raise children not to decide for themselves. We don't teach them that they have the power to make decisions.

One of the first ways a child learns they have control or power in their world is through their control over the entrances and exits to of their body. Any form of child abuse, but especially sexual molestation, causes emotional wounds and it robs people of the very willpower they need to heal. It introduces a disease while at the same time destroying the immune system.

It seems to me that the majority of the clients here suffer from Adverse Childhood Experiences (ACEs), which are known to affect health and emotional function for a lifetime. This was proven through a 10-year study of over 17,000 people through the Kaiser Permanente healthcare system in San Diego headed by Vincent Felitti, M.D. and Robert Anda, M.D. Healing from terrible experiences during youth is a great challenge but it is possible (there are many healing modalities from psychotherapy to reiki and hypnosis and more), and from what I can see, healing through any method that makes a good match for the wounded is completely necessary to moving forward to a better life. (For more information, help and resources, see both **http://tinyurl.com/94sykl2** and **http://www. acestudy.org**.)

After reading Running Deer's autobiography, I cry. His story sounds blaming and full of woe-is-me. But that's just it! I cry some more.

Running Deer makes me consider that we often rob children of their power to choose, the very power they need to live as adults.

SCOTT, MSVA: Monday, March 30, 2009, 2 p.m.

I see Scott from across the room. He is heading over to the Madison Street Veterans Association (MSVA) facilities and invites me to join him.

As we walk the long way around, Scott says, "Tomorrow night they are closing the parking lot of the overflow shelter, which will throw a hundred people out in the streets. Those who have been there for a long time, they will drop them on the street. They will issue new passes for people who have not been there . . . it's a squeeze play."

"Do you think it's that calculated?" I ask, shocked.

"It has to be," Scott replies "Do you know what the second largest industry is in California? The largest is agricultural. Right below that is the California Department of Corrections. And they say crime doesn't pay? Crime pays certain people and it pays very, very well. That's why private corporations have been in it for years and are continuing to build and operate correctional facilities. It's a money making deal. Now for the average cop on the street, crime doesn't pay.

"The system has us instead of us having the system," he continues. Clearly, this is an issue Scott is passionate about. "Systems cannot survive long-term unless they are economically viable, whatever the system is. If we suddenly had a spiritual awakening as a nation and people did not go out and intentionally commit crimes, do you know how many people would be unemployed?"

"Are you implying it's a self-feeding system?"

"Well, there's no money in rehabilitation," Scott counters. "Prisons are paid per prisoner. It's like tobacco companies wanting you to get addicted to their product. Tobacco kills, and prisons kill. In the majority of states, we warehouse our criminals. We do not find the money to rehabilitate them and the reasons are economically based and not socially based."

Scott has become increasingly interested in social issues since his increased involvement in MSVA. And he has a point. Privately run prisons have become one of the fastest growing businesses in America.

We arrive at the MSVA facilities. "Here's what happens," Scott says, sitting down at his desk. "Joe Blow goes to work every day, maybe occasionally gets a traffic ticket, pays his taxes, been with the same company maybe 20 years, retires and grows old with his significant other. He's not a clearly identifiable problem with society. He is one of those pegs that anchor the fabric of society. Joe Blow wants better roads, better schools for his tax dollar, these kinds of things. He doesn't want his tax dollars spent in what he views is a needless or foolish manner. He wants a return he can see. Joe Blow represents the majority of Americans. A politician comes along and tells Sally and Joe that they need to take some of their tax dollars and instead of using the money to improve roads, social services and schools that they need to use the money to teach incarcerated individuals new, up-to-date, marketable job skills. It ain't going to happen."

Arizona's Prison Construction and Operations Fund for fiscal year 2010 is more than 19 times larger than the State Education Fund for Correctional Education. That's 0.08 percent Arizona's total operating budget that's allotted to the Education Fund for Correctional Education.

Scott expounds at a much higher level, "Our problem is at our evolutionary level we should still be involved in small communities. We should still be involved in communal perception instead of national perception. One major flaw in America today is that we are more prone to ask for help from our government than our immediate community."

Scott says many Americans are limited by their experiences, and therefore look for short-term solutions from government rather than slower growth solutions based in the community. If we took some of the billions of dollars we pour into overseas wars every month, he argues, we as a society could develop a system to teach job skills to the incarcerated, dropping the crime rate better than the self-feeding private prison system.

"The greatest lie in America today is we are all equal," Scott concludes, based in his own experiences and countless hours of thought. "That's a great myth."

"That's interesting," I say, "because you are talking about community and here we are in the newly created offices of the MSVA."

Scott picks up something he wrote for the MSVA and reads it:

> In a very real sense, we are a community, one of healing, which provides opportunities for Veterans to take ownership for their healing and lives. The emphasis on Veterans banding together for individual and collective healing and integration back into society makes our entire outreach different and measurably more effective than many other programs. The individual is encouraged to assume personal responsibility in a supportive environment of accountability. This approach gives us advantages over other historical models of recovery where an expert imparts wisdom and tries to control every outcome. With personal accountability the community is not mired in trying to case manage every little thing but rather is freed to embrace and support the Veterans as they fulfill their role in this journey with others who have walked this path before. This approach is a fluid living entity, which addresses the individual needs of the veteran while preserving the mission of the whole.
>
> In this journey of Veterans helping Veterans, everyone is involved in a process of rediscovery and discovery. The "Rediscovery" aspect involves Veterans banding together and moving forward reclaiming those gifts, talents, and skills that enabled them to achieve successes before becoming homeless.

Scott puts the paper down. "A lot of homeless people forget what they had. They need to reclaim that and bring it back with them."

We continue to talk for a long while before I tell Scott I have to leave. He says he'll walk with me back to my car, thanking me for my time as always. I know action is extremely important—but talking seems to be the first step. And it's great to see Scott so involved, so alive.

We descend the steps from small group of MSVC offices, through the open, barred gate, towards the sidewalk. There is a young woman camped on a red sleeping bag on the sidewalk just to the right of the stairs. She is wearing purple sweats and a man's undershirt; no shoes, no socks. It is just her, two items of clothing, in a fetal position on her sleeping bag. She is somewhere in her twenties and sleeps peacefully with her thumb in her mouth. The moment feels surreal, but of course it's anything but that. It's real.

And it isn't just the young, female adult sucking her thumb, sleeping in a fetal position on the street with no belongings or shoes. It is the one item she possessed that really strikes me. There is a jar of mustard next to her. It is sealed, and probably still edible.

A twenty-year-old child sucking her thumb next to a jar of mustard. Where's the family? Where's the bread?

Scott and the girl convince me that short-term thinking will not bring solutions.

THE ROAD BACK

LINDA & JEFF, LDRC CAFÉ: Monday, April 6, 2009, 2:30 p.m.

THE GET GOIN' CAFÉ IS located in the back half of LDRC, behind a glass wall and next to the movie room. The wall helps to create a nice little café area, freed from the volume of the lobby, complete with two round tables and four or five chairs each. Get Goin' Café serves everything from .25 cent Slim Jims, to .50 cent coffee, to breakfast burritos, to juice boxes cheap enough to buy with quarters. Like any café, this one tailors its menu and prices to its customers.

This café, which is ideally all volunteer-staffed, is open Monday through Saturday for most of the morning and afternoon. Jeff explains that they would be open Sundays too, but they already have to use the regular staff to fill in gaps left by too few volunteers.

Linda and Jeff volunteer here every Monday and Wednesday from 1:00 to 4:00PM. Linda explains that they like working the afternoons so they have their mornings to work out. They are both very fit, and together they make for a young-looking, preppy couple defying their true ages, (both are in their late 50s).

I sit next to Jeff in the small space behind the counter, which is packed with inventory. "Jeff, from day one, it's seemed strange to me that there is a café in a homeless services center," I admit.

"That was Nancy's idea," he replies gamely. "She recognizes certain problems. There's no 7-11 store around here. There is nothing around here and these people don't have any transportation."

"Is there any concern for providing healthy snacks?" I ask.

"It's not that simple," Jeff explains. "We though about bananas, but bananas spoil. And we thought about apples, but Nancy said apples aren't good either, because many people here don't have teeth. When you have a crack addict, the first thing that goes is their teeth."

Jeff is dressed in black jeans, blue denim shirt and clean tennis shoes. He strikes an intriguing figure, behind the counter of the only homeless-catering café in Phoenix and perhaps the country.

"So tell me about yourself, Jeff."

"The best way of putting it is, 35 years in the computer industry and early retirement at 55," he begins. "So then I just, ah, imbibed in indolence and then started bouncing around and ended up volunteering here. If you can remember back to kindergarten when you had free play . . . Did you get a truck or a book and play by yourself, or did you play tag with others? If you played with others, then you need to keep working. Early retirement is not for you."

I assumed Jeff liked to play tag, but I ask, "Why are you volunteering here, Jeff?"

"Multiple reasons. I came down here, in one respect, to expand my universe. I think getting old is letting the world fall down in on you and not pushing your limits. This is outside my environment. I'm a normal, white-collar, middleclass guy. So it keeps me young. That's the selfish reason.

"The magnanimous reason," he continues, "is I want to make sure I help people and not necessarily help organizations. You know, like United Way. I don't know where my money is going, but here I donate my time and know where my money is going. And I think as you get older you find out that helping is a reward. You make that realization that giving is better than receiving. At 30, you don't get that."

Jeff gets up from his chair to help a client, and Linda takes his place. I didn't even ask them to switch, but it is perfect timing. They work very naturally together. "Linda, can you tell me a little about yourself?"

Linda thinks for a moment as she sits with perfect posture, then explains that she worked for a hospital for 25 years, ending up in charge of their Meals on Wheels program. Working with the needy and elderly on a daily basis opened her eyes to the fact that people needed her help.

She falls silent and I prod. "Why is it important to help people?"

"Because I like to help people," Linda answers. "Obviously they wanted the food [from Meals on Wheels], but more important was that I came every day, sat and listened."

She falls silent again. "Yeah, but why is that important?" I press.

"Because most of the elderly have no one to speak to, especially if they have no family, and your animals and TV don't talk back to you. It lifted their spirits for one thing, which helped with the healing process, mentally and physically."

I ask why she volunteers at LDRC now, and Linda says it's for the same reason—to help people who need it.

"If somebody wants to vent, I listen," she says. "I like to get to know their background. I find it important to learn their stories. And the really important part is to remember them when they come back, and I do that. I think that is really important to people, that someone is concerned about what is going on."

"How long have you two volunteered down here?"

Linda continues in her perfect posture, perfectly cut short blond hair and neat glasses.

"We volunteered for the first time three years ago at the Christmas party. And we have done other little projects and Jeff does the website for LDRC and works with Laura to put up the calendar, but it's been a year here at LDRC."

"Nancy sucked us in and she still calls us a lot," Jeff adds.

Linda gets up to help a client she recognizes who is pregnant. Linda asks her how she is and the two start chatting. The client explains that her pregnancy was not planned. Four guys raped her, but she is going to keep the baby. Linda, in her lavender shirt and new jeans, compassionately listens and doesn't so much as blink as the tragic story is told. I look down at Linda's feet and notice that her tennis shoes are perfectly white. Everything about this person is meticulous and perfect, yet here she is at the Get Goin' Café.

The girl orders chicken noodle soup, and as she leaves with the steaming bowl, Linda asks her if she has decided on a name for the baby. "Janna or Jella. I'm not sure yet."

Jeff takes the hot seat once again. He, too, has a neat and put-together appearance. His grey beard is closely trimmed, and there is not a hair out of place on his equally grey head.

"When we came in for the [volunteer] orientation, we were out of our element. We were uncomfortable, but not in a fearful way. We didn't feel like this was our nest, I guess."

"And we were the only ones who came back," Linda adds. "Other people signed up for stuff but they never returned."

Dawn has told me before that this is typical. Volunteers show up for orientation and then literally 90 percent of them never return. The initial experience it too overwhelming for them.

"But after two or three times here, it was just as normal as going to a shopping mall down the street," Jeff continues. "I don't want this to sound negative, but everyone gives at Christmas and Thanksgiving, but then doesn't do anything the rest of the year. And I felt that once a year wasn't enough. At a church, everyone will pay for the new organ, but no one wants to pay the electric bill."

This is great point, but I still have to ask Jeff if what he does here actually makes a difference.

"I've come to the conclusion through life experience that you never know what's going to change something," he replies. "Something I did or said twenty years ago might make a difference. Linda's smile 10 years ago might change somebody. You know the old starfish story?"

I do not, so he tells the story.

"There is a tremendous storm and it washes these starfish up on the beach, thousands of them. And a guy sees this kid throwing them back in the ocean. And he says to the kid, 'Why are you doing this? There are too many, it won't make a difference. And the kid throws another one back in and says, 'It made a difference to that one.'"

Linda and Jeff switch seats again, without my prompting.

"Linda, as you admitted, you are very conservative, and yet I see you listening to people talk about rape and drugs," I venture, "and you listen to it in such a non-judgmental way. But I can tell by looking at you that this is 'morally' very distant from who you are."

"It's not my way, but who am I to . . ." Linda's voice trails off. "And you don't even know if all the stories are true, but that's not the point. The other thing is, 99 percent of all the people down here are very polite. They share a lot more down here. Someone in line will give someone else money when they are short. And that's totally not what I expected."

Jeff adds that so much of what's going on here at LDRC is based in the circumstances of people's lives, nothing more. "You are not in control down here. Of course, there are the people who expect entitlement, [but] also those that know they have been dealt a bad hand and want to get out of it."

Linda is still in the hot seat, so I ask her the three questions first. As I explain the concept, I realize again just how small the café space is. This is their little volunteer world, barely enough room for the three of us.

What is the meaning of life?
Being the best and most moral person that you can be.

What are your thoughts about society and/or societies in general?

As of right now, I think our society is definitely headed in the wrong direction, morally, spiritually. I don't know if that is a good answer but that's how I feel.

Who are you?

Um . . . basically, a very happily married, moral, mother and grandmother. Do I need to say more than that?

Next, it's Jeff's turn.

What is the meaning of life?

Well, I'd distinguish between the meaning and the purpose. If you say the meaning of life, I'd say . . . boy that's a tough one . . . the purpose of life is to prepare for death. Death is inevitable and most people avoid even talking about it and you've got to become unafraid of it so that when you come to death's door, you are not afraid. And that includes religion. It includes family. It includes everything. I think if you are afraid of it, then it screws up the rest of your life. If you are focused on that then you can't do anything else. But the meaning of life . . . I'm not quite sure . . . I think it's just to do a good job and be happy. Do the best you can and be happy about it.

What are your thoughts about society and/or societies in general?

I think they work pretty well, but need to be improved. 'Cause I'm sort of a believer in the bell curve, and you always have that 10 percent you have to deal with.

Who are you?

A person on a journey trying to figure out what the right thing to do is. And this [volunteering at LDRC] goes with that . . . I believe it's the journey, not the destination, that's important.

Linda and Jeff make me consider the power of volunteering.

EXPERIENCE

JESSICA, LDRC: Tuesday, April 14, 2009, 3 p.m.

A N OTHER WEEK HAS PASSED. "So it's been a month since we talked in an official capacity," I say to start off this week. "Is there anything you want to talk about?"

"The word 'detachment' has been very relevant the past couple days," Jessica begins. "To just not become so attached to the little things, because I could get upset about the water pipe breaking, or who is in charge of the fundraiser. But I can't fix everything, and I really have to keep that in the forefront of my mind . . . there are things that need improvement. There are always going to be things that are going to need improvement, fixing."

I let Jessica do most of the talking again today. Ever since the shooting incident, she's become the talker between the two of us in these weekly meetings.

"I'm not as excited as I used to be, because everything was brand new, and we were doing things that seemed so revolutionary," Jessica says. "Now, we have open mic poetry events every other week, and we have barbeques once a month, and we have volunteers falling in love with us, coming out of the woodwork, transformations happening and healings happening. So I'm not as shocked by the wonderful things. They are just routine. They are happening all the time.

"Things are working better than they used to be," she concludes, laughing. "Amazing things are normal here, whereas amazing things used to be huge accomplishments that had never happened before."

"I think part of my being overwhelmed is that, now I have amazing staff in charge of these amazing things, and I can't possibly keep up. So things happen and I don't even know about them and that makes me uneasy, because I feel like I'm supposed to know about everything. And the detachment, what I'm realizing is that not only do I not need to fix every detail, but that I don't need to know about every single thing."

As an example, Jessica tells me about a meeting that just took place with two Muslims in the staff lounge. They are planning an interfaith event as a response to 9/11, something that's being planned in 25 cities across the country. This is a cause that Jessica has championed for years, apparently, yet when the meeting finally happened, she didn't even know about it until this morning. Instead, Laura had taken care of everything, and Jessica says she's actually relieved to let someone else take charge of the project.

"So, are you telling me that you have set up things that are self-sustaining within the organization now?" I clarify.

"Gosh, that's what it sounds like."

"Are you telling me that you have directed activities that are now, because of the staff you have selected, running on their own now?"

"Pretty much."

"Kind of sounds like you're directing."

Jessica smiles, then laughs.

"What have you learned in the past month by going through your depression?" I take great personal interest in this question because I feel like Jessica and I have been mirroring each other as of late in our personal challenges. I wonder if our revelations from those challenges will be similar.

"I think for the most part what I've learned [is] just how important it is to take care of myself and to ask for help," Jessica says. "I just need to be very open about what's best for me and what's best for the organization. And I know directors of nonprofits should not stay there forever. Just like you say about your book, not missing the forest for the trees. There needs to be fresh eyes and fresh minds to keep things alive.

"So I just want to make sure that I'm never blind to stuff," she continues. "So whether that's finding a way to do that here or if it's time to find a new director. And I've learned that it's OK to be human and to take time off and to really seriously demand that my staff do that, too."

"So how do you feel now about the shooting?"

She takes a long pause. "I've just been so disheartened." She pauses again. "Disheartened I think is the best word.

"And for some reason, I guess, as we become more organized and more of a structured organization, my expectations have changed. There should be someone in charge of this and that, and it should be clear. And then [Dawn] just reminded me that we're not like that [at LDRC], and that's a great thing. But it's like a fight between the director and the creative human that is OK with chaos, creative chaos."

"Scott once told me, 'You can organize the life out of an organism,'" I offer.

The director just smiles and nods.

Jessica makes me consider that there are amazing things going on all around us, all the time.

TERRY, LDRC, MSVA: Tuesday, April 14, 2009, 4:30 p.m.

Terry Araman is the Resource Developer and Client Coordinator for LDRC. And as far as I can surmise, he is also unofficially in charge of the Madison Street Veterans Association.

Terry explains he'd worked for Motorola for about 20 years before leaving two and a half years ago, taking a "buyout package" in exchange for his own time and freedom.

"I'm used to being really busy and having a large workload and a lot of responsibility, so when I did that I realized that I was going to have to have something else to do," he says.

Hobbies like hiking didn't fill the void, so when Terry saw a newspaper ad for volunteers at LDRC, he took the challenge and volunteered in the mail room for six months. Slowly, volunteer became part-time work became a full-time position as front desk client coordinator. Like many people involved with LDRC, Terry slowly but surely became enveloped in the cause.

"It's a very human place, and I also felt like the staff, the people I worked with at LDRC [and] the other service providers were very dedicated," Terry explains. "I mean, they really had the passion for helping people and I was incredibly impressed by that and I really felt honored to be part of it. And I could see good things happening for people here that otherwise would be sort of tossed aside by society. And I came out of the highest ranks—or fairly high ranks—of the corporate world. I was working with CEOs and CIOs and COOs and all of those kinds of people. So to go from that to working with street people was quite interesting. I was just really drawn to the whole thing."

"And the other things was I realized that something was happening here that was different than other places I had been where they had services and shelters for homeless people," he continues. "And I was sort of amazed by that. And I am just one of those people when I do something I throw myself into it whole-heartedly."

Terry says his knack for communicating with people let him "blend into the whatever" of HSC's special world.

"The other thing that amazed me about the people here on this campus, even though socially they are kinda crude and rough on the surface, it's not much different from what you find in the corporate world or that I've found anywhere else. The same human issues, interactions, way of dealing with people, the politics . . . it's not that different. That fascinates me—there are commonalities about human beings regardless of where they are in the social strata, where they are economically, where they are geographically, what culture they come from.

"To me, it's not so much an issue of homelessness. One of the things I say to people is if I had to make a choice between having a community or having a roof over my head, I would take the community. And I think that is one of the fallacies about this thing is we try and get people into housing and they are sitting in these nondescript apartment buildings somewhere by themselves and surrounded by these four walls. And they feel lonely, they feel cut off, they feel depressed. They've lost their community, their social grouping, their support systems. And many times they end up right back there on the streets. So somehow or other, what I think we need to be doing is promoting more of a sense of community."

Terry hammers this last point home, saying that when staff talks about the evolution of HSC, a big part of the discussion is how much they should focus on putting a roof over people's heads, and how much they should focus on creating a supporting community that helps get the homeless feeling less isolated and disconnected. The two seem completely related to me, but then I remember my conversation with David Bridge at CASS, who hinted that making the campus too comfortable might encourage the condition of homelessness itself.

I voice this to Terry, who recognizes the concern. But his views are different: "So what if people are drawn here and they like being here? There is an element of people who come here and just want to veg out, but it's a small minority . . . what would happen is those people who were just hangers-on, who are just looking for a place to sort of sit and stare at the wall, the energy would just move them out anyway. It wouldn't be comfortable for them after a while, if you have all these vital, aware, energetic people trying to create something positive for people. So I don't think it's something we really need to worry about, but I know that's the fear."

Creating energy is a big reason why Terry says MSVA was formed. Veterans were an unrecognized talent pool in the community, a group that could thrive when given direction, but that rebelled against being micromanaged. Plus more veterans per capita are homeless than non-veterans. The national rate of homelessness is 21 homeless people per 10,000 people in the general population. The rate for veterans is 31 homeless veterans per 10,000 veterans in the general population.

"One of the reasons I got involved in Madison Street Veterans Association is because it's a grassroots organization, a peer-to-peer organization," Terry says. "It's a model we need to start promoting more of. I think a lot of the old models for how to do things, even in the nonprofit sector, aren't working or they aren't working well enough. We need to try new things."

As a Vietnam vet from a poor family, Terry says he felt especially drawn to MSVA's cause. He can relate to the vets on campus; he knows what they've experience, and sort of organization they might need to move on.

"For instance, one of the members of Madison Street Veterans Association is Ross [the veteran in a wheelchair I interviewed some time ago]. And he barely spoke. I sort of knew this guy for months before he even spoke to anybody. He has lots of issues from his veteran's status, probably PTSD and so forth, other things and substance abuse in the background. His day was typically spent sitting in the same clothing, the same jacket that he never took off." I remember the camo jacket well; I also remember the silent need for belonging. "He would sit in the LDRC for hours and just stare, with nothing to do."

Terry says that the peer-to-peer support of MSVA has opened Ross up. He's engaging in intelligent conversation at meetings. He's learning computer skills. He's proud of being in the veteran's organization.

"It's almost like a whole different person," Terry says. "Now, if we had punched him into this program where someone sat him down and told him what to do and when to do it, I don't think it would have served him at all—it definitely hasn't so far. I don't think we would have the Ross we know today if that had happened. So this is a different way of approaching homelessness, poverty and those kinds of things, the kind of lifestyle we have around."

Terry gets frustrated when talking about Arizona, and the lack of support he feels programs like MSVA can get from this state. It's not just a problem of government to him; Terry describes Arizona citizens as "passive" and unwilling to confront society's problems.

"It brings up a lot of anger. I mean, I have a lot of anger." He says, visibly upset now, but without raising his voice or showing aggression. It's a sad, frustrated anger.

"So I haven't exactly taken any anger management class, but I need to find out how to funnel that anger into something constructive," Terry continues. "Just getting angry, you know, bitching and moaning, doesn't do anything. So whatever I do, I need to be a constructive part of something that's effective. One thing I learned from working 20 years in high tech manufacturing is it's very results-oriented, results-driven. The things you are doing are either effective or not effective. For me, that's a good gauge. I tend to look at everything thing from that standpoint. MSVA is not an effort just to make you feel good or warm and fuzzy."

"But it sounds like it is in some way a therapy for you?" I question.

"Well, I don't think I can tie it up for you all that neatly, but it is something that I can feel that I can take some sort of constructive action, rather than just being sad and frustrated and angry."

Terry adds, "The other thing that goes through my mind now that I'm getting older [Terry was 61 years old] and a lot of people that are in my age group have just gone to sleep." The Vietnam vet sighs audibly. "I don't understand it. And I'm certainly not ready to go to sleep. They create these little worlds for themselves. They sort of spin around in a little bit of family and a little bit of retirement activities and every now and then again they go on a cruise and get excited about that, but they are just not really participating in the civic whatever you want to call it. And they're not helping. I'm sort of panicked that I might die, without having done enough to have helped this mess we are in, even if I live 20 or 30 years longer. I watch people and I'm sort of like, 'What are you doing? Is this OK with you? Is this what you intended to do?' And so I decided to become a little different than a lot of people in my age group. But then, I tend to be really healthy too. I always had really good health. And a lot of people in my age group tend to be sort of falling apart. I haven't had that problem."

We talk about CASS budget frustrations, about the loose-but-productive work environment that Jessica and Dawn have made blossom at LDRC. The sort of things everyone here wants and needs to talk about. Eventually, the conversation naturally ends. It's time to end another surprising and enlightening interview.

What is the meaning of life?

Life doesn't have to have a meaning; life just simply is. I don't think it's a valid question. I mean when you say, 'what is the meaning of life,' it's like there's something outside or separate from life that makes it worthwhile and I don't see it that way. It just simply is. It's to be experienced with the grace and ability you can experience it [with].

What are your thoughts about society and/or societies in general?

The thing that has really impressed me most in the past few years, the conclusion I've come to, is that everybody needs some sense of community. And I see less and less of that happening for more and more people. I think that's something we need to focus on more, creating that sense of community that people can move in and out of. That gives them a foundation, a sense of security, and a sense of that belonging. I think that there is a huge lack there.

Who are you?

Who am I? I think I'm a person who is still in the process of evolving. I think that life can be very difficult, but it's also incredibly interesting. It's so interesting! I have a lot of curiosity about things. I have had a very rich experience. I have experienced a lot of it, but I am by no means, by no means do I feel like I'm done yet. I don't know if that really says who I am. But I try and contribute in a positive sense to whomever I meet and whatever I'm doing.

Terry convinces me of the utter necessity of community.

SCOTT, CLIENT FOLLOW-UP: Monday, April 20, 2009, 1:00 p.m.

I wait in one of the MSVA offices. It is difficult talking to Scott because he is so busy with projects. People filter in and out of the office, setting up computers and doing other busy things I'm unaware of.

My interest today is to see if Scott has had further personal insights. He seems to have changed a lot in the past few months especially considering what a brief period of time a few months is in the life of a 54-year-old man. And it seems to help Scott (and others here) when I talk with them in such a way that they hear themselves.

"Up until the last few months, I've lived my life without taking personal responsibility for my actions on a consistent basis," Scott says. "There have been times when I did, but the majority of time I did not. And when I did [take responsibility], those situations were externally influenced or controlled. For example, when I was married there were certain things I could and could not do. I could not go out and get drunk any time I wanted. The internal controls I had at those times were either faith-based, or I had a position as a counselor in a recovery program, or I lived with family members. But there has never been a time—until now—that there has been a deep abiding personal sense [of responsibility]. I don't know what depth it really has, but I do know today I am exercising my personal responsibilities and that motivation is coming from a different internal sense of what I need to do, rather than being forced to do it."

Scott goes on to say he now believes people need that sense of personal responsibility to fulfill their dreams. It's a process: first personal responsibility, then a new vision of the world and finally, action.

"The other thing I'm coming to see is how important and valuable relationships are," he adds. "By coming to understand that, I can look back in my past. I had not, for whatever reasons, had many significant relationships in the past."

He's learned this through his involvement at MSVA. It's also helped Scott get over his fear of starting things that he may not be able to finish. His own sense of responsibility forces Scott "to the legwork" for his projects. He says, "The powers that be, or whatever you want to call it, is responsible for the results."

We talk for much longer about the MSVA and its effect on this man's life. But it's this point about responsibility and results that really sticks with me. In a way, I feel like Scott has helped me begin to connect all my other interviews together.

Scott makes realize that responsibility is about plugging in—not only to others—but to ourselves.

ARTHUR, CLIENT FOLLOW-UP:
Monday, April 20, 2009, 2:00 p.m.

Arthur tells me his spirits are better, but his finances are not. I ask him if he is looking for work or waiting for benefits. He tells me he doesn't think he is eligible for any benefits and isn't interested in receiving any.

As he sits with me, dressed in his clean pressed jeans and t-shirt, he explains to me that he isn't currently looking for work either. And he knows others won't understand. Arthur says, "My head follows my heart, not the other way around. I don't do anything until Mother calls my heart to move. I try and think of God as my Mother and my Father."

Arthur feels he is not just here to get back into mainstream society. He is not just here to learn to make money again and get shelter. He believes he is here to grow spiritually. He is not afraid of hardship.

There is always that ever-present silent intensity to Arthur. I often see him on campus meditating, unwavering, for hours despite the distractions. And you can tell there is no fear in him—none! He is literally willing to die for his beliefs.

"I'm pretty peaceful today," he says melodiously. "My mind is at peace. To me, happiness begins with peace of mind. Peace of mind begets real happiness."

Arthur's speech is punctuated with pauses, but I realize that he is not really pausing to think. He takes his time with speaking. He doesn't rush. He breathes between each sentence. "Learning how to be at peace with the world is the goal."

"What do you mean, 'to be at peace with the world?'"

"Being at peace with the world means learning how to ah, gosh, to have your inner peace in the midst of chaos," Arthur replies as his steely intensity returns. "The world is full of chaos. We have to learn how to be at peace. We have to learn to fight against that chaos in peace. We have to learn how to fight that chaos in peace. There's no bowing. There will always be a conflict between God and the world. They will never unite. You are either of the world or you are of God. That's it! There is no such thing as combining the two. They cannot combine. Light and darkness can never combine. There is no such thing. There will always be that distinction between the two. They are opposites. There is light, which is God and then there is darkness, which is the world. They cannot combine. They can never combine. There will always be that distinction."

"Didn't God create the world?" I wonder aloud.

"Yes. It doesn't matter though. Everything is spirit. Even the devil. The devil is also spirit."

"So you believe in the existence of the devil?"

I love talking with Arthur. These are questions that most people won't give you an answer to, let alone a passionate, unique, soul-felt one.

"I believe in the existence of positive and negative forces! And the devil being the negative force. Yes there is evil. And let's put it this way, selfishness is the beginning of evil. The ego is the creation of evil."

"What if negativity is just a lack of positivity?" I'm baiting him and I don't know why.

"Well it is. And positivity is a lack of negativity. It works both ways."

"I guess Arthur, what I'm questioning is if some people are just lacking knowledge of God and are not actually part of evil?"

Arthur smiles patiently and looks at me compassionately (though still intense). "Light is nearer to God than darkness. OK? Light is more true than darkness. How about that? Nevertheless, in reality, both don't exist. Because both are relative terms, both are relative terms. But this is when we are speaking on an absolute level. Most people don't understand that."

I can't argue with this. I don't agree, but our conversation has become, as they often do, so esoteric, so philosophical that we are pushing the boundaries of words themselves. I love this about Arthur. He is unshakable and quite brilliant. And perhaps most impressive, he doesn't just sit around and meditate all day. He is often volunteering for some church, working long hours.

"What's your dream, Arthur?"

"My dream? My dream is to make a lot of money for the good of others. That is my highest dream. That has been put into me. Because, for me, I don't care for it," Arthur says, and I can't help but believe him. "I have that desire in me for a reason. And it's not mine. Because before I woke up, I didn't have it. It has been put into me. I mean, I always desired to have money, like becoming a millionaire or something. But when I woke up, a whole different attitude regarding that came into me—that with God, I should be able to become a billionaire. Why settle for a million? If that is what He wills, if that is what He desires for me."

I'm tempted to delve into another philosophical fencing match, but think better of it and move on with another probing question. "What's your greatest fear?"

"My greatest fear? That I'm not doing the will of the Lord."

"Why is that your greatest fear?"

"Because I love the Lord. I love the Lord and I don't want to displease him." Arthur looks sad even contemplating this. "I love the Lord with all my heart. If my heart is not true, if I don't please Him, then my life has come to naught."

Our conversation continues on for some time like this, and I think it's important to note that Arthur doesn't preach. I have never seen him discuss these ideas with anyone else. He's much more interested in living what he believes than convincing others of it. I just tend to egg him on a bit. I ask for these conversations.

Arthur makes me think long and hard about how our spiritual beliefs cause us to either work with the world or battle against it. For me, I'm ready to work with it. I'm just not sure how.

RUNNING DEER, CLIENT FOLLOW-UP:
Monday, April 20, 2009 3 p.m.

"So what's going on with you, Running Deer?" After reading his autobiography, I'm more concerned about him than ever.

"Where, I'm at right now is, I'm getting real frustrated." Running Deer looks quite exasperated. "It seems like all of these outfits that claim they are out here to help me . . . buddy, they give me one excuse after another why they can't help me. It's either my charges, my disability, I don't fit in their criteria . . . it's like they tell me not to be negative, but all I get from all these so-called 'helpful' people is a negative reaction.

"I'm being kicked out of CASS because of my alleged crimes back in '92." Running Deer hasn't committed a crime in 17 years. Probations for sex offenders are very often for life. "I only get three months here, then I'm back on the streets which then I'm pretty much guaranteed to go back to jail."

He clarifies that he will be arrested for vagrancy on the streets, and after several arrests, he will be sent to jail for a long time due to his prior record. Sex offenders have few legal options for places to live—and of course aren't supposed to be wandering the streets either.

"I get the belief more and more each day that I'm not considered worthy enough to be treated like a human in this country," he concludes, devastated. "Everybody is very quick with wanting to help me quit drugs, but they don't want to help me with housing; they don't want to help me out with a job; they don't want to help me out with nothing."

Running Deer tried to get into vocational rehab but will not be accepted until his back injury is healed. There is a sort of inbred waiting to social services. Each one is linked to another and you can't work on two links at a time. A social worker down here told me that because of this waiting and running around, "Homelessness is a full-time job."

"It's getting real frustrating because my back's against the wall. Like I said I got to the 15th of next month and if I don't find work I'm done for."

"I know it's bad, really bad, but what do you mean you are 'done for'?" I ask.

"These kind of charges will get me killed [in prison]," Running Deer says. "You see, when somebody in my situation goes into jail, they put you in the general population. And trust me, when you first hit any yard, in any prison, in any state, one thing you have to do is walk on that yard with your paperwork, otherwise you are just going to get your ass beat and killed anyway. Prison is a whole different atmosphere. Anybody coming into the yard, they want to know your whole criminal history, because if you've got any snitch charges or sex offenses, you're dead. You go in there on a murder beef or car theft or burglary or assault and you say I was wrongfully convicted and everybody says, 'I can see that, courts always screw up.' But you go in there with a sex offense or snitch offense and you will get killed."

In Arizona prisons they usually keep all the sex offenders together and out of the general population but that is not true if they return on a different charge.

"Can't they give you fake papers for your protection?"

"It doesn't matter if they do or not. Somebody in there will know me and know my past. When I was in previously it was in another state and I knew a lot of people, so it was safer. Here I don't.

"In prison an inmate killing another inmate is no big thing to the legal system. It's just another problem weeded out. And you learn to keep your mouth shut no matter what you see or you are going to be the next mark."

This conversation is too much; I decide to switch gears and ask Running Deer what his dream is.

"My dream is to get into something that is going to help me with some income coming in," he answers. "I want my own place where I can relax a bit, I can enjoy, I can enjoy my evenings. I can eat what I want to eat that's going to be more healthy for me.

"My dream is where I can meet my own obligations.

"My dream is to get myself in a situation where I ain't got to sweat where my next meal is coming from; where my next bed is going to be. I've been in these clothes for over a week now. I haven't been able to clean up because I ain't got no other clothes. And it's like, it's getting real frustrating . . ."

I've noticed or sensed with Running Deer and many of the people I've interviewed an underlying tone that there is something deeply wrong with them, a metaphorical original sin—something intrinsic. This is different that someone feeling the pain and disappointment that they have made mistakes. It is instead the pain and disappointment that they *are* a mistake.

So I just ask him, "Do you think there's something wrong with you?"

"I always had people tell me that I would never amount to shit, that I was worthless. But as I get older in life and deal with all this crap, the more I start believing it." Running Deer starts choking up. "This is the reason

I always try to show that they are wrong, but I do start believing that something is wrong with me. What it is, I don't know, because I don't see what it is . . . I feel like I'm going to be punished for it the rest of my life. I'm in here talking to people. I'm out there trying to find work. I'm trying to make every effort I can. But it seems like everywhere I go I'm having doors shut in my face. I'm running out of options and . . ." he almost breaks down at this point, ". . . I don't know what to do."

Running Deer makes think that society has to forgive or it creates an unbearable burden for itself.

BILL, CASS, MSVA: Tuesday, April 21, 2009 12 p.m.

Bill Black is a CASS case manager and MSVA volunteer. He is a large man in the teddy bear sense. He has a bushy salt and pepper beard, and a thick head of crazy-wild hair. He is dressed in a white cotton shirt, khaki pants and black shoes. Around his neck is a bohemian-style leather necklace. He looks like a 225-pound Ewok—which in his case is a compliment.

Before we start, I explain the book's concept to him. Bill asks for details about me. He wants to know about my childhood, my heroes, my motivations and loves.

I find myself summing up my entire life for him in about 15 minutes, commenting on my almost perfect childhood in which I was spoiled, not so much materially but never having to face any real struggles or lacks. At the end, he has a very good grasp of what makes me tick. It's fun to be on the other end for a change and I'm reminded how therapeutic it is to just talk.

Bill comments that we are both only children and asks, knowingly, if the world revolves around me.

"Well, of course," I admit.

He lets out a great big long laugh and then as if advising me on this project, "You realize what you've been doing may or may not be successful. Your work may not have any results or it may have results long after you are dead. You may see it; you may not. But you do it because of the rightness of it, not meaning the moralness, [but] because it is the right thing to do."

This really strikes me because maybe that's what my dad meant when he said, "it's the right thing to do." So many things seem to connect here and every moment is serendipitous in one way or another.

"So, you know about me now, Bill. What about you?"

"Often, what I do here is trying to work with people, to stand in the tension between the world as it is and the world as it should be. I didn't make that up. I'm stealing that from others but when something is good, I use it," Bill says, laughing at himself.

I ask him what he would like readers of a book about homelessness to know.

"There's some cynical side to me and some romantic side to me. Part of me thinking of that time that Lincoln met the author who wrote *Uncle Tom's Cabin*. The Civil War was going on and he met her for the first time and said, so you are the little woman that started this big war. If a book can influence a nation, much like *Silent Spring* awoke a generation to the environment, much like *The Grapes of Wrath* awoke a generation to the poverty of the Dust Bowl, then maybe books can reach out and change life. I like to think they can."

"So do I." Writing them sure does.

"On the other hand, the other side of me says there is cheap grace. You know. Cheap grace: Take the grace you can get."

Bill is talking about the social sciences, and the extent to which they can help end social problems. But as he keeps talking, I realize the term "grace" could easily be applied to his own life.

"There was a complication at birth, and this sounds melodramatic, but the doctor asked [my mother] if she had to make a choice, save her or the child? And she said, 'Save the child!' And it was a miracle that she didn't die." However, Bill says, his mother and 48-year-old father were never able to have children again, spoiling him instead as best they could.

"I went to both parochial and Catholic schools depending on, well, depending on how I wanted to manipulate my parents," he explains. "After I went to public school, one of the girls I liked transferred to Saint Mary's, sophomore year. And I liked her, so I convinced my parents that . . . it's really hard to say this with a straight face: 'You know mom, I'm realizing that my religion is important to me and I really miss going to a religious school.' 'Well, then you've got to go to St. Mary's now.' But it wasn't that. I wanted to be near Diana, man!" Bill lets out a full body laugh as he finishes the story.

"I have a theory about only children—and this isn't necessarily for the book, I just offer it to you, that we are very good at splitting ourselves because we put up a front to the dominant parents. You get a lot of attention. You put up a face to deal with that and you hide behind that to get privacy and be your authentic self, because you want some privacy and not just the person they want you to be. You don't have siblings to take the pressure off. And that split is for survival for the child. However, I think once you learn to split like that at a very early age, comes the dark side of that. You get really good at manipulating and lying. You get really good at being a people-pleasing person, because you know how to do it."

"It can keep you from having authentic relationships," Bill adds, voice now solemn. "It can keep you from having the fulfillment of true intimacy . . . it's not that you're a bad person but the world doesn't really revolve around you."

True, this theory doesn't have anything to do with understanding CASS, but I just discovered where my personal sense of homelessness comes from. That split Bill described has kept part of me secret and always alone. This conversation hits a little too close to home, and reminds me that I still need to learn some things about myself before I can come close to understanding 'society.'

It's ironic. This place, or this journey, or these people, have started to shift my liabilities to strengths.

Bill continues, "I went to college and didn't do well. Not that I wasn't smart; I was just busy doing other things. And got married young. I was married at 21." He pauses and sighs. "I was a very bad husband. I didn't take it seriously. I was really too selfish and I didn't have the skills to cope with it."

Whatever wrongs Bill has committed in the past, at least he is honest about them and has learned from his mistakes. He also takes his relative success now with a grain of salt.

"You know, I am basically a talent scout," Bill says of his position at MSVA. "I'm looking for people I can work with. I am basically looking for people I can work with who have anger."

Bill explains that "anger," like the word "angst," comes from the Old Norse word *angr*, meaning a sense of loss for what was or could have been.

"It's not hatred, and it's not madness, but anger, prophetic anger," he says. "And when I look around at poverty or injustice, what I'm looking at is why. What broke and what happened?"

Bill wishes his father, who helped unionize the Phoenix police and paid the price by being frozen at the rank of sergeant, could see the work he's doing now. Like his father, Bill's profession takes hope, faith and courage.

"If I were to die tonight, I think MSVA would continue," he says. "Would it continue exactly the way it would if I were to assist it? No. But it will continue. Something has been begun. There's been fire lit in a lot of people I've been working with. And I don't want to say I lit the fire. I'm a carrier of that flame. People lit my fire and I'm lighting other fires."

I haven't prompted Bill since the beginning and have already left out many interesting detours. He thanks me for allowing the conversation to flow freely as he returns the conversation to his past, and how far he's come ethically since then.

"I believe in redemption," he begins. "My redemption is service to the poor. When I was in real estate, I didn't care how I made my money. We basically worked with companies working in the rust belt to come out here because of cheap labor. And I never questioned it. As far as I was concerned, the poor deserved their lot. That was my attitude. I'm going to make this commission. We are going to help them relocate here and close down 500 jobs in Ohio. And they will come out here to Casa Grande at half the labor costs. Let's do the deal. Tear down a little ma and pa, tear down a little building that's been there for 40 years with little ma and pa tenants in it, put in corporate franchises. Let's do the deal."

Bill pauses for what feels like a full minute before continuing.

"That changed. That changed for me as I formed relationships with people who I really loved and who really got the short end of the stick. And I began to really rediscover personally what it was like to get screwed, or worse, what it was like to have people you love get screwed. "That's when I became more radicalized," Bill says. "It was partially a spiritual journey as well. I think they went hand in hand."

In this journey, Bill says he has seen firsthand the consequences of "deep poverty," and now believes that everyone must recognize where institutions have failed before leaders can emerge to fix the situation.

"When you really get in touch with that in your life, you have to act," he says. "And I think a homeless shelter can be a school where you teach other people to lead people out of poverty."

Bill describes his vision for MSVA. "Twenty other men here can become leaders who will be sensitive to the suffering of others because they have experienced it." Pondering for a minute, he continues, "But how to build a platform from which they can act, so that they can seed their communities with leaders?" He looks at me as my hands catch up on the keyboard. "And that's just the beginning," Bill concludes after talking for two hours while belly-laughing through both joy and pain.

What is the meaning of life?

42. [He's quoting from The Hitchhiker's Guide to the Galaxy, *in which author Douglas Adams uses the number 42 to be the answer to this kind of a question.] I'm going to quote someone else. "The exercise of vital powers along lines of excellence in a life affording them scope."* [often attributed to Aristotle]. *Or 42. I don't know.*

What are your thoughts about society and/or societies in general?

Well, we are social animals. We have a dualistic nature. One of the things I learned in philosophy and understanding into the duality of our public and private selves is we are social and individualist. Suspension bridges are held up not by balance. They are held up by tension, and that is the only way to bridge the gap. You have to stay in that tension long enough for the surprise. The tension is the act of creating. Community is an abstraction. You can't get your hands around it. So society occurs in named institutions. Every scientist knows you don't just deal with the essence of an idea. It has a reality. It's institutions that matter, that really have staying power. I'm not saying it doesn't have sometimes consequences, but that's not the level I'm working on. Institutions are the way.

Who are you?

"I am Dionysus, the son of Zeus, come back to Thebes, this land where I was born. My mother was Cadmus' daughter, Semele by name, midwived by fire, delivered by the lightning's blast. And here I stand, a god incognito, disguised as man."

That's the opening lines of The Bacchae. *I love that. I think all of us are Dionysus. See Dionysus was half god, half man. It's the proto Christ. You are both animal and spirit. I'm not a scholar; that's my disclaimer, but we are all that, we are both divine and dust.*

Bill makes me realize that living our philosophies is the right thing to do.

FATHER ERIC, ANDRÉ HOUSE: Tuesday, April 21, 2:00 p.m.

I walk across the street to the warehouse-like building that is André House. I have been here once before—on my immersion, to eat dinner after my long walk to the Human Services Campus.

When I meet with Father Eric, Director of André House, he is running the showers. They have three and offer them to clients on a first come, first serve basis. Soap and other standard amenities are provided. Father Eric asks someone else if they can take over monitoring the showers for him while we chat.

"One of the people who was a founder for Helping Homeless in South Bend said we have to stop talking about the poor," he begins in a remarkably soft, quiet voice. "That's why we don't call the people here clients: They are our guests. That's the foundation of who we are as a Catholic place. We believe we are all created in God's image and likeness."

Everybody has human dignity, Father Eric says, and their mission is to recognize that and treat every person like every other person. I ask Father Eric how long André House has been around, and he says it began almost 25 years ago as a small flophouse elsewhere in central Phoenix. Quickly, the mission realized they needed to feed their guests as well.

Father Eric explains that he had arrived on the scene about one year ago. It is common for the Congregation of the Holy Cross (founders of Notre Dame) to rotate persons through locations.

Father Eric admits that originally, "I was in denial of my vocation," after earning college degrees in chemistry and theology. He resisted becoming a priest for some time, which surprises me because now he looks the prototypical campus priest: Birkenstocks, Bermuda shorts, a white t-shirt, and a large cross hanging around his neck.

"The idea that I should be a priest was in the back of my mind, but I didn't want to do it," Father Eric explains. "And what made me enter the seminary was, I had been thinking about priesthood for about eight years and I found out that less than half the guys who went into the seminary become priests. So if less than half the guys become priests, the odds were in my favor." He flashes a little smile to acknowledge the joke. All of Father Eric's gestures are small, quiet and unobtrusive.

"Why didn't you want to become a priest?" I ask.

"My vision of my life was getting married, having some children, and working in a chemistry lab," he replies. "I didn't see getting married in the priesthood being an option—It's not. And I didn't see working in a chemistry lab as a priest. Again, that's rare."

He finishes and sits quietly.

"So what happened in seminary, then?" I have to prod.

"Well the first year in seminary as a candidate you're just getting to know the place, and learning from prayer and spiritual life. At the end of that first year, I realized that I kinda liked it. I went on to the second year, [which] is semi monastic, and I started falling in love with God, per se. And thought, maybe this is what God wants me to do. At the end of the second year, you make temporary vows of poverty, celibacy and obedience."

"Temporary?"

"Yeah, church law says it has to be temporary for at least three years until you make it forever. It's kind of like a three year engagement," Father Eric answers, flashing another brief smile.

During those three years, Father Eric worked on his masters of divinity, but took a break to serve overseas in East Africa for over a year before finishing the program. The religious calling felt right because of the mission he now serves in life.

"We are educators in faith with a preferential option for the poor," Father Eric explains. "We tend to have schools and then things flourish around the schools. We offer scholarships to people so that the poor can come to the school. The school does outreach to the community. We are educators—what does our faith mean and how to put it into practice?"

"So tell me about this place. What would you want a reader of this book to know about André House or the Human Services Campus?"

In response, he explains that though they share a mission, the two entities are very separate. HSC invited André House on to campus, even setting aside space for them, Father Eric says, but "philosophical differences" kept the mission from accepting the offer.

"We don't have security guards over here," Father Eric says. "Most of our security is taken care of by our guests. We try and get to know the people who are around—you build that relationship as we take care of each other. You shouldn't have to come to a sense where you need to put a gun on campus."

"Are there other differences?"

The security guard issue was "one of the biggest" differences. Father Eric says André House also feared losing autonomy or a sense of its own unique mission when it entered the HSC. Also, the mission does not take government money while CASS and other agencies do.

Father Eric says André House has also been accused in the past by other agencies of "coddling people and enabling people." This is because André House does not screen anyone before offering showers, shelter or meals.

If you study the history of homelessness in America, this has been the central social argument for over a century. Should aid be given to all, or only to those who are deemed worthy? How do we determine the worthy? In the past, homeless persons had to perform work to prove they were worthy of being fed and sheltered. Ironically, the work was often useless in nature (think rock-breaking).

"And that's an anathema to us," Father Eric contends. "Who deserves this? Are you a human being? Yes, then OK. You deserve to get a shot. If someone does something on our property, if somebody pulls a knife in our parking lot, they are going to be banned from our services for six months. But I'm not going to say that you might have been tripped up last week by something else that has nothing to do with us, so therefore you can't use our services."

I verify that he means that they don't want to have to deny services to an individual who has an infraction at another agency, but not with André House. This differs from HSC policy, where an infraction at one agency can lead to dismissal from the entire campus.

"And I can see the argument," Father Eric says, "but I would also say a lot of the problem comes from desperation, so if you further put someone in a position of desperation you are also causing the problem. It is the process of dehumanization that leads to violence. And whether that violence is physical or emotional or spiritual, violence is violence and we don't want that."

This conversation makes me think of the recent shooting. I ask Father Eric if he thinks the campus culture had something to do with the violence.

"Well, mental illness definitely had a big factor in that one," he replies. "Whether that was exacerbated by culture, I can't say. I can say we have not had any stabbings or shootings on our property in 25 years. I'm not aware of any, [and] definitely no fatalities. I've been here since July, and we've had three, maybe four fights."

To me, that sounds like a pretty low number for a place that serves 650 to 750 meals a night.

Changing the subject, Father Eric explains that they serve more meals toward the end of a given month, when Social Security checks and other welfare payments have run out.

"If you say you're in need, then you are," Father Eric emphasizes. Some André House guests have jobs and housing, but not enough left over to put food on the table, especially by the end of the month.

It occurs to me (for the first time) that people doing drugs might not be the only reason for the lower service numbers across campus at the beginning of each month. Many probably just find better—but temporary—living arrangements.

Next, I have to ask the priest: "Where do you get these volunteers? I have never seen 13 people so happy to serve me as the night I ate here." He laughs and I continue, "If anything would make me come back to the church, it might be those volunteers' attitudes that night. Are they all Catholics?"

"A lot are Catholics, but not all," Father Eric answers. "Every other Monday, there is an Episcopalian group that comes. We need about 25 volunteers every night to serve the meal." That's over 9,000 volunteers in all the nights in a year."

The seven André House staff members rotate each night, one of them in charge of the kitchen. All food is bought from St. Mary's Food Bank. André House pays about $12,000 a week, and St. Mary's "roughly matches that," Father Eric says. I can't help but think that in total, they are spending and or receiving over a million dollars a year to provide roughly a quarter of a million meals a year.

It isn't the cost, which seems quite reasonable. It is just the sheer volume of it all. Father Eric, however, acts nonplussed about the endeavor as he quotes from the Bible.

"What we do here is right from Mathew 25: 'When I was hungry, you gave me food. When I was thirsty, you gave me drink. When I was naked, you clothed me. When I was in prison you visited me.'" After all, the André House does not just feed people. They provide showers, lockers, clothing provision and laundry services.

"But why the great attitudes with the volunteers?" I still have to ask.

"The volunteers have built up over 25 years," Father Eric replies. "There's a culture. Relationships have built up with other parishes and schools. People can choose to do service wherever. There are lots of opportunities for people to serve. But when they find something is pulling at their heartstrings, even if they are afraid of this environment . . . What is this place? Who are these people? And serving in the soup line [behind a counter] is relatively safe. And that is actually part of our mission—bringing people who would never have the experience of meeting our guests who are poor. So we can reduce the stereotypes, and humanity can meet humanity."

What is the meaning of life?

Besides the Monty Python movie? The Catholic Church used to have these questions in catechism. And the first question was, who made you? Well, God made me. Why did God make you? Well, to know Him and love Him in this life and to be with Him in the next . . . and we do that by knowing and loving our neighbor. The scripture says, if you can't love the person you can see, how can you love the God you can't see? Just to know and love God and to share that.

What are your thoughts about society and/or societies in general?

They exist! [Laughter.] Um . . . people need community. And that's one of the things that I see here. For people who are feeling isolated and being kept out community, the loneliness and struggle is that much deeper. So societies form, hopefully so that people can be in community together. But too often you get the 'us versus them.'

Who are you?

First, a child of God, Priest of the Holy Cross. And from that comes how I live and interact with others, but those two are first. If I honestly believe those two, then I have obligations to fulfill and lots of graces that I receive. I think one of the goals in this life is ultimately to see all is grace. If we could live out of that, things would be very different for a lot of people. Ultimately all is gift. My Protestant friends are going to think, is he really Catholic? But that is what Catholics believe. It's all gift. Because it's a gift we have obligations. But we start with all is gift; all is grace.

After the interview, Father Eric gives me a tour of the facility. It's two levels and it is massive. The entire basement of the André House, approximately 4,000 square feet, is a clothing bank. Guests can get two new outfits a week. André House also has many washers and dryers and does weekly laundry for guests. All this on top of serving several hundred meals a night.

As we walk out of the building, we see a man crying outside. He asks Father Eric in Spanish for help and so Father Eric speaks with him about a dental problem for a few minutes. At least I think that's what they are saying.

"Father, did you tell him that you can't help him and he needs to wait till he can get into the dental office over at CASS?"

"Yes," he replies.

"How do you deal with that, with not being able to help everyone?" The man was obviously in great pain.

"We'll . . . I'm just one man. I'm not Christ, Mike."

This statement really seems to sum up Father Eric's philosophy on helping others. Do what you can for all humans and do it with respect—but also respect that you are only human.

Father Eric makes me decide that we are all guests on this tiny planet and therefore, who am I to judge?

RESURRECTION

TODAY, I SIT DOWN WITH Arlene Pfeiff, the Director of the Human Services Campus, in a meeting room next to her office above the New Arid Club. The room has a row of windows on one side, allowing us a view of the street that leads into campus. Natural lighting floods the room. We sit in high back, leather swivel chairs at a wooden table that's as long and thick as a Buick and definitely as corporate.

I explain to Arlene that I know little about what she does or her vision for the campus, but that she has come up in many conversations I have had with others. People think she is on to something, and I want to find out what that "something" is.

"Well, there is only so much we can do here in this little self-contained, 13-acre place," she begins.

I think this place is gigantic. Arlene apparently sees things differently.

"We have to involve the community. Because what we are looking at is sustainable solutions that will end homelessness, not just make people who are homeless less miserable or get their teeth fixed or get them a job and still have them . . ." She trails off, gives me a look that says 'our mission should be obvious to everyone.'

Then, with a hint of exasperation, Arlene adds: "It's about ending homelessness. That is our intention. That's what we are dedicated to."

Before taking on this mission, Arlene had spent the last ten years as a vice president for American Express. "That was my thing: corporate America," she explains. I'm not surprised, because Arlene has the angular persona of a successful businesswoman. Though she loved the corporate life, Arlene decided the travel was too tough on her 4-year-old daughter Fayelee.

Arlene says she knew her next step had to be in the nonprofit world, so she began scouting organizations while wrapping up at American Express.

Her sister Amy, Director of St. Joseph the Worker, encouraged Arlene to check out the group and its mission.

"She told me about this amazing place and I was always kind of like, 'You know, that's great, Amy. Good luck with that. You go, girl.'" Arlene says, showing off her sarcastic sense of humor.

But the former corporate star decided to volunteer a little, if only in the interests of learning about the nonprofit world.

"My first day walking onto the soil of this campus, I will never forget, because I knew that there was something else going on here," she says. "And as I, you know, started to participate and get involved with meetings . . . these people that had stories that were off the chart amazing. And to see these transformations occur, I was transformed in the process."

When "the opportunity to become the managing director" of Human Services Campus presented itself to Arlene, she took it. There was an internal battle—this place was hardly what she expected right off the bat, after being an American Express VP—but Arlene says after three months, she trusted her soul and took the plunge.

"You know, I'm a corporate girl," she says, describing her internal battle. "This [HSC] is not nice and clean. It's front line. It's ground zero for what is going on—on the planet."

Despite this story, Arlene's personality seems a bit sterile to me. But I feel that she is sincere. This woman has a big, warm, caring, sensitive heart. She goes on: "It's kind of like I could feel the pull. And you know, when you are pulled, you want to resist. But I could feel every fiber of my body being pulled in a way that my brain and my intelligence and everything else was just wanting to resist . . . at some level, I knew this is where my soul wanted to be and I could wimp out and live with that for the rest of my life and live in just an unengaged, half asleep manner or I could just do this cause it's what my soul wanted anyway."

Arlene finishes this story looking vulnerable for the first time in our interview. Maybe that's it. Arlene is so sensitive that she has to be a bit guarded and sterile-seeming in person.

I decide to ask my most pressing question: "What's your vision?"

"It's been evolving over time," she replies. "We are learning together over time. It's not carved out in stone because we are going to be creating this vision together as a community, because that's what's going to make it sustainable."

Arlene wants HSC to be the "epicenter" for a far larger net of public involvement that will serve as a model for other communities. This begins, she says, by embracing the value of help that anybody can bring.

"But by separating ourselves from the rest of the community with this big fence that you see around here, that looks like a prison, it sends the message that the way to make this work is to separate," Arlene admits. "And it's not. Like I said, you can make homeless people a little less miserable by the current approach that we have, but you cannot end it and this vision is about ending homelessness."

I had heard people talk about this dream many times now. Most admitted that they felt it was nothing more than a dream. Arlene, on the other hand, has a four-point plan (how 'corporate' of her!) to actualize this vision. She shares this plan with me: Sustainable Campus—releasing the campus from external food and energy sources—then taking that knowledge to the community. Growing their own food, reducing energy needs, creating renewable energy.

Arlene wants to get the campus "off of the grid." Ideally, Arlene says clients will become experts on permaculture, gardening and all the green technologies that they are going to be using. "They will be the experts on how to choose it, how to install it, and how to maintain it. And in the process they will be able to begin to contribute. And not only to contribute, but to lead the way for a transformation that needs to occur, in this community and in this world."

"Some of this will sound crazy to other people but this vision . . . I don't even feel like it's mine," Arlene says. "I feel like it came through me. I wasn't into homelessness or green technology, until I came here."

I ask Arlene flat-out if she's a nutcase. She says no, but admits that she might have called this plan nutty even two years ago. "I actually see my old self as being nutty [now]," she adds, before going on to the second part of her plan, which is: Sustainable Economics—releasing the campus from a need for outside funding to become an economic development engine.

"This is very controversial, but there is an absolute place for charity and for the kind of support that has allowed our nation to grow and become the great nation that it is of loving caring people, all supporting each other," Arlene says. "But at some point we have to eliminate the need for that. And one thing that is very important to me is transforming the Human Services Campus [by] releasing it from a reliance on donor contributions. And in the process, [we will be] role modeling for our clients the very principles of self-sufficiency."

It's controversial, but I like it. I would feel far better contributing money to an organization if their ultimate goal was to arrive at a place where they would not be asking me for more money.

For example, Arlene is working on partnering with a company that has a new green technology for recycling tires. Typically recycling tires is anything but green. Arlene is looking into many such projects where the campus would provide connections and resources in exchange for job placement and profit sharing. "And it's hugely profitable and profit is good. Profit is good," Arlene says, chanting the corporate mantra in the heart of this Phoenix nonprofit. "People who don't think it is a good thing are hugely confused."

"Dependency needs to leave our vocabulary," she says, talking about donor contributions. Arlene doesn't want the risk of running out of funding to hang over HSC. She wants to redesign the place in a way that supports health; independent living for the homeless community. This mission dovetails with a belief that the way money is made in many industries is inherently wrong.

"There are so many artificial revenue streams out there right now," Arlene says. "People are shipping things; all kinds of middlemen making money. And it's so that people can make money. It's not that it's actually needed. It's artificial. And that's why everything is breaking down right now. It's because all of these artificial solutions are, you know, wearing out."

Arlene just changed my worldview of economics in three minutes. In my opinion, we are never going to bail ourselves out of the artificially created "housing crisis" with money based on a system that requires artificial growth to continue. And I've come to that understanding about the housing crisis at a homeless shelter. Go figure.

The third part of her plan is called Service Innovation, which is to identify the causes of human dependency and eliminate them. "We are really good at arresting people; as a matter of fact, Arizona is fabulous at it," Arlene begins. She is not one to mince words. "We have the highest number per capita of incarcerated individuals, anywhere. So we are excellent at it. We are fabulous. We arrest people who are making a bad choice [and] throw them into prison, thereby eliminating them, isolating them from society. And then when we're done there, we throw them back out onto the streets with no identification and no money. There is only one thing that can happen with those people. That's dependency, and they end up here. It's a feeding system. We have got to find a better way.

"I mean who in their right mind would design a system that says 'OK, you did something bad so now I'm going to warehouse you and then throw you out so that you have to commit crimes'—more crimes to stay alive? Or you have to become dependent on the rest of society to live after that. So that is your punishment, a life of dependency where I then need to fund your life. I don't understand why—if you break into my car—I have to pay for that and to take care of you for life. Now why not create job systems behind the walls and train those people to come out and be productive members of society? So that you and I and everybody else doesn't have to support them?"

Arlene contends that "it's a hell of a lot cheaper" to support life through nonprofit service work than to throw countless individuals into a self-serving incarceration system. "It is more expensive to have someone spend a year in prison than to have them spend a year at Harvard. Nothing about this makes sense."

Like my friend Scott, Arlene makes the distinction between short-term fixes that don't work, like criminalizing the homeless (especially veterans), and long-term solutions that might just be worth the effort, like the slow-growth programs at HSC.

Arlene proposes a "holistic infrastructure" at HSC, which includes taking all the separate agency databases and creating one campus database. She says this will streamline their efforts, get agencies working together and create an information source that can be extended to the criminal justice system.

Once that happens, Arlene says she hopes to get experts from nearby Arizona State University to analyze the data, "the entire service chain," and give advice on where and how money is best spent. "If we have a dollar to reduce recidivism . . . here's where we should spend it," is how she explains the ultimate goal. We need to look at the entire experience of these people so we can determine the real costs and the way out of it. And it's very doable."

This lady makes kindness cost-effective.

Finally, the fourth pillar of her plan is Community Engagement—taking the model of "sustainability" to the rest of the community. "It's not rocket science what needs to happen here," Arlene says. She describes her mother's childhood: They owned chickens, so they provided eggs to their community. "And down the street was the guy with the horses," Arlene says. "And up the street was the people with the milk. And someone else with the vegetables. And they had, they wouldn't have called it this, but their own sustainable community."

Arlene says this natural cooperation, this interconnectedness, is what HSC is striving for. "We need to learn what each other's names are, and I need to learn what that guy across the street is doing, so that I can figure out how to help him be more successful and how he can help me be more successful," Arlene says. "And we need to document this transformation so we can share it with people. [So they can] see the evolution, the messiness of it all and the mistakes we make along the way."

Arlene says social media will play a huge part of how the Human Services Campus shares its story going forward.

"What's happening right now is supposed to be happening," she says. "It's time to seize this opportunity and redesign and incredible, wonderful existence for ourselves. Four years from now, people are going to be coming to the campus not because they want to see the world's largest, most comprehensive, progressive homeless shelter. My dream is, it'll become a distant memory that this used to be a 'homeless place.' What people are going to be coming here for is to get their organic fruits and vegetables, and to figure out how this place got off the grid, and to see our green water system and to see all these energy efficient choices we have made. And our clients are going to be the ones showing them those solutions. And it will be a model. And you see that will end homelessness, because we will provide a place where they can come and be productive."

And Arlene doesn't just mean the campus. She means changing the world so that people fit into it once again.

I like this new Arlene—softer, less guarded, and full of ideals. Not the sterile businesswoman I first suspected her to be.

What is the meaning of life?

I think it is just to have experiential knowledge of what it's like to be a human being, a growing human. Because I think we choose to come here and we all have different things we want to learn and experience when we are here and I think some of those people out on the street corners, ah, living what we would call, horrible, impoverished lives are some of the heroes, because they teach us things and have chosen to sacrifice their lives and do that for us. I think that is the case for many people and they chose a really brave existence; they wanted to really experience, it. What am I made of? What is love? What is pain? How deep can I get into the hole and how far can I pull myself out of it? I feel like we constructed our lives, we chose to come here and have these experiences. I think we are just creatures that need this time and space, [this] continuum to be able to feel what it means to be human. And so we come here and do this for kicks and to learn and it creates depth that you couldn't have just flying out there in the atmosphere with wings on.

What are your thoughts about society and/or societies in general?

Well, we've gotten lost. We've gotten a little confused and distracted about what's really important. It's really just simple stuff. So we've gotten just a little bit lost and confused. And uh, I think we are going to figure it out, because human beings are resilient, amazingly. You know you don't ever stop trying to figure out, until you die. We are determined. So we will figure it out and we will be better for having had this little, you know, experience with what's going on in the world right now. But we need each other.

Who are you?

Shoot! I am constantly figuring that out. I don't think I know yet but, you know, I'm a mom and I'm a leader and, you know, I'm wounded just like every other person walking around on the planet. Because we all are, and we're all going through our lives working on how to, you know, heal those wounds. And for whatever reason just opening myself up to people and my community and, greater and deeper love is incredibly healing and just beautiful to me. And so that's, you know, what has me making some of the choices and following the path that I am following.

Arlene just convinced me that great change really can occur, and it will come from getting back to basics.

A community garden managed by the Human Services Campus staff and maintained by clients is an example of the kind of sustainability that can be created in or around shelters for people who are homeless. Photo by: Steven Sable.

CHAPLAIN DAVE, HIS HOME: Thursday, April 23, 2009, 11:00 a.m.

Chaplain Dave is a large man by any standards, mainly width-wise. He works in a small office off the main lobby of LDRC, next to St. Joseph the Worker.

At the time of our scheduled meeting, Chaplain Dave was at home, sick. Sick enough that he had just gotten home from the hospital minutes before our appointment. He had instructed me to just come to his home.

I find him in his living room, taking up all of the allowable space of a large recliner, with a catheter still in tow. Chaplain Dave asks me to explain this book before we get started and I find that I still can't fully explain this project. I tell him the book is searching for an answer to what is homelessness, but it seems to be so much more and is definitely a journey of sorts for me. He nods and smiles knowingly. I tell him, in an attempt to build rapport, that the necessity or power of faith has become reoccurring theme in my interviews.

This 64-year-old responds with a laugh. "Oh, let's not get into that faith crap! You can get carried away with that bullshit!"

I was not expecting that from a man who looks like Moses with glasses.

"I haven't always been a chaplain," Dave says, in response to my astonishment. He then goes on to explain that this chaplaincy started with a man named Reverend Jerry Roseberry who, along with his other community roles, was a cofounder of Hospice of the Valley.

"Everybody was helping the homeless: food, clothing, whatever," Chaplain Dave begins, "and he [Reverend Roseberry] had one question: Why are they still on the street? What do they need to get off the street? And so what he did one day was that he locked his door behind him, put some soot from his grill on his hands and face, and walked down Central Avenue with a walking stick. And everybody he met, he would [ask], 'Do you know where there is a homeless shelter in this town?' And nobody knew. People threatened him. People were afraid of him. Police told him, 'Move on, move on.' Finally he ran into another homeless man and he told him about CASS—the old CASS. Now this is over 20 years ago that Jerry lived on the street, for a month, as a homeless man."

"Now I'm old and sick and I'm a combat veteran, but I'm not sure I would have had the *cajones* to do what he did," Chaplain Dave concludes.

I now know 30 hours on the streets is hard enough. I can't imagine 30 days. We return to talking about Reverend Roseberry's story. "At the end of the month he realized [that] every time he turned around, someone had asked him for identification. To get services, to get help, ah, for anything.

And he said, 'I don't have it. How do I get it?' Well, nobody knew. If they knew he would go there, but nobody knew how to pay for it. And, um, you need a birth certificate. And so he started the chaplaincy with a small stipend from a wealthy friend."

Ever since, the chaplain's office has helped people, mainly the homeless, get identification documents. An ID is required for most any basic services: food stamps, ACCESS [health care], a job application. Clothing and food banks usually require a state ID, Chaplain Dave adds. To top it all off, in Arizona, you can be arrested for vagrancy without a state ID card.

"You need to get an ID to get a birth certificate, but you need a birth certificate to get an ID," he says. "No one is interested in addressing this dichotomy and the hardship that results from it. Even the Supreme Court, in arguments this year about voting rights, concluded that IDs are available to anyone, anywhere. They are not!"

This really strikes me, after talking with Arlene about sustainability of the service campus on such a grand scale. What Chaplain Dave and his office staff do is of equal importance.

From his recliner, Chaplain Dave says recently they have seen a big increase in people asking for their help. Before, they'd settle 10 to 20 birth certificate questions a month. Last month, that number was 131. He credits the increase to more people realizing they need identification to receive basic services—and realizing they can go to him for help, no matter what state they were from originally.

Chaplain Dave is understating what his office does, by the way. He and his staff are considered so good at obtaining birth certificates that homeless persons come to him from other states. He is considered the best in the business. Stories abound of homeless persons traveling hundreds, thousands of miles for his services, because no one else can get them a birth certificate.

"Now there are times, several times a month, where I have to sit there and say, 'I have no way to help you,'" he says. "What it really means is that you are sentenced to life on the street! No birth certificate means no ID. And without both there will be no services and no jobs. End of story."

Chaplain Dave pauses to stare into me with that last statement. His is the smallest office on campus, and yet in many ways, the most indispensable. He says, "I have met perfectly employable individuals on campus who had been waiting over a year to get a birth certificate so that they can start looking for work."

Problems often occur with people who were home birthed and never reported to Social Security. Or, as is sometimes the case with Native

American clients, their births were reported to the tribe, not the state, and the tribal record is not accepted without a baptismal record in tow. The climate of fear instilled after 9/11 certainly hasn't made getting these birth certificates any easier.

"It's life, liberty and the pursuit of happiness . . . if you're a citizen and the birth certificate is the proof of citizenship," Chaplain Dave says. "We also have people who lose their green cards and it's $370 to replace. Naturalization papers are $380. But you can't work without it."

"Do you do this alone?" I ask, once again astonished by this cynical, sailor-mouthed, inarguably good man.

"Hell no," the Chaplain replies. "In my office, we have myself and one part-time employee. And we also have many volunteers who work like every Monday for say four hours. Most of our budget is spent providing direct services to clients."

That budget includes $4,000 each month for obtaining IDs and documents (mostly birth certificates), $1,200 a month for replacement documents for legal immigrants and naturalized citizens, and . . . not much else. Dave says his office has to turn people away due to lack of funds. They receive no government funding. "We don't even get quantity discounts from the Motor Vehicle Division or any state vital records office."

Sometimes, the process of tracking down family members in order to obtain birth certificates solves more problems than intended.

"Sometimes they say, 'We've been looking for him for years. He has a place to stay if he comes home.' Sometimes we [can] send him that day on a bus," Chaplain Dave says. "A lot of people think that the last word yelled when the door slammed was the last word and it rarely ever is. I used to work in the Fort McDowell Substance Abuse Program on the reservation and there was drug addiction and the problems of other communities, but they were never homeless unless they left the reservation."

Chaplain Dave says his organization looks for small missing, but extremely important links to the service chain; IDs being just one case in point. It seems like such a small thing, but every other link requires it. Another example is recent efforts to reach out to the elderly homeless population, which is chronically underserved.

"Many agencies were willing to assist families and children, but senior citizens don't make such attractive press and fundraising," he says. Chaplain Dave and others (including Nancy's minister husband) have established the Justa Center for this purpose.

"On average, they get one person each day out of homelessness into and appropriate living situation," Chaplain Dave says. "As far as we've been able to determine, it's the only facility of its kind in the country. The people they see have usually been turned down for services by other agencies because they have issues that no one is willing to address. Those could be very old outstanding warrants, mental health issues including SMI, additional issues, credit problems, whatever. The staff at Justa Center has had to blaze new ground to deal with each situation. They have developed relationships with landlords. They don't just place someone and forget about them. They follow up and are available to deal with any situations that may arise."

The LDRC has a similar housing program that visits clients in their residence every month for a year just to make sure things go smoothly and they stay in their housing.

Half of the senior citizens they help at the Justa Center are veterans, a fact that disgusts Chaplain Dave. "Many, if not most of the guests at Justa have been productive most of their lives," he says. "They are the victims of illness, mental and physical, loss of jobs late in life, and lack of family to assist them. One day I had an 87-year-old woman in my office crying, saying, 'Is it my fault I have outlived every member of my family?' In our society, we have stopped caring for our elders. We have stopped caring for our sick if they are poor, or the cost of care is so expensive that they become homeless. We have stopped being grateful to the veterans who have given, protected and maintained our freedoms."

I'm reminded again that this man was not always a chaplain, and I ask Dave about his past life.

"I used to be a raging atheist," he says, "and atheists know that there is no God. And my life was proof, because if there was a God he would have squashed me like a grape."

"Are you trying to make up for that now?" I ask because it feels that way to me.

"I have guilt from past mistakes," Dave replies. He stops, gets very teary eyed, and tells me of two mistakes he made that he feels are unforgivable and then requests that I not put his confession in print.

"In 1984 my life was such a mess, I killed myself. I failed obviously. My wife at the time saved my life and all I could think was, 'How could she do that?'"

Dave says he had "a series of profound spiritual experiences" that, slowly but surely, turned his life around. It began with a return to church in 1991, weighted with guilt. He began to get involved, and his involvement with community seems to be what saved him.

"In hindsight, it seems like a dramatic change," Chaplain Dave says. "And it was. But I'm still a bit of a curmudgeon." He laughs. "Everybody knows a lot of people who know the right things to do, but every once in a while I meet someone who does the right stuff."

"Why do you do this work?"

"How do you see this and not do something?" he replies. "If you were driving along and saw a train wreck, you would stop and get out and help."

Dave waves his hands around, as if he is actually trying to alert me to a train wreck ahead. Perhaps he's right, and we just don't see it yet. Suddenly, his voice quiets and softens:

"I have been down. I have been very down. And it's not, 'There before the grace of God go I.' It's, 'I've been there, done that.' But most of us don't want to associate with things that are unpleasant. We don't like to identify with the feeling of homelessness, helplessness and powerlessness. We don't want to need somebody's assistance. Yet for most of us, the beginning of change is saying, 'Hey, I need somebody's help.' I knew a guy who came from Denver to Phoenix just to get an ID. They couldn't help him in Denver and somebody told him about us. Obviously, he really wanted that ID."

What is the meaning of life?

I'm going to take the meaning of life as the purpose of life.

I have learned that the purpose of life it to love God and all His children, all His children. That's it. That's all there is. I'm trying just because it means so much to me. It's . . . I have so much to make up for, so much that was horrible. Most of us beg for mercy, are terrified of justice. And some of us get grace and that's what I have. I have been given grace to undo as much as I can.

What are your thoughts about society and or societies in general?

We have lost our compassion, not just in this society but in other societies. And that doesn't mean doing everything for everybody. But it means helping them to do. You know that story, give a man a fish or teach him to fish and he will sit in a boat and drink beer . . .

Who are you?

I was first asked that question in October of 1984 and I said: "I'm on this board, I'm on this committee, I have this wife, I have these children, I drive these cars." I didn't know . . . I know today, and it goes back to the first question. I am just a man who tries to do his very best to love God and all His children.

**Chaplain Dave shattered my ideas of scope and
showed me the importance of identity.**

DAWN, LDRC: Monday, April 27, 2:15 p.m.

Dawn Shires is the Volunteer Coordinator at LDRC and the inspirer of
many of its more creative programs (such as the movie workshop), although
I only discovered this through the course of this investigation because she
never talks about originating anything.

I had already chosen to use the 12 steps as outlined in the hero's
journey as chapters early on in this project. As time unfolded, this decision
proved to be prophetic. My experiences have fit all too well into the hero's
journey and the seeming magical connections have been far too numerous
to note them all in this book. And as Dawn outlined in greater detail
the significance of each step, I was in awe that there really did seem to
be a heroic journey to it all—for me, for everyone—one that sort of falls
together in this 12-step order, if you continue to show up for it.

In our one-on-one interview, Dawn as always exhibits her humble,
passionate and stern New York manner. "It sometimes sounds like an
internal fight, but I really think it's much more of an alignment issue than
a fight," she says, talking about having your heart, mind and will aligned.
I ask her to define these terms.

"Will is a force. Heart is trickier: It is experienced through emotions
but I think it is your sense of spirit.

"I think most people are tortured when their heart has told them
something for a long time and they've chosen consistently to ignore it,"
Dawn continues. "I think they are miserable people. And they end up
shut down. I think that heart aspect is a guiding force of where your soul
wants to be directed, what you want to be doing. And what does that is
your mind: Blah, blah, blah, blah, blah; about what you should do, what
you shouldn't do, what's right, what's wrong."

"But what ends up happening is the mind is used more for memory,
pattern framing. And it's not shifted. Patterns are probably started early on
and then just go on repetitive. And it's dominant with our culture. So we
listen to the tapes over and over, rather than the heart and the will, which
is where it [the mind] needs to be directed."

All conversations with Dawn make me think. I ask her if she thinks
the mind needs to follow the heart and the will?

"No. Think of them as a circle," she replies. "There's not a hierarchy. They all have valid parts to play. It's the relationship of the parts which is where the dysfunction is."

This sort of human development stuff is of great interest to us both, and Dawn and I could go on for hours. For the sake of the interview however, I change course.

"You asked me a little while ago if I might be interested in heading up a Women's Group here at LDRC," I say.

"I feel it's obvious that we have different groups that come down here, and I feel that each group has [a] unique need. And I think the women on this campus have a uniqueness to them that needs to be addressed in a particular way."

Dawn pauses and looks me square in the eyes before continuing.

"I am absolutely positive that I am not the person to do this!" she exclaims. "Our whole society is not set up to support the feminine. I'm not meaning to sound like a feminist. I'm saying the concept of how 'feminine' attributes are dealt with. We are not designed as a society to work with those."

I would agree.

"They need to be able to express in a venue that is not going to tell them what they have to do," Dawn continues. "They need that therapy. They need to be able to release that to be able to come to their own conclusions."

"But they are not willing to sit in a room to do it though," she concludes, clearly frustrated—not with the women, necessarily, but possibly with her own inability to solve the problem.

"They will not come to a meeting or something even though they know it would be good for them if the 'guy' they've been, you know, hunting, is somewhere outside," Dawn says. "They will drop everything. It's a total self-sacrifice. They don't know how to meet their own needs. Their expectation is to meet the needs of somebody else [a man] and then you will give back and take care of me. And that doesn't happen. What happens is people keep taking and then they are the depleted victims. And the love of the drama—they can't get out of."

I think we've all been guilty of this sort of thing at some point in our lives, if not every point. I voice this idea to Dawn: "But humans love drama: movies, plays, stories, etc."

"There's a difference between pursuing excitement and emotional stimulation, which is what we are looking for, which is why we go to the movies versus, for the lack of any other stimulation, having to jump in front of a train to feel alive. You know what I mean? And so they will leap in front of a train and get hurt for the attention. And it's so draining. They can't ever get to what they need to get to."

Clearly, Dawn has no tolerance for this lack of independence. Perhaps she was right when she said someone else should lead the Women's Workshop. She talks about her attempts at this very thing.

"Just to get them to show up . . . the first time getting them to talk was not that difficult, but then getting them to come back after the first-time exposure to that conversation," Dawn says. "The most frustrating part is, all's you ever wanted was someone to listen to you, then the first time someone listens to you, you run out of the room because you can't handle someone listening to you. How do you continue to get listened to if you just run? You know what I mean?"

It's rare to see Dawn this flustered, because it seemingly only happens when there's a problem she can't solve. Dawn's job is to solve people's problems—or, more accurately, teach people to solve their own problems—and normally she's very good at it. But in this case, she is reaching out for help.

Dawn explains that while it sounds strange to have a man lead the women's workshop, she thinks I have the particular skills to make it work. And it hasn't worked so far to have women lead them.

And it hits me. She's right. I do have the particular skills to make this work. I've done it before, in a way, as a manager of 65 women at my old job.

"I'm just the man for the job."

Dawn smiles. "I don't envy you for one minute."

However, I want to return us to the interview. "Do you have anything to tell the future readers of this book?" Dawn sits and thinks for a minute with no response. "I also have some questions to ask you that I ask everyone I interview."

"OK," Dawn agrees. "Ask me some questions because nothing is coming to mind right now."

What is the meaning of life?
To evolve.

What are your thoughts about society and/or societies in general?
About society or societies in general? Structured insanity. I'm not a fan.

Who are you?
I still don't know yet. I don't know. I just think a whole bunch of things. How do people normally answer that question?

"I'm delighted to say that there is no 'normal' answer," I interject. "Everybody says something different."

Dawn takes this opportunity to neatly sum up the power these final three questions have come to possess in my interviews. "If you think about it, you are asking a bunch of homeless individuals or staff who work with homeless individuals, who they are. And everything about who they are has been stripped away and has to be reevaluated. Who you thought you were—and who you've come to realize you are—are bound to be miles apart at this point.

"You thought you were the doctor; you thought you were the father; you thought you were the construction worker; you had all your labels. And you lose it all, but you're still here; so who are you? You definitely don't know now."

Dawn convinces me that there is a path for everyone and if you choose to accept it, then it becomes the path of the hero or heroine.

WOMENS' WORKSHOP, LDRC: Tuesday, May 19, 2009, 9:30 a.m.

Dawn and I both felt it was a radical approach to have a man teach a woman's workshop, but at this point anything was worth a try. Dawn really believes that women are under-represented on the male dominated campus and I would have to agree. Further, homeless women quite possibly suffer greater abuse than homeless men, if such a thing is possible.

Anyway, I'm intrigued by the challenge. I believe women are equal, if not superior to, men in many respects. I think it only appears to be a male dominated world and men actually rise up to or lower down to the standards women set for us. Heal the women and you change everything. And, I'd previously written an unpublished book titled *Reflections—The Mosaic of You in Mortal Time*, about empowerment. I want to share this book's material with my students-to-be.

I prepare heavily for the first class. My spirits are high and my expectations low, but in a good way. I don't expect to have a room full of women hanging on my every word or to change lives in our 90-minute session. Instead, I hope they feel valued and cared about, appreciating that a male volunteer took the time to share, learn and grow with them. If anyone picks up pearls of wisdom along the way, it would just be icing on the cake.

Earlier, Jessica gave me free reign to approach the class in whatever way I saw fit. Her trust and faith inspired me all the more. First off, I changed the title of the workshop due to the previous failed workshops. What homeless woman wants to go to an "empowerment workshop" when she doesn't have a place to sleep? What homeless woman wants to get in touch with her "inner child" when she's depressed, lonely and scared? So I changed the title to "Women's Workshop: Getting What You Want—Men, Money and More." Jessica was surprised, to say the least.

"Who doesn't want sex, money and love?" I ask her as I explain my thesis. Supportive, but uncertain, Jessica says I have a point.

An hour before the first class, I walked around the campus lawn, inviting women to the workshop. In general, they are not receptive, suspicious of my motives. Two women simply say it won't make a difference. I tell them that I completely understand their feelings, but headstrong thinkers like them are exactly what we needed in the workshop.

Seven women show up, including the two headstrong women who said it wouldn't make a difference. The staff told me that I'd be lucky to get three for a first class. None of them are smiling and most of them look pessimistic at best. But they're here.

I buy everyone drinks from the Get Goin' Café, then ask the women if they know why I did that. They say they don't know—maybe to be nice.

"Well yeah, I want to be nice, but it's to schmooze you."

They laugh. Good start.

"I promise not to lie to you about my motives. I'm trying to build a relationship with you all, and this is a start."

The course, in my mind, it's really to be about exploring and strengthening the relationship these women have with themselves, and then with others. As the other, still unpublished book I wrote states, *everything is a relationship.* I know now that homelessness is more about a state of mind and heart than anything else; a reflection of the relationship we have with our society and ourselves.

I continue the momentum by giving them all roses, and in their choice of colors: red, purple or yellow.

"And why do you all suppose I am giving you a choice of roses to pick from?"

Silence.

"Because it is always important to make choices. Even the wrong choice is better than no choice. Oh, how much time I've wasted in my life sitting on the fence. And you know what that gets you?"

Silence.

"A fence post up your ass."

They laugh louder.

"And I won't even tell you about the splinters."

They are roaring and I, surprisingly, actually am the man for this job.

"But seriously, why do you think I gave you roses?"

One woman meekly says, "Because we're special."

"Absolutely! And because you are ladies. It's my commitment to you that in this class you will be treated as such."

I can tell by their faces that they like this. They sense that I mean it. I knew I had to. I remember how much I missed recognition from the opposite sex during my brief homeless immersion.

Next, I go over ground rules for the class.

"You are not here to agree with me. You are here to argue with me when you don't agree."

They like that—who wouldn't?

"We don't talk about the past. Not because I don't care. I really do care, but because we can't change the past."

I do another crowd check. They seem to still be on board.

"We do talk about thoughts and feelings in the present that most likely came from the past because we can and will change thoughts and feelings in this class."

With the intent to stay in the present moment out of the way, I ask the women what they want. They mention things like money, a job, a home, a boyfriend. I ask the lady who mentioned money why she wants money. She looks at me as though I'm stupid. It should be obvious. I explain that nobody wants money. They want what they think money will give them.

"So what will money get you?" The woman explains with money, she can get a home.

"Why do you want a home?" Again, she looks at me as though I'm a bit slow on the uptake. Eventually, we find she wants a home because it will give her a feeling of independence and love. I continue to do the same with every woman's response. We are able to trace all their wants back to a desire for love and independence (a form of self-love, as far as I'm concerned).

I had anticipated this sort of thing, but did not know this was exactly where we would arrive. And that's one of the points of the class. I am exploring ideas with them. I have a process, a magic to share with them, but because they are a part of this process, in relationship with it, with me, I don't know exactly where the process will lead or what the magic will produce.

I ask the ladies to sum up our discussion so far. After some debate, one student says, "It all seems about this self-love thing. She says 'house' or she says 'money' but in a way, they mean self-love." The student finishes with a perplexed look on her face, as though she senses the connection but hasn't totally wrapped her mind around it yet.

I drop the subject. The idea is to keep the class entertaining and thus always moving, always changing. Deep, but light.

I throw a large box of chocolates out on the table. They just stare at it.

"Well, aren't you going to open it?" I ask.

"You didn't tell us to."

"Nothing happens in life if you don't look inside."

My students open the box and start to sample the various chocolates. As they do, I ask them: "What is the one factor that has been present in every aspect of your life, in the ups, the downs and the middles?"

I get no response except for the sound of chewing. Finally, a woman who hasn't said a word since she walked in meekly suggests: "Me."

"That's right! You!" I reply in my extremely animated tone, reserved for public speaking. "You are the one factor that has been present in every aspect of your life. There is nothing in your life that you did not contribute to. In fact, you have contributed 50 percent to every situation in your life. Don't you all agree?"

Silence.

"Hey, if you don't agree, tell me I'm full of shit." They laugh. A good sign, even if they're still a little reluctant to engage. "But tell me something. Yes, no, maybe, anything!"

One student says she agrees, but 50 percent isn't always enough to make a difference.

"Well, I applied for 20 jobs and I only got one. That's five percent. I've dated a hundred girls and only have one girlfriend. That's one percent." They nod their heads, seeming to get the point. "Fifty percent is more than enough to tip the scales in your favor, coupled with a little persistence."

I turned to one of the two 'headstrong' ladies in the workshop and ask her how she likes the chocolates.

"Well, I've bitten into five and haven't found one I've liked yet," She replies, sarcastic. Her friend laughs.

"Then why do you keep biting into them?" I shoot back, smiling.

"I keep hoping to find one I like," she answers, still sarcastic.

"Exactly!" I literally yell. "You can't find what's inside unless you bite in. That's the point of this workshop. You have to try looking inside to find something you like. You have to look behind or beyond the outer layer of things, from a house to love of self, from the chocolate covering to the creamy center. So many of us just give up after trying five. I'm glad you're not one of those kinds of people." My toughest student smiles, perhaps a bit proud of herself.

And as for the large box of chocolates? It's empty.

We discuss concepts for a while more, but I feel like I might be losing the class's attention. I throw out a big box of dominoes, and direct each woman to take a pile. We make those tenuous domino lines, ready to fall at the slightest push, like we are kids again. While the class is full of deep philosophical ideas and hopefully heading towards deeper ones, I also want to keep the mood playful and comfortable.

Next, we connect each line of dominoes with everyone else's so that there will be one continuous line. The line gets long quickly, but the students have trouble completing the task. Invariably, a domino gets knocked over, taking out the entire chain. I watch silently, pleased they are so involved in the assignment.

They finally successfully complete the full chain of upright dominoes. I ask them what they learned and they essentially say, teams are good for taking on large projects, but you do have to deal with the mistakes of others when you work in a team. I also point out that my headstrong student came up with a strategy to get the best of both worlds. She takes over and explains that she left a connecting domino out between her part and the rest of the chain and then placed it last.

As we approach the end of class, I ask the students to pick out a favorite colored pen from an assortment I offer. Again, choices. I am struck by how much pleasure they get from being able to choose the color of their pen and more struck by how much I still have to learn here. I didn't fully appreciate how empowering even little choices are to one's individuality. Once you are homeless, it feels as though your choices evaporate. In actuality, I suspect this feeling, in part, is what leads to homelessness.

I also hand out paper and envelopes with the LDRC's address already on them. I ask the women to write themselves a letter.

"I will not read them, and I will not have you read them next week to the class," I say. "The letters are for you alone." I recommend that they say nice things to themselves in that letter, but insist that they have to be true.

"If you can't write, then draw yourself a pretty picture. The point is to send yourself something nice. And even that is just my recommendation. As always, do what you want to do. Choose what you want to do."

The group loves that I don't insist on them doing anything my way. And the workshop is a success whether they agree with my ideas or not. Either way, they are making choices. Either way they are thinking; they are engaged. And it adds to their trust in me.

I need this workshop to be empowering and trust-building, because where I will be heading in the weeks and months to follow is a place my students cannot go if they do not develop the ability to consciously make choices and decide what is right for them.

After they finish, I collect the letters and tell the students I just want them to remember two things for next week. I write the first item on the board.

"Bring a friend. Get a gift."

Again, I ask the class why I am doing this. Again, they don't know.

"I'm bribing you!" I yell. More laughter ensues.

"I want you to bring other women to this workshop so badly that I'm willing to bribe you! It's a referral program, but to be honest, it's bribery. I won't lie to you."

One lady shrewdly asks what the gift is. I tell her it will be Go-Getter Bucks. This seems more than acceptable, and I now know firsthand why Nancy introduced this concept.

I write the second item on the board: "Write down your thoughts and feelings during the week."

My students ask what they will write with and I explain they are to keep the pens they picked out. I'm surprised how happy this makes them. It's amazing what a colorful .20 cent pen can do. They ask, but what will we write on? "On the notebooks I got you all." You would have thought I bought them all ponies. This is so much fun! I feel like Santa Claus. I then let them choose a notebook in their favorite color.

As my students leave with huge smiles, I feel it was a huge success. It's as though all of my life's experiences and skills came together to help me teach this class. I can't remember the last time I had so much fun.

Now I have to think up a lesson for next week.

WOMEN'S WORKSHOP, LDRC: Tuesday, June 16, 2009, 9:30 a.m.

There are 16 women at the fifth workshop, more than double from where we started. It is quite obvious by now, to myself, and the staff, that the workshops are a success.

Also, today is a special day. It is my 40th birthday. And on this 16th of June, 16 women show up to the workshop. How far I have come in the past several months, it seems. My life felt as if lacking something essential, and now it's overflowing.

So what better place, what more appropriate group, to celebrate my birthday with than my women's workshop? In fact, this class is my only birthday plan, aside from time with my kids later in the day. And I know what you're thinking; I'm not avoiding the whole 40-year-old thing. I'm just . . . content. I'm content with things the way they are. I don't know if I've ever felt this way. I feel settled in me; at home with me.

Birthdays cause me to reflect, this time on the past five classes. I started them all with drinks and roses, reminding them each time why. I threw every trick in the book at them and have more ideas to come. One week, I brought a helium balloon and asked them why it floats? A very shy lady in the class said, "Because it's got helium in it."

"Wrong!" I yelled. I then reassured her that in a way she was right, but not completely. "You all have helium in you. Why don't you float? There is helium in the air right now. We're all breathing it in along with oxygen, hydrogen and carbon dioxide. So why don't we all float?"

They didn't have an answer.

"The balloon floats because of what it keeps outside of it. When you keep the heavier stuff outside of you, helium is the only thing that's left and you effortlessly float."

Many of the lessons were multileveled like this, to speak to the different aptitudes of the ladies. For some, this lesson was as simple as getting them to consider the importance of what or who they let inside them (physically or emotionally) and if these people are uplifting for them or if they weigh them down. For others, the metaphor made them consider what ideas they let inside of them by agreeing with them.

We carried the balloon analogy even further, pointing out that every time you say yes to something it implies millions of other no's.

"Don't think you are being nice by saying 'yes' to spending time with someone who doesn't deserve your time, because that 'yes' means you are saying 'no' to hundreds of other people more worthy," I said. "It's a 'no' to them and you. Often the nicest thing, the best thing we can do for others and ourselves, is to say 'no.' A 'no' to one person or thing means you can say 'yes' to another."

Of course that lesson and all the others spoke as much to me as it did to them. This place has taught me to say no to a lot of the self-defeating baloney in my head. Most of it just doesn't hold water anymore when faced with real problems. When your world expands, your problems get smaller in comparison. And by saying yes to the right people, to people who really need my time, like these ladies, I did start to float.

Each week had been filled with these sorts of thought-provoking stunts and much group discussion. I could fill a book with lessons from the first month of classes alone.

At the end of every class I always ask them to write themselves a letter. I mail the letters back to them each week. I also write personally to each member of the class every week. In class, I ask new students how they felt about the letter they got from themselves. They always say it made them happy and I always ask: "Why? You already knew that stuff about yourself? So why did it make you happy?"

Nobody seems to know why, but the personal messages make everyone happy.

Back to today—my birthday. These 16 homeless women surprise me with a cake, flowers, and a card signed by all of them. Think about that. These homeless women got a cake, flowers and a card for me.

They sing the happy birthday song. And is if that isn't enough I realize my real present is the gift of my students' appreciation, enthusiasm and insights. They and this place gave me the gift of freedom—freedom from bemoaning my life and thus the ability to appreciate the gift of me. In this moment, I somehow recognize in my heart what I always knew in my head: Everyone is a gift. Everything is a gift.

Photo by: Ashton Romano

I think back to the many people I interviewed, what I learned and how they all helped me to teach this class:

- I wouldn't have done the class in the first place but my father taught me to do things because they are the right things to do.
- Jessica and Dawn both taught me the first day I met them, to be passionate.
- Jessica taught me that politics and rules are not solutions. So our class only had one rule: Don't talk about the past. Relationships are solutions and that's what we always focus on.
- The shooting incident taught me the sanctity of life and the fact that everything is in our backyard. These are my sisters. This is my backyard.
- Dawn taught me that there is a path and if you choose to accept it, then it becomes the path of the hero or heroine.
- Don reminded me of the importance of letters from loved ones and so I made that an integral part of the class.
- Clarence taught me how to connect to the ladies—through and with humility.
- Dwight taught me that faith is a choice and it was the choice I made from the very first class.
- Scott taught me spirituality couldn't be intellectualized so I needed to make the class playful. The girl on the street with the mustard taught me that we simply cannot afford to not think long term anymore.
- Ross taught me how important it is for us to be included and to feel loved which is why I give the ladies flowers and buy them drinks.
- David taught me that we are anything but independent. And these workshops proved that to me. Again, I am getting as much out of them as the attendees.
- Running Deer taught me that people aren't disposable and it is this conviction that I founded our classes on, the conviction that everyone is important.
- Larry and Ronnie taught me how well relationships work when we celebrate the differences of others and I used this to manage our group sessions. I don't arbitrate conflicts between members—I celebrate them!

- Amy taught me how important the other things besides money are. And so our workshops instill dignity and encourage the participants to help one another.
- John and Matt taught me how important our stories are to us. But knowing we can get lost in them, the workshop for women focuses on rewriting those stories, not reliving them.
- Clarence and Tony taught me that it's not about helping; it's about cooperating. I don't play the Good Samaritan. I work with the class members, exploring better, more effective ways of living and learning. And they work with me.
- Tony taught me that I don't have to be healed or be perfect to help and helping might be the perfect healing. And was he ever right!
- Nancy taught me the dangers of arrogance. These ladies will eat me alive if I'm even the slightest bit arrogant. Confident, yes; arrogant, no.
- My homelessness immersion taught me that I don't know what it's like until I've lived it so I don't talk at the ladies. I listen to them. I don't know who they are or what they need. They do, or they're here to learn that.
- Hector taught me that the only real help we can give another must contain dignity. It must be through helping another to help themselves. For this reason I never try to fix anyone in our workshops, because that would be robbing them of their dignity.
- Laura taught me that this world is my home and taking care of it should be fun. She was right. I haven't had so much fun in years. We can heal and grow through play.
- Michael taught me that we usually only fool ourselves while trying to fool others. Now, knowing this better than anyone, I act as a loving witness, a loving mirror, often just repeating back to participants what they just said, and with surprising effects.
- The people in the AA meetings taught me how home and acceptance are synonymous—or should be. For this reason we work on accepting others so that everyone has a home, at least for those 90 minutes. We work on accepting ourselves so we might all have a home beyond those 90 minutes.
- Every individual taught me the sheer necessity of cooperation. These workshops work because they are a tiny piece of a very large pie. Often, ladies would comment, "This is kind of what Dawn

showed us in the movie workshop," or "Nancy said something about that."

- Arthur taught me that regardless of the path, we need bravery and conviction. It takes bravery to take on challenges greater than ourselves, and conviction to see them through.
- Sergeant Freudenthal taught me that you don't have to have all the answers to work the solutions. Self-help book or not, I don't have all the answers, but I have some and that's what I work with.
- Lieutenant Connolly taught me the importance of seeing things through other people's eyes, so that real solutions can be found. I tried to do this in every interview, and now in every workshop.
- Julia taught me that we can never fully understand another's challenges and therefore should have deep respect for everyone.
- Linda and Jeff taught me the power of volunteering and I can't say enough about it. I don't recommend you volunteer because the world needs your help, even though it does. I recommend you volunteer because you need the world's help.
- Terry taught me the utter necessity of community.
- Bill taught me that living our philosophies is the right thing to do. If I really believe all the things I say, then I have no choice but to act.
- Father Eric taught me that everyone deserves dignity and help. Who are we to judge? After six months and five workshops, I would have to agree: Who am I to judge?
- Arlene taught me that great change really can occur and it might just come from getting back to basics: Relationships, families, communities.
- Chaplain Dave taught me the importance of regaining one's identity—on paper and in person. He also taught me that size doesn't necessarily equate to effectiveness. One person can make a big difference.

Six months ago, I thought turning 40 might be be lonely and empty. Instead I am at the LDRC, on my birthday, feeling at home, here and with myself.

We finish the cake. I am given hugs, thanks and praise. And of course it feels wonderful. But the most interesting thing is that it feels natural. My life feels natural, organic, in flow.

I end this workshop like all the others:

"Ladies, thank you for coming. I say this every week, but it bears repeating. You are sharing the gift of you with me and no greater gift could I receive. You are choosing to spend your only truly non-renewable resource with me, time. Time is the only thing we can never get back. Money or anything else can always be replenished, but not time. Who we chose to spend our time with is one of the most important decisions we make in life. Thank you. I can't tell you how much it means to me that each of you chose to spend 90 minutes of your life with me."

And again, I mean it!

The women's workshops taught me how gifts are transferred from person to person; how they combine, change, grow and continue endlessly.

RETURN WITH THE ELIXIR

BEN, CASS: Monday, June 22, 2009, 1:00 p.m.

B EN ZACHARIAH, DIRECTOR OF PROGRAMS at CASS, is a short man with a pleasant soft face and an Indian accent who speaks clearly and simply.

Before his current position, Ben was a client for several months after losing his business in Los Angeles. He left town because he "was tired of people feeling sorry" about him, and quickly realized that other clients in CASS were in much more dire straits than him. Ben took up kitchen and cleaning duties, hoping to help those around him.

"I was basically cleaning the cobwebs of my own mind," he says. "I grew up in very poor surroundings in India, and then I came over to the States and I attained riches. And in a way, it was too much for me to deal with."

Ben's feelings about money now are very different from the profit-minded man who made it and lost it all in L.A.

"When you are poor, you want to have money," he says. "You want to be rich and want to be noticed. You want everything that you never had. And that means everything that you see in the movies, everything that you see in the newspapers, every single fantasy. And when you grow up, then it becomes bigger, and you realize that it's a fantasy but you try and do it anyway."

Not knowing what to do with his newfound riches as a successful businessman, Ben says he simply spent and spent. Still, he wasn't happy.

"You constantly strive to be on top of the mountain," he says. "And when you reach the top of the mountain, you don't have anywhere to go. And it leaves you feeling empty. And you look down one side and there are things you did to get there which you are not really happy about. Because business is cutthroat. You had to cut corners in order to get there. You made your money, you have pains. It leaves you feeling empty."

Ben says that no matter what his bank statements said, he was emotionally bankrupt. While it gave him status and buying power, business was not good to him as a person:

"It made me have the spine of a Gummi Bear."

Ben means that he thought all problems could be solved with money. People hit him up for $100, $200, even $1,000 at a time. Ben always said yes. After all, wasn't money the root cause of any problem? Now he feels this behavior made him spineless.

When his business went under, Ben took the first plane out of L.A., which happened to be Phoenix-bound. The journey, he suggests, has been his healing process.

"Change has been a constant friend," Ben says.

In the CASS kitchen, he learned stories from people in the community, figuring the best way to help is to listen. One day, he noticed a shelter manager having a hard time with the paperwork and numbers. Ben offered to help, and the manager noticed his talent for such work. That was 16 years ago, and he has worked at CASS ever since.

I suggest that after such a long time, this place must have changed Ben's character.

"I think . . . it has not changed me from the sense that I am still able to hold to my humility," Ben replies. "This job, after you do if for many years, you become cynical to it. Suffering becomes a constant. Suffering doesn't engage your soul anymore. But by practicing humility, every new suffering that I see is a chance to address it again. It's like a wound that never heals."

After talking some more about active listening and how much it helps in a place like the Human Services Campus (a sentiment that many volunteers and staff here seem to share, knowingly or not), I ask Ben to talk about homelessness in general.

"The way I look at it, the only difference between the person who has the helping hand and the homeless person who has the outstretched palm is a twist of the hand—at any point, anyone can be the recipient," Ben says. "I made up my own philosophy about how to approach homelessness. It started out as a theory of meeting people and giving them something to hope for or attain, because that way, you are not letting homeless people be a recipient. It's more that you are giving them a choice to stand up for something. That means I will not hand out a sandwich to their hand; they have to at least walk a step to me. And that takes practice because we are so used to giving everything, because it's easy for our egos to accept that we helped somebody. It's harder for us to believe that other people, who don't have enough, have dignity. They have dignity even though they are unshaven, un-bathed, and lying in the filth. They still have dignity of some sort, they just haven't exercised it yet."

Ben says this philosophy has not been universally loved by other members of the CASS team. He has heard criticisms that he was not cut out to be a social worker.

"If somebody came and got five pairs of socks two days ago, and they come back today, I would ask them what happened to the five pairs of socks when you don't have any shoes?" Ben smiles as he relates the story. "Asking questions like that was taboo, because there's this perceived notion in social services that we have to be Christ-like. But at the same time, we have no problem accepting paychecks in the name of the homeless." He pauses; this last point seems to bother Ben. "That's still prevalent."

"I hear some criticism of CASS as though it's the old school, heavy-handed, less caring agency around here," I press. "Do you want to address that?"

"The people that I hire subscribe to my philosophies," says Ben, who is sometimes considered a rebel within CASS. To describe the relationships between agencies, he compares them all to a big family.

"CASS is the patriarch," he begins. "[CASS] enforces the rules, the disciplines and some sort of structure for the mere fact that we have been in existence for 25 years. We have survived for the last 25 years. LDRC is the youngest child. It is loved, but it needs its freedom to grow. It is artistic. It is more dreamy. The Clinic is the matriarch. It is the nurturing one. It takes care of your boo-boos. Same with Saint Vincent de Paul's and André House. They are the first-borns and the elders. They are the responsible ones. They feed everybody and take care of everyone. So the kids don't necessarily want to listen to their parents. NOVA [a mental health agency] would be one of the aunts; like that caring aunt that gets you when your parents don't. But like the natural order of events, when things go bad, the person everybody goes to is the patriarch."

Ben says without this "family unit," none of the agencies would be able to do the amazing work they do. But the drawback is that each agency has its own identity crisis to deal with, and sometimes, those identities clash with one another.

"So while we are going through this identity crises, we all revert back to the things we know best," Ben continues. "The patriarch reverts back to saying that it's the rules and the structure that makes everything better. The matriarch says that keeping everything quiet and taking care of the wounds is what makes it better. The youngest child says that breaking the rules and free-thinking and new horizons is what makes it better. The aunt, she does what she normally does, she patiently watches to see if somebody falls and if they do she will be there to help them out. I think embracing the uniqueness of the family is the glue that holds it together."

What is the meaning of life?

Doing what you were born to do. We all yearn for greatness, to belong, and a better place to leave behind. So by doing what I am born to do, and the only place I can connect is by helping others, because for every human being I touch, I hope to leave them in a better place. So I give my children a better world. Each one of us is chosen to do certain things, amazing things. There is some order in which people are, everyone is, everyone has a sense of purpose, has a divine purpose. And so to me the Rwandan killings were as necessary to life as me being in Phoenix helping the homeless. Anything that happens has some sort of purpose.

What are your thoughts about society and/or societies in general?

I think societies are essential for human development. But in general, societies are failures because of the lack of it [human development]. Anytime you break the chains of morality within the constraints of society, you are branded a traitor. That means the society is the one who made the rules in the first place. If you were not supposed to break them, you should not have made the rules. Rules are meant to be improved. Society terms it as breaking. It's just trying to improve. If the rules are fence posts and you see you cannot cross this because of unknown dangers, then there would not be a word named explore.

Who are you?

I'm a healer. I'm a healer. Loving someone who repulses you is the ultimate gift that you can give yourself, because that will show you what you've been afraid of.

Ben taught me that strength and identity is created and maintained in family relationships. And, we are all family.

TILLIE, CLIENT, LDRC: Tuesday, June 30, 2009, 11 a.m.

Tillie is a beautiful, huggable, vivacious, boisterous woman, and a regular member of the Women's Group. What better interview subject could I ask for?

In her singsong voice, Tillie says there are gaps in her life story that she can't remember, she'll try to start from the beginning. I nod in agreement, and she launches into a scattered but engaging storytelling style.

"So, um, when I was little, my mother—I'm the baby of five—and um, my mother was wonderful, fabulous, but she was an alcoholic," Tillie says. "Uh, we moved like gypsies. And uh, I hated it. I hated that we moved all the time, because every time I really liked where we lived, we had to move."

It wasn't until later that Tillie identified this as a possible reason for her homelessness as an adult. As a child, she'd never had the chance to be rooted in one place and grow.

"So um, my mother was an alcoholic . . . but she was a functional alcoholic." Tillie has a peculiar tendency to fluctuate the tone of her voice, especially at the end of a sentence. "We always had clean clothes. We always ate. And um, she worked for a while. And then she got um, welfare. We call it welfare back East. Or public assistance; that's the really nice name for it. And um, so um, I don't know; at about eight years old I realized, this woman, she drinks a lot and um, I'm going to take care of her. I'm going to watch out for her, because I love her."

This arrangement worked for a little bit; Tillie's mom was "on top of it" for a time. But seeing people take advantage of her illiterate mother [her parents were sharecroppers] made Tillie dream of an education for herself. But she continued to take care of her "promiscuous" mother instead, and hid this fact of her life from others.

"I don't cry about it anymore when I talk about it, because before I used to cry because I was so ashamed and so embarrassed," she says. "And I just really felt like God had dealt me a raw deal. I couldn't understand what I had did to deserve a parent like this, but I loved her. I never said a harsh word. I never cursed. And God forbid I ever raised my hand!"

Now, Tillie is OK with telling people about her past. Maybe a better way to say it is that Tillie is tired of keeping her past a secret.

"It really affected my thinking," she says. "It affected the way I lived. It affected my relationships . . . and it took all this time for me to learn that. You know? To be honest, um, taking the class [Women's Workshop] really helped me to say what I'm saying now. 'Cause I could tell the story. You know what I mean? Because telling the story is nothing. You know? It's when you get tired of telling the story that something begins to happen."

This realization makes Tillie smile, and when Tillie smiles, you can see every tooth. She smiles with all her teeth and laughs.

"I would always get to this point," she says now, with increasing passion, "where I'd think everything would be going great. I would have the perfect job, the car, the apartment, even a man sometimes." But Tillie says she always set herself up for failure, never letting herself take that last step into lasting success.

"I was always afraid to believe in me," she says, shaking her head. "That's what it was! It's good now, but it's just so sad when I think about it."

Tillie says she married "a man from Liberia" who was very successful and educated, thinking that would solve her problems. That his success and intelligence would rub off on her. But it didn't work out that way. Tillie is now divorced and spent time in a battered women's shelter for the verbal abuse she endured from a string of bad relationships.

"Yeah, verbally, not physically, because I'd have to bust them up if they ever tried to hit me," Tillie clarifies. She makes a fist and I believe her. While Tillie has a great, radiating warmth about her, she also looks like someone you would not want to mess with. "So, um, they never tried to physically hit me. But they knew, here is this bright fabulous person, shining like a star, and they would just try and kill my light. Oh my God, they would kill my light! You know?" She smiles and laughs. There's a sense of comic relief in her laugh, as if it might help mute the pain these stories still hold for her.

Tillie has been bouncing from shelter to shelter for some time now, cleaning up temporarily only to revert to drug and alcohol abuse when her self-esteem fails.

"It was a rebellious act," she says of the substance abuse. "You do the drugs because you have to transform into another person. You are in this world and putting on this facade that everything is OK and it's fabulous. But you are wounded. You are hurt. You are all beat up from that world. And when you are out there doing drugs and alcohol, for some reason, those people out there accept you. They understand you. They've been through what you've been through. They know exactly what you are talking about. And of course, they are eating you alive all at the same time. But who cares? You have somebody there nurturing you."

From here, Tillie describes the family roles people take on for each other on the streets.

"Like if you are a 'mom,' that means like you have big clout," she says. "That means like you are the head of it. They think twice before saying anything to you or before they come up on you, because you've got back up if you're the mom. A mother got kids. A mother got daughters. If you try and mess with the mom, you can best believe that some kids or some daughters are going to come and help that mom. Daughters.

"Sisters—not daughters—are just that: They [sisters] come and they go," Tillie continues. "A mom is something you've got to earn. Like when I first came on the scene, I met this guy and so I knew if I charmed the big drug dealer, I would be his girlfriend. I would be a mom and nobody would bother me. See, I'm a big charmer and I knew that."

This isn't just talk. When Tillie is feeling good about herself, she can charm the socks of a snake.

"Aunts are cool," she goes on. "They ain't always on the scene. They come and they go. You know what I mean? Like you are happy to see her when she comes cause she gots some money. She just comin' and livening up the party and then she goes. You know?"

Tillie says it's a matriarchy created for women, by women. The men may deal the drugs, but his girlfriend often draws the customers. And the girls can fight: to defend themselves, to defend their friends, to win a man.

"The men are too busy thinking that they run the show, but really they don't," Tillie says, her singsong voice replaced with a street edge. She spends some time describing the entire hierarchy of "the scene," a complicated web of gender, race and money-based status.

"And why don't men fight over the women if certain women are the money makers?" I finally have to ask.

Tillie's response isn't shy. "You want to know why men don't fight over the women? I think it's because there are so many women—so many women with low self-esteems, who feel like they're nothing, garbage. You know what I'm saying?"

"And why do the women fight over the men?" I ask.

"As a woman, speaking from a women's point of view: I was always taught that the man is the head, you know what I'm saying, and I was made from his rib," Tillie says. "And I'm his help maiden. And if I've got a man, everything is possible. You know? And if I just got me, something is missing. But that's a lie. We think that—well, I used to think that we need a man to make us complete, that we are not complete unless we have a man. And then, of course, if you've got a man, that's protection, that's like a covering out in the street. You know what I'm sayin'? If you've got a man, you've got cover."

"Do you think 'needing a man' is pretty common thought?"

"Oh yeah, most definitely."

"So most women out there would tell me that if they could articulate it?"

"Even if they couldn't articulate it, I know they would tell you that," Tillie says, flashing one of her enormous, disarming smiles.

Tillie has had good jobs in the past, but also "been to a million rehabs." They didn't help, she says, because recovery group meetings only make her want to use more. But now, Tillie says that lifestyle can't keep on anymore. Instead of listening to others' advice for her (whether that be "go to rehab!" or "use drugs"), Tillie is trying to learn to trust herself.

"I don't need people to make my decisions for me. I can do it and be confident. So what, I made a bad decision. It ain't the end of the world anymore."

I'm personally thrilled, because this is a concept I teach often in our Women's Workshop. "And now you're here," I say. "Can you talk about that? What's going on now?"

"Freedom," Tillie replies. ". . . I could cry, because I wasted so much time." In fact, she does start to cry. "But now I don't have to waste any more time. I'm so glad that I'm not wasting time anymore."

"What freed you?" I ask.

"I think a combination of things. I was so tired. Being here . . . well, right before I came here I was living with some friends. They had a beautiful condo. I had my own room and it was everything that I wanted. So I just woke up one morning and I got a clue and I said, 'Guess what, I'm leaving. I'm out of here.' Because I want my own. I don't want anybody else's. I want my own. And what's the difference between me and this girl [the friend who owned the condo], for real? You know what I mean. No difference. No difference at all. So I left.

"Do you know that this is the very first time in my whole 46 years that I ever paid attention to me?" Tillie asks aloud, maybe more to herself than to me. "I'm praying that I get another 46 years to just do me. Now I'm so conscious of me and I'm so good to me!"

"And now I'm looking so forward to taking it to another level, like you talked about. I'm looking so forward to taking it to another level!" Tillie continues, her voice returning to that delightful singsong tone and raising two octaves along the way. "I'm a little afraid, but I'm ready to take it to the next level. And it's like I know my destiny now . . . I don't know how to explain it. The only way I can describe it is, [in the workshop] you used 'magical.' It's just so good to share love . . . I just didn't know how to distribute it. I'm learning how to distribute it now. You know? Because I was so busy giving it all to one person at one time that there was none left for me."

"There are these successful happy women here like Nancy and Jessica and they are like a magnet," Tillie concludes. "You know, they've got something for you when you see them. It's just so good. People would pay for it if they could."

What is the meaning of life?

What is the meaning of life? I want to say the meaning of life is breath. The meaning of life is love, most of all! The meaning of life is life itself. That's it. That's the meaning of life.

What are your thoughts about society and/or societies in general?

My real thought about society is . . . I love society. I do. I don't think society loves itself, but I love society. I think I want to help society love itself. You know what I mean? Like all society want is some love . . . for real. And to be honest, that's really all it needs. It would be a great society if it could just love itself more. You know what I mean? Because everything else would have no choice but to fall into place.

You know what I learned a long time ago? You know how people tell you things and we never take heed to it or we never . . . until like it's 40 or 50 years later? Well one time a man gave me a piece of paper at one of these millions of rehabs I went to. He drew a woman on a paper like this. [Tillie draws a stick figure of a woman on a piece of paper.] *And he drew a circle around the woman and he said that the circle represented the world.* [She completes her picture by drawing this circle around the stick figure.]

And the woman was inside the world. So then he tore it up. And he told me put it together. And so I said OK. And when I put it back together, he asked me, 'what happened?' And I said I don't know. And he said, 'You mean to tell me you can't look at that and tell me what happened?' So I said no. He said, 'Once you put the woman together; the world fell into place.' That blew my mind! And now, going to your class, doing all this stuff, I'm putting the woman together; I'm putting me back together! You know what I'm saying? And the world ain't got no choice but to fall back into place. Mike, it's so cool!

You just don't know what you do for me! Like, I was all broke up and now I took your class. And I'm not saying like it's the cure for everything, but it's like the major ingredient.

As Tillie speaks, I'm thinking about how pleased I am to receive this sort of feedback.

Who are you?

Whoever I want to be! But I am love though . . . for real. That's who I am. For real Mike, that's who I am. People just don't know it. I didn't know it. But I do now.

Tillie convinced me that we can have a profound effect on others when we love ourselves first, and there is great joy in experiencing even the possibility of that.

JESSICA, LDRC: Monday, August 3, 2009, 9:00 a.m.

"Jessica, I've learned so much in the past eight months thanks to everyone down here," I gush in our final meeting to discuss this book project. "And every time I read over my interview notes I learn new things. What have you learned since we met?"

"I think a lot of the past six months have been about Kevin Collins [the staff member who was killed] and everything that came with that," Jessica says. "There were things that were starting to shift before in terms of empowerment, in terms of people living in condition of homelessness. You and I talked about that in January, and I think things were just starting to get solidified at that time. And I think that there were several things that happened when Kevin was killed and some of it was about security, obviously, and some of it was about collaboration and supporting each other as staff. And then maybe the most important piece was about just client empowerment and client's voices."

Jessica says there has been better communication between the agencies about how to empower the clients as much as possible. Both points boil down to how people treat each other on campus. For instance, she and Ben at CASS have talked about how to make the metal detectors at the shelter less intimidating. So far, the solution is manning them with "friendly people." But at least the discussion is happening now. The campus-wide focus is now to treat clients with dignity.

"I don't know if you've spent a lot of time there [CASS] or seen it, but there's been a lot of moving staff around so that their skills and passions are matching their job descriptions," Jessica says. "And having client volunteers at the front desk creating a surrogate family atmosphere, because that's probably the biggest common denominator."

"Other changes include uniforms for staff members, so clients can identify them, and the creation of the Campus Leadership League, composed of representatives from the New Arid Club, MSVA, and the Men's Volunteer Corps. Hopefully, what comes next is a more supportive political climate and more help from the community." Jessica is hopeful.

"There's definitely been a culture shift on the campus, and nationally there's been a culture shift, and my personal life has had a shift, but I don't know how significant that is for the book," she says with a self-deprecating laugh. "But I'm also taking life more seriously. It's not a rehearsal. People die."

"This is a very different reaction to Kevin's death than you and others had at first," I point out. As director, Jessica is used to listening to everyone else. She's not used to someone listening to her.

"Yeah," Jessica agrees. "Right away, within a couple of weeks, we talked about security and this philosophy of treatment. I mean, we don't really know how George, the shooter, was or wasn't really treated. But we need to make sure everyone is treated beautifully. Not that every person has the capacity to shift into becoming a murderer just because they're angry, but our first job needs to be able to lower tension. And I think you do that with love and listening. And yes, at the same time, discussions went to security. They go together. In fact, they totally need to go together. And that goes back to what I said about family, that experience of being unconditionally loved and secure."

"You did a great job summing up the past six months," I say finally, "but it's interesting to me that you didn't mention your depression."

"Honestly, when I was talking before, I forgot about it," Jessica says. "The other thing that came out of Kevin's death was my becoming very depressed. Crises are an evaluation time, an assessment time. So I think . . . well . . . you know, the murder happened and my parents came to visit the next day for two weeks and without my really thinking about it, I just went into this mode of trying to convince my mom not to worry, and as the director, I went into this mode of trying to protect staff security-wise and trying to make sure everybody was OK. And I know I felt like, I don't know how to do this and I'm feeling scared and sad and overwhelmed and so how am I supposed to lead the way forward for a team?

"I suppressed a lot of stuff I should have learned how to express, that I should have been focusing on how to express," Jessica admits. "And I really had a hard time and felt depressed, like I hadn't felt in years, and stuck and disheartened."

"What's wrong with people taking care of you?" I ask. "What does it say about you?"

"I don't know," she replies. "I guess it's just about being vulnerable and showing people my weaknesses. But I think when I was younger, I thought my parents wanted to take care of me too much. Yeah, I think for some reason, I used to make up that if someone was taking care of me, it meant that they thought I couldn't take care of myself. And in a lot of ways, what I learned [this year] is what I am trying to teach staff and clients."

"So this tearing you down made you more comfortable with being . . ."

"Human." Jessica finishes my sentence, with laughter and a sense of relief.

This place adds humanity to everyone it touches, one way or another. I have been waiting eight months to ask Jessica the questions.

What is the meaning of life?

Oh, that's so easy! [Sarcastically.] I think it's a lot of what I said this morning already. Um, it's about just connecting with the world and people around you and in your life and having meaningful relationships. And figuring out what your truth is and living that . . . I think. Or maybe it's about connection.

What are your thoughts about society and/or societies in general?

There are certain rules that get established and if we don't pay attention, they can be dangerous rules. But if you do pay attention you can really . . . I think you can really have a positive impact on those rules. It's interesting to think about that in relationship to homelessness, because if you think about it it's really insane that as a society we accept homelessness in this country. I mean we expect people to live on the street. And we expect there to be people with cardboard signs at intersections. If you step back, it's just completely insane that we allow that! The same way I hope that it is completely insane in a few years, when we look back, and at this point I think in every state, that we voted for discrimination in terms of bans on gay marriage. I imagine . . . not just

I imagine society will change, I know society will change, because society has always changed. I mean there used to be laws that a black person was 3/5ths of person compared to a white person or something like that. So I imagine that in a few years we will look back and find it insane that in all of the states, especially California, which is fairly hysterical, voted for discrimination.

I think a lot of stuff that's happened in the past six months is significantly affecting our society, the campus society as well as the national society. You know again, there is going to be an Office of Social Innovation and Civic Participation that would not have happened a year ago. And this Vista program that has been around . . . [a client volunteer training program] *I think Reagan started it, maybe. And now we have six Vista volunteers who are homeless individuals. I mean one person decided to try and make a car that wasn't totally dependent on gas and now last year Prius was the biggest selling vehicle in the United States after Chevy trucks were the biggest selling vehicles for 15 years, or something like that."*

So I guess my point is [laughing], *that if you really pay attention you can have a really big impact on society and really a society is this set of sometimes invisible, indescribable rules that hold us together as a community and if we care, we're pretty obligated to speak up, because we can make a difference! Seriously don't you think I should be able to go home now?*

Who are you?

I'm seeing these pictures that I have around my office and I think I'm a combination of them. OK. So there is this local artist her name is Lisa Aubinger and there's this ah . . . how would you describe that painting? There's a lot of wind in it. Anyway when she writes about this character, her name is Penny. [Jessica reads the caption.] *"A girl accepting the elements around her. She knows that having a life under construction enhances her character. How boring it would be otherwise." So, uh, I'm like Penny in that I always want more knowledge and growth and connection.*

And then Wonder Woman, of course. [She turns to a picture of the original Wonder Woman, Linda Carter, on her wall.] *She has always been one of my heroes. You know she's this strong, sexy, independent woman who ah, lassos people and forces them to tell the truth. I mean I don't think she ever hurts anybody; she just forces them to tell the truth. And I really admire that.*

"Jessica is there anything else you would like to tell me or have readers read?" I ask at the end of this, our last interview together.

"When someone sees a homeless person desperate on the street that somewhere, they can remind themselves 'this person is part of my community' and if they are broken, then know 'my community is broken.'

"And it's not an easy answer about how to help that person, and it's certainly not about giving them a dollar or buying them a cup of coffee. Not that those things are bad. But if we all just treated each other with a little bit of dignity, I think that goes a long way. I think that's what we all try to do here. I mean imagine being on the street and asking for money because you are so desperate that you don't know what else to do and people literally ignore you, as if you are invisible . . . and then you start to feel invisible. Just help someone not feel invisible and it might lead to them changing their life. That's it."

After she finishes speaking, Jessica just sits at her desk for a few minutes, quiet and sad. Then, she pulls herself out of it, and a little girl's genuine smile rolls across her face.

"What if every person started their Monday like this?" she asks. "Starting your day, starting your week with someone coming and asking you essentially to talk about why you matter. And giving you back that energy that you do matter. That's the society that I want to live in. How can we institute that? The government should pay . . . I don't know. What you are doing? I mean, I know you're writing a book, but you're doing something else. They really should send out people to do this."

This was Jessica's way of thanking me, and it was probably one of the greatest compliments I have ever received.

Jessica makes me realize that people need to be seen. This is one of the things relationships do for us, our families and our communities.

The other side of the Homeless Hero. Photo by: Steven Sable.

ME, HOME: Thursday, December 31, 2009, 5:00 p.m.

I don't really think a conclusion for this book is necessary, nor is one entirely possible. My study and understanding of the subject continues. And already, so much has changed here with the people, the LDRC, and the Human Services Campus as a whole. I could write another book about all the amazing things hinted at, just started, that are now in full bloom.

When revising this material, I removed almost another book's worth of my own personal notes that I wrote along the way. While they added to the material, they also detracted from it. I realized that each person I interviewed had plenty to say and I didn't need to add copious commentary, my experience of their experience. While I originally noted many easily missed concepts and a magical sort of coincidence running as an undercurrent through the material, I decided I didn't need to point all that out in this version.

In the end however, I knew, it's not all about me. That said—it still involved me.

This book started, just like my life, in great part because of my father. He led me to question what homelessness is. Now, at the time of writing this conclusion almost a year later, I think I have an understanding of that. And it truly was the journey, not the destination, that brought me to that understanding.

And what is my understanding? It is now one of intellect, feeling and imagination. My understanding of homelessness is in my head and in my heart. And the answer was always there. I don't mean I always knew it. I mean the path to the answer was always there.

I am still teaching and learning with the women in our Women's Workshop at the Lodestar Daily Resource Center on the Human Services Campus. I now also teach ballroom dance at LDRC (the first homeless adult version of the international children's dance program known as Dancing Classrooms) and use it as a vehicle to build self-esteem, teach social skills, and to rebuild a sense of community. And of course it was Dawn's idea to try such a radical approach. I run other workshops for the staff and coach many of them as well. Angels need help as much as anyone else, if not more. The toll on the staff here is heavy, as they strive constantly to address and solve this communal ill. All in all, for me, volunteering has become an essential ingredient to a fulfilling life, to being whole.

I don't volunteer to be a good guy, although I would have at the start of this project. I volunteer, like my father, because it's the right thing to do. It is the natural, organic thing to do. It is the human thing to do, and the thing that makes us more human by doing so.

Humility was a big part of this learning process. I now believe that humility is the knowledge that you are unique and unmatchable, but so is everyone else. Without humility, you can't fully experience humanity, because it is the recognition of the divinity in everyone. And before experiencing this, I was truly homeless, even though I have always been blessed with four walls, a roof and food on the table.

In fact, whatever walls you place around yourself may ultimately take your sense of home away, if those walls separate you from others. My connection with humanity and myself is my sense of home. In a very real way, they are one in the same.

And Jessica is right that we are all connected, all one. I have always known this somehow, but had never fully experienced it. Volunteering has shown me that. I can't explain it, nor do I need to, because I can feel it when I participate with others. If one person is broken, then my community is broken; and if my community is broken, then so am I, because we are all one. Home is a feeling, a knowing of wholeness, oneness. To the extent that anyone is left out, to that same extent we have less of a whole, in a very real sense we all become homeless.

"Homelessness" is not a disease. It is a symptom of a disease, the dis-ease of not feeling at home with one's self, not feeling whole. It is a symptom of a disconnected person and a disconnected community.

I don't see any problems in the world that are the result of anyone recognizing that we are all one. And we can all think of numerous environmental, social and economic problems that are the result of thinking the opposite.

Homelessness is the result of a society that does not believe we are all one.

The choice is simple. Live as one and be home. Live as less than one and be home-less.

Facilitating the Woman's Workshop and teaching the ballroom dance class has shown me an amazing thing. When I spend time interacting with, getting to know and to understand 'unusual' people, they become less unusual and more individuals in my mind and heart. They become more human to me. And for them, when they are included, they learn from me and from others. They learn to relate in a healthy manner, and a community is just a network of relationships.

Of course the opposite is true. Exclusion fuels prejudice and extreme behavior. So if the problem is disconnection, then the solution is reconnection. In order for homelessness to end, the Ordinary World needs to meet the Special World, in order to become Our World.

I used to ask, what can one person do? Well, a hell of a lot! They can do a hell of a lot like Arlene by thinking and directing big movements. And they can do a hell of a lot by doing one small thing very well, like Chaplain Dave and his office. They can do a hell of a lot by getting to know one stranger. Scope really is an illusion. It all starts at home.

Our gifts are endless. My father didn't think he helped much at the shelter he worked at in Albuquerque, but he sure has made a difference in Phoenix—through me.

I will finish by answering the three questions I asked every interviewee. Obviously, my answers would have been very different at the start of this book's path. But I am now different. I am now a mosaic of the many people who have shared themselves with me. I am now so much more whole.

What is the meaning of life?

You get to decide! You give life its meaning, not the other way around.

I think the better question is: What is life? It's a relationship. So get involved.

What are your thoughts about society and/or societies in general?

Society is family.

Who are you?

I'm a romantic. Miguel de Cervantes Saavedra, the author of The Ingenious Gentleman Don Quixote of La Mancha *(who was one of the greatest romantics) wrote, "Too much sanity is madness and the maddest of all is to see life as it is and not as it should be." Romanticism is the only religion that has ever made sense to me.*

EPILOGUE

THE LDRC IS THE MOST creative and alive organization I have ever known. It's a great honor and privilege to be associated with them. Its small staff is full of global thinkers—courageous and outrageous individuals. This handful of people work for the homeless clients they serve; they also work for the community—for you.

While much emphasis has been placed on the need to change how we see ourselves, each other, and our community, as opposed to money solving the problem of homelessness, I must mention that money is still a necessity to running the organization.

Money doesn't solve the problem of homelessness. People, programs, and institutions are the solution, but money funds those efforts. I donate both my time and money to LDRC. I don't see it as charity. I know that each dollar I contribute will save hundreds of dollars down the road for me and for you. I think it should be obvious by the end of this book that we as a society tend to spend copious amounts of money trying to fix problems that we could have prevented in the first place and for so much less money, not to mention pain.

I hope you will consider helping us to end homelessness instead of just dealing with it. It's the right thing to do, and, it's the cheaper thing to do.

And as for you, dear reader, how would you answer these three questions now?

What is your meaning of life?
What are your thoughts about society and/or societies in general?
Who are you?

Lodestar Day Resource Center
1125 W. Jackson Street
Phoenix, AZ 85007
(602) 393-9930
www.lodestardrc.org

EDITORS' NOTES

TYE RABENS

W HEN MIKE FIRST APPROACHED ME to edit this book, I was struggling to get a creative writing class off the ground at Lodestar Day Resource Center. I'm still not quite sure what motivated him to trust such a personal project with me, a virtual stranger more than 10 years his junior. Maybe he just wanted to make sure *Homeless Hero* was "in the right hands," or, in the hands of another full-time writer who'd experienced the Human Services Campus up close.

I harbored more reservations about my editorial skills than Mike did. What qualified me—an Arizona State University student (at the time) with no professional editing experience—to take on this project? I could barely keep the writing class afloat, and was secretly thinking I should bail out on even the meager two hours a week I contributed to LDRC. At the time, I was working, taking an overload schedule of college courses, and frankly frustrated by how little impact I seemed to be making.

The decision to edit a book about this place that might never make it to print was difficult, but inevitable. In the end, Mike's passion for *Homeless Hero* and its cause won me over, despite the time commitment.

I now realize how happy and lucky I am to have stumbled into this project. And it's funny how much my journey began to parallel Mike's as soon as I came into contact with *Homeless Hero*. The LDRC has a way of sucking you in. By the end of my seven-month editing stint, I volunteered three times as long per week as at the beginning. Besides helping out in the LDRC Library, the Writer's Workshop (as I now call my class) has taken off in attendance to the point that we've split into beginner and advanced groups.

But more basically, LDRC sucks you in because you start needing to be there. The emotional highs and lows are intense; every moment is important. I've seen my students leave to get housing, jobs or the college education they've always dreamed of. I've also seen students disappear for less positive reasons. In the library, I've had intellectual conversations about Alice Munro, Miles Davis, the Bible, Joe Frasier and everything in between. I've watched clients enjoy the magazines I've donated, been verbally threatened and watched a man's mind fall apart before my eyes.

My chess game has improved.

I used to tell people who asked why I volunteered that LDRC was "my weekly reminder of how lucky I am." This is still true, but "lucky" means something different now. I'm lucky for the type of person this place makes me, and for the people I've gotten to know here.

Don't think I'm trying to sugarcoat life at the Human Services Campus. This community is still assaulted by desperation, fatigue, misery, a sense of failure and, above all, frustration. I don't focus on the assaults here partially out of optimism, but mostly because many of you already assume this aspect of homelessness. Mike understands this decision, too, as *Homeless Hero* clearly shows.

Why *not* focus on solutions? Why feel helpless?

Mike's story is first and foremost a personal journey, but he also has a knack for encapsulating the nuance and dirty beauty of this place and time in American history. The moments I'll always remember from my 18 months as an LDRC volunteer are the ones I still don't fully understand:

- Jumping over a sleeping client en route to first base during an impromptu Wiffle ball game on the HSC front lawn
- Seeing a student of mine inside the Cronkite building at ASU, and watching CNN with her between classes
- Seeing the same student on the street as she smiles, waves and breaks into a flawless soprano
- Seeing the same student and, after a year of writing classes, having her forget my name
- Watching a hungry sparrow hop through the gravel, trying to find crumbs among the cigarette butts
- Girls flirting with me when they find out that I volunteer, and not being able to flirt back
- Editing this book

Most of the edits I've made to *Homeless Hero* were to eliminate repetition, streamline the longer interviews and lop off the occasional tangent. I left the book's structure, chronology and tone untouched. My contribution is making this book a more intuitive reading experience—no more.

To finish, I'll honor Mike's "Three Questions" obsession by answering them myself, though you will undoubtedly find the responses of the clients, caseworkers, clergy, cops and other volunteers he interviewed more insightful and interesting.

What is the meaning of life?

Mercy is the most powerful and meaningful gift one human being can give to another. You don't need religion to believe in that. My life's talent is writing, or more broadly, understanding one person's ideas and explaining them to others. My life's goal is to help peoples' lives be less shitty. The meaning of life, I guess, is to translate one's talents and goals into acts of mercy.

What are your thoughts about society and/or societies in general?

Societies are the structures we build when our wants and needs as a community grow bigger than person-to-person relationships alone can handle. They are neither good nor bad nor fair nor unfair. But all the macro-level structures—economics, government, religion, art, science—are rooted in the micro-details of how individuals treat one another. Like relationships, societies will always have flaws; someone always gets hurt. But also like a relationship, a society becomes healthier the more we care, the more we're committed to it, and the more selfless we can all be.

Who are you?

I am an evolving pattern of stardust and subatomic particles, just like anyone else.

MARY L. HOLDEN

After Tye Rabens (who I never got to meet) did the work of the first edit, Mike let this book sit while he studied the best way to get it published. It has been said that all things happen in just the right time—all the time. I believed this before, but now I believe it with the brain of my heart and the heart of my brain.

The year 2012 was supposed to be filled with doom—for the world. For me it started with an invitation to join a group called 12 Women for 2012. The idea for the group came from a woman named Janneke Koole, who happens to live in Phoenix. Using the Internet, she suggested to women across the world to come together in groups of 12, find a project to work on that would improve their community and in the process improve their individual self through service. Learn more here: **www.12women2012.com**.

The Phoenix 12 Women for 2012 was initiated by a remarkable young woman, Sara Regester, R.N., BSN. Through her leadership, I joined Terry Duffy, Mary Westheimer, Kris Floor, Kim Harris, Lara Rosenberg, Catherine Genzler, Jennifer Kittoe, Betsy Davis, Lisa MacCollum, Sherie Hayes, Martha Wolmedorph and Jessica Berg.

Our first assignment was to find a service project. Many ideas were suggested but then Jessica said something like, 'I don't want to seem self-serving because I work there, but the Lodestar Day Resource Center's women's restroom needs to be remodeled.' All other project ideas went by the wayside as visions of the artists, designers and architects in the group caught fire on the restroom idea and ignited a mass consciousness in the group. Giving *relief* to a community through a design-and-build remodel in a place of the most basic *relief*, a public restroom for those in our society who need it on so many levels, seemed very right to all of us.

Each of us toured the facility; some of us attended the Women's Group led by Mike Tapscott on Tuesday mornings. Over the course of 2012 we studied designs; sought donations; made our own donations of money and materials; found contractors to help; held fundraisers (a show at a comedy club, an event at a yoga studio where proceeds were donated to the project, and, an auction); raised awareness of the LDRC through social media and the press; crushed tiles, rocks and mixed glue; learned how to make a mosaic; manifested new stalls and got to know one another and our community better.

As this book shows, miracles happen at the LDRC. All those miracles, along with the many personal miracles all 12 women experienced in their own lives during 2012, add up to One Big Overall Miracle. One of these 12 women even conceived and gave birth to a new baby during 2012 and created a bunch of honorary aunts and grandmothers!

The women who use the restroom at Lodestar Day Resource Center are greeted with these words on a mural along the back wall: "Amazing changes blossom with HOPE DESIRE PLANNING PERSISTENCE GRATITUDE and LOVE." The creator (and donator and installer) of the stall doors and partitions, Rich Roberts of Steel Krazy in Phoenix, embedded those same words onto each steel panel. Roberts himself lived without a home and in a van for four years, so that he could pay child support. When his children would visit, he made their stay into a camping adventure. The exact opposite of the deadbeat dads who are portrayed in the media, he wanted to give something back out of the gratefulness he felt when his life got back on track.

I didn't even know that Rich existed until the 12 women met in August at Lodestar while creating the mosaic with guest artist and mosaic expert Kathy Milazzo. In the midst of discussing how sad it would be to have to keep the existing stalls (which were so very beige, over-painted and institutional) in light of the bright mosaic and mural, something took over me and I stood up and said, "Let's create a miracle here. If we can create a miracle with *toilet stalls* we can create a miracle with *anything.*"

A week later I got a call from Rich. He said, "My girlfriend Vessa was delivering a donation of water bottles to Lodestar and she heard that you might have something for me to do. I own a company called Steel Krazy, and I work with steel."

Miracles, large and small, lined up all over the place in 2012! The Miracle Of The Toilet Stalls matched The Miracle Of The New Floors; The Miracle Of The Mosaic Design And Creation; The Miracle Of The Graphic Design; The Miracle Of The New Mirrors; The Miracle Of The Donated Paint; The Miracle Of New Lighting; The Miracle Of Toilet Paper Rolls Inside Each Stall As Opposed to One Roll Outside Of The Restroom Where Each Entrant Had To Make A Public Display Of Their Guess And Take The Amount They Might Need.

When the *toilet stall* miracle had come to pass, it became my desire to help get the miracle of this book into the world. I met Mike Tapscott when I toured Lodestar Day Resource Center in February 2012 and said something like, 'The story of this place needs to be written!'

He said, "I already wrote a book about it."

Hmmmmm. In 2011, I signed a contract with Abbott Press to self-publish a novel I'm still in the process of finishing. It will do nothing to help the world. After I read *Homeless Hero*, I decided to donate my contract to Mike and publish *this* book (which I see as being far more valuable than my novel) to the reading public and to the social policy makers of both Arizona and the United States.

Mike and I hope that *Homeless Hero* will touch the hearts of both individuals and policy makers, allow them to better understand the plight of those who are homeless and hurting and then . . . *PLEASE improve our world in any way possible from knowing and loving yourself, seeing humanity in a new way, expressing both gratitude and compassion and... creating miracles.*

My answers to Mike's three questions? Well, after my experiences with 12 Women For Lodestar 2012's project, reading, editing and publishing this book, I know that single individuals (all of whom were created in a moment of intimacy equivalent to the 'big bang' that most likely created the universe) equal the 'allness' of mass consciousness. And all of these people contribute to my three answers…in one word.

Love? Love. Love!

Mike Tapscott Photo by: Steven Sable.

Made in the USA
San Bernardino, CA
08 November 2013